Language Politics, Elites, and The Public Sphere

PERMANENT BLACK MONOGRAPHS

The 'Opus 1' Series

This series comprises outstanding first-time academic monographs in the broad area of South Asian Studies. It is intended as a publishing forum for *the first important books of a younger generation of scholars* in the disciplines of History, Politics, Sociology, Literature, Cinema Studies, and related disciplines.

Consulting Editors

Books in the Series

SUNIL SHARMA

PERSIAN POETRY AT THE INDIAN FRONTIER
Mas'ûd Sa'd Salmân of Lahore

VEENA NAREGAL

LANGUAGE POLITICS, ELITES, AND THE PUBLIC SPHERE
Western India Under Colonialism

MRIDU RAI

HINDU RULERS, MUSLIM SUBJECTS
Religion, Identity Politics and the History of Kashmir

CHARU GUPTA

SEXUALITY, OBSCENITY AND COMMUNITY
Hindu and Muslim Identity in Colonial India

Permanent Black Monographs: The 'OPUS 1' Series

Language Politics, Elites, and the Public Sphere

VEENA NAREGAL

Published by
PERMANENT BLACK
D-28 Oxford Apartments, 11 I.P. Extension,
New Delhi 110092

Distributed by
ORIENT LONGMAN LTD.
Bangalore Bhubaneshwar Calcutta Chennai
Ernakulam Guwahati Hyderabad Lucknow
Mumbai New Delhi Patna

ISBN 81-7824-005-X
First published 2001

Typeset in Adobe Garamond by Eleven Arts
Printed by Pauls Press, Delhi 110020
Binding by Saku Binders, Khanpur, New Delhi

for Appa

Contents

Acknowledgements

Many people have generously supported me in completing this work. I recount all the help I have received with deep gratitude, though it is not an easy task to translate that appreciation into a neat list of acknowledgements.

Foremost among the people who have contributed to this study, I owe thanks to Sudipta Kaviraj, who was adviser for the dissertation on which this book is based. His perspicacity and encouragement were challenging and utterly valuable and made working with him a rich learning experience. David Taylor read my drafts with thoroughness and his comments have helped me sharpen some of the comparative points. Thanks are due to him also for helping with administrative matters through my years at SOAS. I owe a special debt to Homi Bhabha for the generous support he showed towards my work. His comments on an early draft provided me with inspiration at a crucial point in the writing process. I thank Sheldon Pollock for his prompt comments on an earlier draft and for allowing me to read his unpublished work. He and Homi Bhabha made it possible for me to present my work to the South Asia Department at the University of Chicago in 1998. The suggestions and comments received there have been important in shaping my arguments: in particular, I thank Anne Hardgrove. I am deeply grateful to Ram Bapat for being so magnanimous with his time, books and ideas and being ever willing to share his deep understanding of the cultural and political history of Western India. I am deeply grateful to Professor Sumit Guha for helpful suggestions and the interest he has shown in this study.

It is with pleasure that I recount several other debts I have incurred: to Sudhir Chandra for several stimulating and critical discussions and the warm support he has shown towards the project; Thomas Blom Hansen for interest and generosity with his time in commenting on the original thesis; John Sidel for his enthusiasm and detailed comments in engaging with a study strictly outside his regional specialism; Tejaswini Niranjana for inspiration and support; and an anonymous referee for the most judicious criticism on the arguments and materials presented here. I have profited immensely from discussions with Professor Jayant Lele. I thank him especially for being such a receptive and keen listener, qualities that are inestimably precious to a young scholar. Sincere thanks also to Dr Rosalind O'Hanlon for valuable criticism and suggestions.

The research for this study was supported by a fellowship from the Felix Trust, additional and timely support was provided by the Charles Wallace Trust and the Leche Trust. My thanks to all these funding bodies. I am also grateful to the School of Oriental and African Studies and the Central Reserve Fund, University of London, for financial support towards fieldwork; the Research Grants Committee, SOAS, especially Professor Lawrence Harris, for assistance with a conference-related bursary. Finally, the London Goodenough Trust provided amenities and a comfortable working environment.

I gratefully acknowledge comments and other inputs received from participants in various sessions where parts of this work were presented: the workshop on 'Print, Readers and Listeners' at Wolfson College, Cambridge; the Colloquium on 'Translation and Community' at the University of Sheffield; the panel discussion on 'New Literary Histories' at the 15th EASAS Conference in Prague; the seminar organised by the Department of English at SNDT University, Mumbai; the conference at the National Museum of Ethnology, Osaka. I am especially grateful to Professors Kotani and Fujii and to Dr Fumiko Oshikawa for the support they extended.

Several friends and colleagues at SOAS read and provided supportive comments on draft chapters. Among these, special thanks are due to Prathama Bannerjee for her critical and insightful reading of my drafts. John Game and Rashmi Sadana offered themselves as 'readers' in the early stages of writing. Francesca Orsini has been a warm and relentless critic as I made my way through successive drafts. Special words of thanks for friendship and encouragement to Srilata Mueller, Raminder and Bhargavi.

This study provided an occasion to discuss my ideas with several people in Kolhapur, Pune and Bombay, too numerous to name individually. Many of them know so much more about the region than I do and I would like to thank them for sharing their enthusiasm and information with me. In particular, I have learnt a great deal from my discussions with Professor A. R. Kulkarni, Baba Adhav, Dr Sadanand More, Dr Vora, Ashok Kelkar, Y.D. Phadke, Sitaram Raikar, Vasant Moon and Raja Dikshit. Dr Sujata Patel commented on some earlier drafts: I owe her thanks for probing questions. I would like to acknowledge Dr Milind Malshe's encouragement in the early stages of this project when I was a research student in the Department of Humanities and Social Sciences in IIT Bombay.

This work would have been impossible without the help and support of various libraries in London, Edinburgh and India. I would like to thank the staff of India Office Library for their unfailing efficiency and service. My deep gratitude to Shailaja Jadhav and Nilkanth Gurav at the Shivaji University Library, Kolhapur; Malvika and Mrs Potdar at the Bombay University Library; the Director and staff at the Bombay Archives; the Librarian and staff of the Bombay Asiatic Society Library. My work in the Ferguson and Deccan College libraries in Pune would not have been possible without the cheerful assistance of the staff at these places. I am grateful to the staff and scholars at the Bharat Itihaas Samshodhak Mandal for help with *modi* documents. Special thanks to Mr Phansalkar of Tilak Smarak Mandir and Suneela Jani of the VJTI library for giving me access to microfilm-reading equipment. I thank Sunil Kumar for helping with references at short notice.

Thanks to Chris Gutkind for being a special friend through our stay in London, helping to alleviate anxiety at times when progress was slow. Special thanks to Eddie Rodrigues, Gita, Sridhar, Vrijendra and Mahesh Gavaskar, my friends in Bombay, who have provided much animated discussion over the years and significant help in acquiring materials for this project. I warmly recollect the debts owed for providing hospitality and good cheer to Anil and Ashwini during the long stints of fieldwork in Pune and to Umadikars and Professor Tigadi while preparing the script for publication.

This book owes much to Rukun Advani's sharp editorial skills: my thanks to him.

Last but not least, my family has been a source of strength in sustaining me through this work. I have to thank Anish, Ramdas, Bibbi and my parents for never allowing my work to seem a lonely burden; their love and understanding has meant much to me over the years that this book has been made.

Introduction

Much has changed in the study of colonialism since the time when the history of colonial India was plotted in terms of economic drain or the history of administrative change. From a predominant emphasis on economic issues, there has been a visible shift towards the ideological, cultural and political dimensions of the colonial encounter. Earlier, even if questions about colonial power were raised, they were discussed mainly to document official measures and administrative shifts in the structures of the Raj. Such economic and statist approaches were common to both colonialist and nationalist historiography. They were unsuccessful in addressing the complexity of colonial power, especially its cultural construction and modes of dissemination.

The first rumblings of discontent against a historiography that did not substantially admit the possibility of contestation came from Marxist historians who critiqued the self-representation of nationalist historiography but did so mainly by deriding its ideological nature as 'false consciousness'. A historiography that aspired to address the enormous complexity of colonial transformation needed more than this. It needed a refined theory of ideology which would begin by specifying the structures and modes of contestation introduced through colonialism.

Here the contributions of the 'subaltern school' towards theorising the possibility of a history from below from a post-colonial perspective, at a time when the intellectual legacies of colonialism still endured, must be acknowledged. Though it was not held together by an ideological core, the work of this collective redefined colonial historiography as a project that needed to trace the emergence of contesting narratives of modernity through the mutations of liberal discourses as colonial ideology. In doing this, it has drawn upon post-structuralist and post-orientalist critiques of modernity and introduced new levels of sophistication into an inquiry about the modes through which modern ideas spread outside the West, and the profound implications of these processes.

We now accept that a history of the making of colonial power requires a theory of ideology which recognises that colonial domination operated by altering the structures and categories of discursive production. Attempts to analyse the making of colonial discourse have focussed attention on how both the 'deep structures' and 'surface forms' of discursive production were altered by the introduction of new conceptual languages through colonialism. The introduction of modern normative categories redefined and displaced existing cultural and cognitive hierarchies and generated new indigenised forms of regarding and representing the social and natural world. These ideological and cognitive shifts were the result of processes that were historical and contingent, and which took shape through struggles between elite and non-elite groups differentiated by disparate levels of cultural and linguistic capital. With the construction of colonial power being underwritten by such complex cultural, institutional and political shifts, it is appropriate that much of the promise within the field of South Asian colonial studies in the last decade has emerged from the dialogue between anthropologists, historians, political scientists, and literary scholars. Questions about the hegemonic nature of the colonial enterprise, the connections between colonial power and its forms of knowledge, its technologies of rule, and the influence of modern norms through complex layers of dissemination and displacement via colonialist and nationalist discourses—these have been among the major issues.

Today, colonial studies have also advanced significantly beyond general insights into the construction of identity and difference offered by the cultural imperialism argument. In this respect, two methodological insights have been particularly productive. First, the analytical necessity and benefits of treating colony and metropole as a shared field are now well recognised. Similarly, the need to separate the political impact of colonial rule and the structure of anti-colonial responses from their representation in nationalist narratives is also readily acknowledged. However, if we are to make the most of these lessons as well as take colonial difference seriously, much remains to be done. The diversity of ways through which the liberal imagination underwent vernacularisation outside Europe needs to be mapped in order to understand the divergent trajectories of non-Western modernities. Market economics, the universalistic categories of modern reasoning, and modern cultural practices have travelled great distances to redefine not just ideas of society and self, but also the possibilities and hierarchies of production, knowledge, communication and contestation. If the field of colonial studies is to retain its political relevance, we need micro-historical studies that plot how the dissemination of modern discourses and cultural norms effectively structured the boundaries of inclusion and exclusion in different areas of the globe.

Some writings of the 'subaltern school' attempt to theorise the relations between colonial discourse and the structure of the emerging political world in South Asia. A powerful early stimulus to the debate was provided by Guha's thesis that colonial power ruled through dominance without hegemony.[1] His arguments, claiming that colonial ideology signified the limits of bourgeois social rationality, are well-taken, as also his observations on the severely elitist nature of the efforts of the colonial state to cultivate an ideologically amenable native intelligentsia. Clearly, the Western bourgeoisie could not remake the colonies in the image of post-Enlightenment Europe. Yet, a view such as Guha's does not fully acknowledge the enduring ways in which colonial intervention altered discursive and political hierarchies in many parts of the world. Colonial intellectuals have been the subject of much ironical comment, some of it self-inflicted. Nevertheless, despite their politically subordinate and numerically marginal position, they were able to acquire an influential position through their re-inscription of cultural and political norms. More recently, Partha Chatterjee's writings[2] have addressed questions about the position of the intelligentsia

[1]Ranajit Guha, *Dominance without Hegemony: History and Power in Colonial India*, Cambridge, 1997.

[2]See especially the chapter on 'The Nationalist Elite' in Partha Chatterjee, *The Nation and its Fragments*, Delhi, 1993, pp. 35–75.

within the emerging public domain, and the complexities of mediation given the disjunction between 'public' and 'private' within colonial modernity. Similarly, the discontinuities and differences between the political meanings underlying the nationalist elite-led freedom movement and their reception by subaltern participants have been among the important themes of Shahid Amin's work on Gandhi.[3]

However, there have been few direct attempts to analyse the local intelligentsia's self-definitions, especially in the early period before anti-colonial thinking articulated its hegemonic claims as nationalistic discourse. The introduction of English as the 'high' language through a bilingual educational policy and the efforts to re-shape the 'native vernaculars' signified the colonial administration's intentions to define arenas that would determine access and marginality *vis-à-vis* its ideological project. These measures altered the universe of communicative and cultural practices on the subcontinent, and introduced crucial hierarchical and ideological divisions between the newly-educated and 'illiterate', 'English-knowing' and 'vernacular-speaking' sections of native society. The making of a bilingual relation between English and the native vernaculars was crucial to both the construction of colonial ideology and the emerging cultural and political hierarchies. Print was basic to the making of colonial literacy, and to initiating a shift in the nature and substance of the relation between 'high' and 'low' languages in South Asia from previously existing ones. Print was not simply a new communicative technology; it also signified a shift from prevailing assumptions about the distribution of cultural and political power. Although the principles of publicity and the idea of general access underlying the use of print were subject to the rule of colonial difference, even the nominal possibility of a laicised literate order radically altered the means and modes of social contestation. Colonial bilingualism neither presumed, nor was capable of conferring symmetric capabilities in English and the vernacular upon native intellectuals. Inevitably, the bilingual divide was a crucial factor structuring the options open to the new intelligentsia in their use of intellectual and cultural resources to achieve a hegemonic position. This book proposes

[3]Shahid Amin, *Event, Metaphor, Memory: Chauri-Chauri 1922–1992*, Berkeley, 1995.

an argument about the links between educational policy, colonial bilingualism and the strategies of the native intelligentsia in Western India to realise their hegemonic aspirations within the sphere of colonial literate politics.

Educational policy in the Bombay Presidency, the entry of print, and the making of modern expressive forms in Marathi through its association with English are all important themes. However, I shall not trace any of these strands exhaustively. They figure as elements in a larger analysis of structural links between the cultural changes introduced through colonial rule and the options available to the intelligentsia within the political domain.

As a work on the making and implications of colonial bilingualism, this book traces the hierarchical relation between English and vernacular spheres in the Bombay–Pune region between 1830 and 1881. This time-span is important in the emergence of a public sphere in colonial Western India. Initiatives to establish the first native Marathi newspaper, the *Bombay Durpan* in 1832 signified the beginning of the intelligentsia's efforts to disseminate the new discourses among wider audiences and to establish a sphere of critical exchange through the vernacular.

Most studies of colonial culture in India have focused exclusively on the making of a 'high' literary culture. However, colonial Indian intellectuals first tried to explore their 'middling' position within the emerging social structure through their initiatives to establish a newspaper press. Later attempts, from the 1860s, to aestheticise vernacular discourse by creating 'high' modern literary forms were undoubtedly important in enhancing the intelligentsia's hegemonic claims, but they also corresponded with crucial shifts in their self-perception and ideological orientation. By the early 1880s, the upper-caste intelligentsia had renounced even the minimal scope that had existed for them to act as agents for a more egalitarian cultural and social order. In analysing the conditions under which the intelligentsia in Western India was able to achieve a position of ideological influence, this book raises questions about the displacement of the meaning and spaces for hegemonic articulation within colonial modernity.

1

Textual Hierarchies, Literate Audiences and Structures of Patronage

Language and Power in Pre-Colonial Western India

Introduction

One of the important, if indirect, consequences of the orientalist critique of colonial knowledge has been the overdue plea that relations of culture and power before colonialism need to be systematically theorised. This raises theoretical questions about applying modern cognitive frameworks to pre-modern worlds. But the task is imperative if our ideas about pre-colonial cultures and polities are to be rescued from the restrictive, even fanciful, frameworks of nationalist and Indological scholarship. Before elaborating on my main aims, it would be apt to recount some of the main strands within contemporary cultural and political theory.

We now have a fair understanding of how colonial power altered notions of political space, subjectivities and collective identities in South Asia, displacing and appropriating existing notions of authority, self-identity and collective belonging. Despite being criticised by scholars of non-Western nationalisms,[1] Benedict Anderson's idea of imagined communities[2] has acquired wide currency in studies on the

[1]See Partha Chatterjee, *The Nation and its Fragments.*

[2]Benedict Anderson, *Imagined Communities: Reflections on the Origin and Spread of Nationalism*, London, 1991.

making of the political imagination. Anderson's use of the term was specific to the modern context of the emergence of nationalism and national communities. Nevertheless, without undoing his specificity, the idea of a political community as an imaginary construct can be used as a starting point for how boundaries of inclusion and exclusion underlie definitions of community and hierarchies in pre-modern contexts. Alongside Anderson, work on the emergence of modern reading communities and audiences has shown how special uses of language, particularly those valorised as 'literary', along with the production and circulation of printed texts, have formed means of advancing ideas of subjectivity and community.[3] Habermas' influential analysis[4] of the emergence of the bourgeois liberal public sphere in the West has pointed out the connections between communicative practices, literary audiences, and the political public within modernity. Although Habermas' project explored these relations within the history of modern Europe, his work has proved suggestive for the relation between norms of communicative rationality and the distribution of political power in the making of non-Western modernities. To invoke Habermas in a study of pre-modern notions of the literary 'public' may appear to disregard definitive shifts underlying the emergence of *modern* audiences based on notions of publicity. In response, one may point towards recent work[5] that explores state–society relations in pre-

[3]To mention some important titles from the literature on modern book history: Lucien Febvre and Henri-Jean Martin, trans. David Gerard, *The Coming of the Book: The Impact of Printing, 1450–1800,* London, 1976; Roger Chartier, *The Order of Books*, Cambridge, 1994; Roger Chartier, trans. Lydia Cochrane, *Cultural History Between Practices and Representations*, Cambridge, 1990; Robert Darnton, *The Kiss of Lamourette: Reflections in Cultural History*, New York, 1990 and *The Business of the Enlightenment: A Publishing History of the 'Encyclopedie', 1775–1800,* Cambridge, Massachusetts, 1979.

[4]Jurgen Habermas, *The Structural Transformation of the Public Sphere: An Inquiry into a Category of Bourgeois Society,* English edn., Cambridge, Massachusetts, 1989.

[5]I refer here mainly to the currently ongoing work as part of the Chicago project on pre-colonial literary cultures and history of South Asia, some of which was presented in the workshop on 'Literary History, Region and Nation in South Asia' in December 1993 and published in the special issue of *Social Scientist,*

modern South Asia[6] by looking at the links between culture and polity, especially at questions about structures of patronage, the languages of literary expression, and audiences.

Such attempts to explore links between literary languages, the sites of literary composition, and the boundaries demarcating 'cultivated' audiences from political community in pre-modern South Asia provide welcome correctives to interpretations of the pre-colonial past within nationalist narratives.[7] The dominant interpretive paradigms until now have viewed the pre-colonial South Asian literary past and its textual traditions either as evidence of brahmanical dominance or as signs of the overwhelming religiosity of traditional Indic civilisation. More generally, most attempts to theorise the nature of pre-modern state power here have attended to questions of culture only peripherally, perhaps out of a misplaced sense of allegiance to Marxist historiography. They have expended much academic labour on questions such as whether the pre-colonial Indian past showed 'sufficient' signs to 'deserve' the category of feudalism.[8] Deviating from such attempts to plot the pre-colonial past against categories derived from European history, Burton Stein's

---

Vol. 23, Nos. 10-12, Oct.-Dec. 1995. I am grateful to Sheldon Pollock for permission to cite from his recent drafts for the project.

[6]The essentially fuzzy nature of identities before modernity would mean that the state–society distinction can be applied to pre-colonial social formation only imperfectly. Yet, the term is used here in preference to 'indigenous' categories like *'raja'/'praja'* as being more amenable to the analysis of pre-colonial cultural and political hierarchies.

[7]For work that proposes an argument about the need to separate narratives of community from the self-representations of the nation state, see Prasenjit Duara, *Rescuing History from the Nation: Questioning Narratives of Modern China*, Chicago, 1995.

[8]See R.S. Sharma, 'How Feudal was Indian Feudalism?', Hermann Kulke, ed., *The State in India 1000–1700*, Delhi, 1995, pp. 48–85, and Harbans Mukhia, 'Was there a Feudalism in Indian History?', *Journal of Peasant Studies*, Vol. 8, No. 3, 1981, pp. 273–310. For a critical account of the literature on South Asian medieval political structures see also B. Chattopadhyaya, 'Political Process and Structure of Polity in Early Medieval India' in *The Making of Early Medieval India*, Delhi, 1994.

work[9] described the nature of the state in medieval South India as 'segmentary'. This helped to place the question of state power within the context of medieval social formation. However, being mainly interested in assessing the degree of economic integration and coercion displayed by the Chola state, Stein's terminology remained conceptually resistant to questions about the relations between cultural production, literary languages, and pre-colonial state power.

Given the significance of processes that distribute the cultural sphere into 'high' and 'low' realms, it is astonishing that such little exists on the socio-political dimensions of the division of labour between and within languages, even for the colonial period. We know that colonial rule was able to alter textual norms, networks of patronage, and dissemination, and the ways in which natives described and assessed their world. But we know little about the specific ways in which colonial literacy engineered shifts in indigenous textual hierarchies and vernacular forms, and the redefinition of ideas of cultivation, learning and the 'literary'. The introduction of English as part of the colonial literate regime saw it being invested with several 'high' functions: it was the language of an alien government and a new political arrangement. But it also represented the cultural and intellectual repertoire against which the native languages, including the erstwhile 'cultivated' languages like Sanskrit and Persian, were now measured. Elsewhere,[10] I argue how the project of a standardised education policy, especially the introduction of English along with print, led to the reinscription of existing political structures in Western India. However, an analysis of the ways in which the entry of English and print saw a *radical* shift in indigenous textual hierarchies and the nature of literate communities needs to be contextualised within an understanding of these relations in the pre-colonial period.

Although the emergence of a distinct cultural domain and non-coercive modes of power are characteristics of modernity, the links

[9]Burton Stein, 'The Segmentary State: Interim Reflections' in Kulke, *The State in India 1000–1700,* pp. 134–61.

[10]See Veena Naregal, 'English and the Politics of Language: The Emergence of a Public Sphere in Western India 1830–1880' Ph.D. thesis, University of London, 1998.

between textual practice and political power remain a vital condition of the life of civilised societies at all times. The coding of 'high' and 'low' functions of form—what may be termed the linguistic economy of a society—is crucial to the making and distribution of moral and political norms. Languages are invested with the authority to carry out 'high' social functions such as worship, literary cultivation, the pursuit of knowledge, official and political communication, and business or administrative record-keeping. All these represent instances of how culture and power intersect even before modernity. These processes establish the realm of the permissible and the legitimate in the interaction between rulers and ruled, even as they serve to demarcate the 'political' from the realm of 'everyday' life.

It may be argued that to regard textual production as a primary site of pre-modern social contestation is to overemphasise a domain that may not have had such relevance within pre-modern political structures in South Asia. Let it suffice to say that to accept the rationale for the significance of oral histories is, surely, not to refute the power of writing and its role in demarcations of marginality. Importantly, it can be pointed out that the emergence of vernacular polities, from the end of the first millennium onwards,[11] suggests that there did exist

[11]Describing the cultural imperial formation in the first millennium in South Asia as the Sanskrit cosmopolis, Sheldon Pollock has argued that the clear decline of Sanskrit as the language of religious discourse and communication of public-political meanings from roughly 900 CE marked a fundamental and historic shift in the definition of political boundaries through the subcontinent. These developments saw Sanskrit being displaced from its monopolistic status as the trans-regional 'high' language of inscriptional, sacral and literary texts. From around the end of the first millennium, Pollock argues, the local vernacular forms emerged as the chosen language of political and literary expression both within court culture and outside. Poets and dynastic rulers all over South Asia, from the Cholas in the south, the Chalukyas of Vengi, the Yadavas in Maharashtra, and the Rashtrakutas in what is mostly present-day Karnataka, to the North Indian courts of Gwalior and Malwa increasingly exhibited a discernible tendency to forsake the use of Sanskrit and, instead, employ the local vernaculars for inscriptions, epigraphs and courtly/eulogistic verse. See Sheldon Pollock, 'India in the Vernacular Millennium: Literary Culture and Polity 1000–1500' in Shmuel Eisenstadt *et al*, eds, special issue on 'Collective Identities and Political Order', *Daedalus*, Vol. 127, No. 3, 1998 and 'The Sanskrit Cosmopolis, 300–1300:

strong links between the linguistic/ literary past and the political history of South Asia. This is apparent both in the increasing tendency for the vernacular to be used as a medium of courtly/ eulogistic verse, and non-courtly textual idioms such as bhakti.

Evidently then, the making of the textual domain had much to do with the regulation of religious and social practices and the legitimation of political claims and ambitions. I begin by exploring the story of pre-colonial Marathi textuality and literary and literate practices for insights into linguistic hierarchies and the intersections between structures of patronage and political legitimation in Western India before British rule. The literarisation of the vernaculars, which goes back to the early medieval period, shows two main dimensions. Scholars have persuasively argued[12] that the start of the second millennium saw the break-up of the Sanskrit cosmopolis, resulting in the vernacularisation of the South Asian political world and the emergence, alongside, of vernacular textualities. Almost miraculously, during the period 900–1500 CE, throughout South Asia, vernacular cultural production supplanted and displaced Sanskrit's position as the pre-eminent trans-regional language for public-political expression—such as inscriptions and courtly literature. However, not all the emerging vernacular writing was of an official-political nature; the period also saw the growth of a body of devotional verse in the regional languages. Of course, the adoption of localised idioms for literary and political textual functions in the regional courts and the work of the bhakti poets necessarily occurred under the dual normative influences of Sanskrit, Persian and Arabic. The period after the twelfth century saw the emergence of a body of Marathi devotional verse.[13]

Transculturation, Vernacularisation and the Question of Ideology', in Jan Houben, ed., *Ideology and Status of Sanskrit*, Leiden, 1996.

[12]Pollock, 'The Sanskrit Cosmopolis, 300–1300'; Pollock, 'Literary History, Indian History, World History', *Social Scientist.*

[13]Although Dnyaneswar, Namdev, Tukaram and Eknath are names most familiarly associated with Marathi bhakti, in a world of pre-standardised languages they could not have been exclusively 'Marathi poets'. Thus, besides having compositions in regional varieties of Punjabi and Hindi to his credit, Namdev finds mention in the *Gurugranthsahib*. Also, the *mahanubhav* cult apparently

These tendencies towards vernacularisation were in evidence in Marathi writing[14] earlier than was the case with its southern neighbours—Kannada, Telugu and Tamil.

A political culture based in Marathi, seen most clearly from the time of Shivaji in the latter half of the seventeenth century, was the next stage. An important dimension of the emerging vernacular corpus of bhakti compositions had been its social critique. However, the rise of a vernacular polity under Shivaji saw a recession of such overt critical impulses within the vernacular. As is well known, Shivaji's reign coincided with the life of the religious figure of Ramdas. Ramdas' alleged role as Shivaji's guru has been a favourite theme in the ideology of political elites in Maharashtra (including the Shiv Sena, whose name derives from the first Maratha king). For our purposes, Ramdas' actual political significance can be understood somewhat differently from what such accounts suggest. Generally speaking, the links between pre-modern religious and political power were manifest more directly than their arrangement within modern state–society relations. The revivalist strategies, which characterised Shivaji's reign, and his support to Ramdas and other holy men,[15] are examples of this. Yet, Ramdas' inspiration seems to have been quite distinct from the impulses underlying the work of the bhakti poets. His prolific compositions reveal that, by the late seventeenth century, vernacular devotional expression was patently less anti-hierarchical and more inclined to uphold the benefits of institutional structures in the religious and political spheres. Viewed alongside what has been termed the 'royalisation

---

spread to the Punjab region in the seventeenth century. See Shankar Tulpule, *Classical Marathi Literature from the Beginning to AD 1818*, Vol. IX of Jan Gonda, ed., *A History of Indian Literature*, Wiesbaden, 1979, p. 372.

[14]For work on the devotional idioms of bhakti, see especially Guy Deleury, *The Cult of Vithoba*, Poona, 1950; Jayant Lele, ed., *Tradition and Modernity in Bhakti Movements*, Leiden, 1981; R.S. McGregor, *Devotional Literature in South Asia: Proceedings of a Conference held in Wolfson College*, Cambridge, 1992; Charlotte Vaudeville, *Myths, Saints and Legends in Medieval India*, Delhi, 1996.

[15]Although probably aware of Ramdas from earlier on, Shivaji met him around 1672, when he made grants to the Chaphal *math*. It seems Ramdas spent the last years of his life at the royal fort of Sajjangad. See Setu Madhavrao Pagdi, *Chatrapati Shivaji*, Bombay, 1974, p. 50 and p. 91.

of religious practices',[16] these concurrent shifts in vernacular textuality towards the legitimisation of kingly power throw up important questions about the cultural politics of the medieval Deccan. Moreover, from at least the time of Shivaji, varieties of Marathi were increasingly used for purposes of record-keeping, business and political communication. These developments had an impact on 'literary' uses of the vernacular. This raises questions about the equations underlying the pre-colonial political formation, especially the degree of integration between the realms of 'high' and 'low' culture, and elite and popular forms.

Marathi Textuality Until the *Peshwai*: Dissent and Political Legitimation

The origins of Marathi textuality lie amidst the intellectual ferment and political turmoil that marked the last few decades of Yadav rule. The first textual evidences in Marathi date to the closing decade of the thirteenth century, around the time when the Yadav capital of Deogiri was conquered and renamed Daulatabad by the Tughlaqs. These evidences come both in the form of royal epigraphs and inscriptions, and as the compositions of the *mahanubhav* and *varkari* sects that emerged during this time, founded by Chakradhar and Dnyaneswar respectively. The credit for the invention of the cursive *modi* script (which continued to be used in hand-written Marathi documents like private letters long after printed texts became common currency) is apocryphally attributed, to a prominent minister at the Yadav court, Hemadri.[17] Alongside, it is claimed that he composed learned, exegetical treatises, including the *Chaturvarga Chintamani*, a text that attempted to

[16]Indrani Chatterjee and Sumit Guha, 'Slave Queen, Waif Prince: Slavery and Social Capital in the Eighteenth Century', *Indian Economic and Social History Review* (henceforth, *IESHR*), New Delhi, 1999, Vol. 36, No.2, p. 166.

[17]See G.S. Sardesai, *A New History of the Marathas 1606–1707* (henceforth, *NHM*), Bombay, 1946, p. 23, and V.K. Bhave, *Maharashtra Sarasvat* (henceforth, *MS*), Pune, 1954, pp. 48–9. Like many brahmanical accounts, Bhave's too is prone to exaggerate the contribution of powerful upper-caste personages to the historical record and therefore deserves to be used with caution.

establish an orthodox code of vows, charities and pilgrimages, in keeping with the prescriptions of the *Dharmasastras.* Whatever the extent of Hemadri's erudition, his simultaneous connection with the deity worshipped by the *varkari* sect, Vithoba, evident through the inscription on the foundation stone on the temple at Pandharpur, is certainly significant.[18] The concurrent association of Hemadri's name with an orthodox text and as a patron of the deity of the emerging radical *varkari* tradition speaks of latent complex tensions of political legitimation. For, clearly, doctrinal ideas such as those espoused in the *Chaturvarga Chintamani* were the main target of the unorthodox teachings of the founder of *varkari* practices, Dnyaneswar. These apparent early links between the ruling classes, new devotional orders and the emerging vernacular literacy point to significant intersections between the domains of textuality and political authority. This trend of royal lineages extending patronage to popular deities continued through the precolonial period, indicating that relations between the ruling elite and emerging dissenting devotional practices were more complex than can be defined simply by antagonism.

While conceding that a generally understood, standard form of the vernacular was an impossibility before print, it seems that by Chakradhar's time it is possible to identify a 'core' Marathi speaking area.[19] However, many questions regarding the *mahanubhav* sect and its practices, especially its hostility towards other dissenting sects and its links with political authority, remain unresolved. Despite their own strong iconoclastic views, it is not entirely clear why the *mahanubhav* sect remained hostile to the *varkari sampradaya.* Or why, despite Chakradhar's own anti-Sanskrit stance and the considerable following for the *mahanubhav* creed, including a widespread network of *mathas,*

[18]V.K. Bhave, *MS*, p. 48. For a detailed history of the cult of Vitthala and the Pandharpur temple, see G.A. Deleury, *The Cult of Vithoba.*

[19]Chakradhar's writings contain a minute record of his journeys, which help in estimating the approximate boundaries of the Marathi-speaking medieval world, as the limits of the area he covered apparently correspond quite closely with places where Marathi inscriptions have been found. See M.G. Panse's essay, 'Regional Individuality of Marathi' in V.K. Bava, ed., Aspects of Deccan History, Report of Seminar held in Hyderabad, 1975, pp. 139–40, quoted in Stewart Gordon, *Marathas, Marauders and State Formation*, Delhi, 1994, pp. 192–3.

subsequent *mahanubhav* religious poetry and philosophical treatises were encoded in secret scripts which have been deciphered to reveal a highly Sanskritised idiom.[20] It seems reasonable to propose that, despite their use in the public–political domain, pre-colonial vernacular forms existed precariously in the shadow of Sanskrit, forever haunted by the possibility of being reappropriated into the fold of 'high' textual traditions. Similarly, one can surmise from the Hemadri legends that the rise of vernacular textuality was mediated by the 'high' textual traditions of Sanskrit. Mediated powerfully by norms of Sanskrit textuality, the intelligibility of the new medieval vernacular literacy was likely to correspond with the literacy limits of existing audiences.[21] This would seem to corroborate Pollock's point that the work of vernacularisation was not necessarily a subaltern process, but actually represented attempts by political elites to re-articulate their authority in localised idioms.[22]

These arguments are important in assessing the political impact of bhakti and its opposition to the authority of 'high' scriptural traditions. Scholars have pointed out that the general shift towards vernacularisation and the textual tradition of bhakti owed much to the relativising impact

[20]See V. B. Kolte, *Mahanubhav Samshodhan*, Vol. 1, Malkapur, 1960, esp. pp. 79–81.

[21]It is worth asking to what extent the bhakti poets might have been familiar with Sanskrit reading and recitation. The stories about Eknath indicate that he had an erudite and rigorous understanding of the Sanskrit tradition. Although his learned commentary on the *Bhagavata* in Marathi challenged brahmanical codes, apparently Eknath was able to more than hold his own while defending his 'translation' before the Varanasi brahmins. Claiming not to be a deviant, he justified his writing in the vernacular as a popularisation of the high religious texts. The precarious ambivalence of such claims is underlined when placed against the fact that Eknath's son and later his grandson, Mukteshwar, rejected the importance of using non-elite idioms; Mukteshwar's own rendering of the Mahabharata stories are highly influenced by Sanskrit.

[22]Pollock, 'Literary History, Indian History, World History' in *Social Scientist*, p. 131. This pattern was reiterated during the second phase of vernacularisation in the nineteenth century, when the emergence of a colonial-modern vernacular literacy was primarily impelled by the desire of ruling elites to re-create the 'high' discourses in local idioms, rather than the need of 'organic' intellectuals to reach a popular audience.

of intellectual forces like the sufi influence that entered the Deccan with Turkish rulers. The idioms of these texts show the influence of Persian and Arabic.[23] In Maharashtra, the main practitioners of bhakti verse lived between the thirteenth and the seventeenth centuries and came from an array of ordinary backgrounds. Born into a *shimpi* (tailor's) family, Namdev (1270–1350) celebrated his devotion to Vitthala of Pandharpur through his compositions. Dnyaneswar apparently lived between 1250–1350 and his contemporaries included Visoba Khecara, a staunch *saivite bhakta*; Gora, a potter; Narahari, a goldsmith; Chokhamela, an untouchable; Joga, a *teli* (oilman); Kanhuputra, a dancing girl.[24] The best known among saint-preachers of the second phase of Marathi bhakti was Eknath (*c.* 1533–99), who apparently composed his *Bhagavata* in Paithan and Banaras between 1570 and 1573, besides his *Bhavartha-Ramayana* and the shorter *bharudas*.[25] Similarly, Tukaram (*c.*1598–1649) came from a low-caste family from Dehu near Pune. Apart from the fact that their dissenting sects attracted the attention of powerful nobles—either by way of donations for the building of temples or by inviting their violent wrath—little is known about the structures of patronage extended to

[23]G.S. Sardesai notes a greater lexical influence of Persian and Arabic in the work of Eknath than in the idiom of *Dynaneshwari*, composed about two centuries earlier. See his *NHM*, p. 33.

The presence of linguistic influence may not be a sufficient indication of deep cultural influence. Scholars have argued that despite the emergence of syncretic devotional idioms like the bhakti compositions and a composite culture, especially among political elites during the Mughal period, there remained deep lines of division between Hindus and Muslims in pre-colonial South Asia. While accepting these arguments, it may be generally acknowledged that the coming of the Islamic ruler lineages represented an important relativising force that precipitated the need for political/religious elites and ordinary people to rearticulate their world-views in face of new circumstances.

[24]For more details see A.N. Deshpande, *Prachin Marathi Vangmayacha Itihaas,* Vol. 2, Poona, 1966, p. 115 and L.R. Pangarkar, *Marathi Vangmayacha Itihaas,* Vol. 1, Nasik and Poona, 1932, p. 623.

[25]The *bharuda* was a shorter verse-form with much realistic detail. Hindus, Turks and *mahars* figured as major characters in Eknath's *bharudas*, which give vital insights into contemporary social structures and interaction. See Tulpule, *Classical Marathi Literature,* p. 357.

the performance and dissemination of these texts from royal or mercantile quarters during this period. Legends even attribute the end of Yadav rule to Hemadri's opposition to Chakradhar. Be that as it may, it appears true that Hemadri had Chakradhar killed in the year 1272 because of the threat posed by the latter's teachings.[26] Evidence also shows that the deliberate assertion of the equality of the vernacular with Sanskrit often led to the persecution of the bhakti poets at the hands of the custodians of religious orthodoxy.[27] Unlike the later *ramdasi sampradaya, varkari* bhakti gained a substantial following. Thus, in voicing the devotional aspirations of ordinary people, the bhakti tradition expostulated against social hierarchy, especially that practised under the sanction of institutionalised, dominant religious beliefs. In doing this it defied Sanskrit's monopoly in interpreting and ordering the world and articulated ideas of the equality of all *bhaktas* in a limited way.[28] Through their use and defence of the vernacular for devotional practice, these texts raised the possibility of a laicised religious faith.[29]

However, we need to be careful when theorising the exact nature of the challenge to hierarchy and scriptural exclusivity in the bhakti corpus. In applying categories derived from the European Reformation

[26]G.S. Sardesai, *NHM,* p. 23.

[27]Among the most frequently mentioned episodes of the opposition the *sant kavis* faced from brahmins is the story of Tukaram's confrontation with the learned brahmin, Rameshwarbhat, of Vagholi. Legend has it that, greatly irked by the *sudra* poet's great popularity, Rameshwarbhat had orders issued for Tukaram to leave the village. Thus tormented, Tukaram is said to have flung the entire *pothi* containing his *abhangs* into the Indrayani river, from where they apparently resurfaced miraculously. See Bhave, *MS*, p. 373.

[28]See Kumkum Sangari, 'Mirabai and the Spiritual Economy of Bhakti', *Economic and Political Weekly,* Vol. 25, Nos. 27 and 28, July 7 &14, 1990.

[29]While defending his rendering of the *Bhagavatpurana* into the 'lowly' Prakrit in the following way: 'In the richness of the regional language, things in the world get different names, but the names of Rama and Krishna do not change ... with such blessings have I described the *Bhagavatpurana* in Prakrit in all its true, pure and intended meaning. Learned people may enjoy the various works in Sanskrit / A cow may be dark or brown, and yet the milk has no better taste.' Quoted in Madhav Deshpande, *Sociolinguistic Attitudes in India*, Ann Arbor, 1979, p. 74.

to this body of South Asian vernacular devotional texts, one must avoid a naive historicism of the kind that characterises their representation within nationalist narratives. Of this, Ranade's account of the Marathi saint poets is a good example. Writing under the dual pressures of Eurocentric historicism and the demands of constructing a nationalist ideology, Ranade conceptualises the significance of the bhakti corpus in the image of the impact of the European Reformation:

> The struggle between claims of the classical Sanskrit and the vernaculars of which we hear so much these days is thus an old conflict, the issues in which were decided in favour of the vernaculars or living languages long ago and whatever scholars and antiquarians may urge to the contrary, there can only be one answer to the question—the answer which was given by the saints and prophets when they laid Sanskrit aside as useless for their work, and spent all their energies in the cultivation and growth of their mother tongue. It may safely be said that the growth of the modern vernaculars in India is solely the result of the labours of these saints and the provinces, which showed the most decided tendencies in the way of reform ...[30]

Ranade's purpose was not to foreground the cultural politics underlying the bhakti tradition; rather, it was an attempt to construct the antecedents of Marathi literature in such a way that the vexing challenges confronting the vernacular sphere, especially with regard to issues of democratisation, were seen as the 'well-settled' questions of a distant past. Using colonial assumptions of the essentially 'apolitical' and religious character of South Asian society, this paradigm views the emergence of vernacular textuality as primarily impelled by religious imperatives; it ignores the other important evidence, namely epigraphs, inscriptions and vernacular texts authorised by ruling powers. Bhakti texts represented one dimension of the shift towards vernacularisation. They were only part of the larger story of the intersections between Sanskrit–vernacular hierarchy and strategies of political legitimation. Deviating from such derivative logic, therefore, what we need are accounts that theorise the *difference* between these

[30]M.G. Ranade, *The Rise of Maratha Power*, Bombay, 1900, p. 161.

analogous processes of vernacularisation in South Asia and early modern Europe.

It would be worth asking if vernacularisation in South Asia led to a redistribution of the sites of textual production, networks of dissemination, and a redefinition of prevailing aesthetic and intellectual norms grounded in the authority of Sanskrit. To what extent did the bhakti tradition lead to a re-distribution of cultural and political power? The fact that many of these saint-preachers, who sang their faith in the languages of everyday life, came from humble, artisanal backgrounds is not sufficient reason to infer that vernacularisation resulted in a drastic widening of the literate base, or in a redefinition of the meanings of literacy and cultivation.[31] Despite their wide following and influence on the popular imagination, these medieval devotional texts did not enunciate any explicit challenge to existing structures of authority, and processes of vernacularisation in medieval South Asia did not result in a radical alteration of the structure of state–society relations or the place of religious knowledge within it. Even if the emergence of vernacular textuality corresponded with shifts in the boundaries of literate and political communities, these changes did not redefine the structures of pre-modern cultural production and their relation with political power. What needs to be ascertained is whether the vernacular textual traditions elaborate upon their tacit opposition to the esoteric status of Sanskrit. In fact, despite its relative disuse, political elites were able to effectively invoke the normative influence of Sanskrit right up to the Peshwa period. The dissemination of devotional compositions through performance and recitation did, however, create a lasting impact on popular beliefs and practices and opened the possibilities for forging ideological and cultural links between elite and non-elite discourses.

As Maratha power consolidated itself in the Deccan, it needed ways of accommodating itself to local cultural practices and belief-systems. Stewart Gordon has argued[32] that the emerging Maratha political–military elite created a space for itself by foregrounding signs of their

[31]See fn. 22.

[32]Stewart Gordon in 'Zones of Military Entrepreneurship 1500–1700', in *Marathas, Marauders and State Formation,* p. 193.

links with the dress and life-style of rural communities rather than by symbolically identifying with the courts of the Deccani sultanates. But, in addition to embedding itself in local practices and emphasising regional cultural bonds, the new monarchy also needed to signal its superiority through a display of its 'cultivation', authority and claims to righteousness. Shivaji's patronage to the 'Maharashtrian' brahmins living in Banaras, one of whom, Gagabhatta, was expressly summoned to devise an innovative coronation ceremony,[33] can be understood in this context. It is also thought that Shivaji patronised the compilation of an influential critical edition of the *Mahabharata* in Sanskrit by another brahmin, Nilakantha Chaturdhara, living in Banaras in the last quarter of the seventeenth century.[34] Similarly, he commissioned the *Rajvyavaharkosh*, a dictionary of administrative terms in a deliberately Sanskritised Marathi idiom,[35] besides following a policy of extending state patronage to holy men, places of worship, popular shrines and local festivals and celebrations. Alongside attempts to maintain centralised control over his territory through a policy of cash rewards and gifts, rather than through the granting of hereditary fiefs,[36] these strategies helped Shivaji present himself as a righteous and orthodox monarch with a deep regard for ancient texts.

Significantly, these revivalist strategies of legitimation under the first Maratha ruler coincided with important shifts in the vernacular textual domain. Besides Ramdas, Shivaji's reign coincided with the life of Tukaram, the last famous practitioner of the important variety of medieval metaphysical verse, *varkari* bhakti. Despite the continuing appeal of the bhakti tradition, the fact that there were few major successors to Tukaram suggests that, at this time, conditions were not fertile for its reinvention as the idiom of social and religious dissent.

[33]For an account of Shivaji's coronation and his attempts to claim a 'true' Kshatriya lineage through the special rituals devised by Gagabhatta for the occasion, see G. S. Sardesai, *NHM*, p. 209.

[34]Sheldon Pollock, draft entitled, 'The Death of Sanskrit in Four Movements', (ms.): see fn. 5.

[35]See Madhav Deshpande, *Sociolinguistic Attitudes in India*, p. 79.

[36]H. Fukazawa, *The Medieval Deccan: Peasants, Social Systems and States*, Delhi, 1991.

If the radical idiom of bhakti had emerged through the stimulus of the sufi and other Islamic orders, it was not surprising that the tradition lost some of its potency as the 'neo-Hindu' Maratha kingdom consolidated itself as a regional power. The decline of bhakti needs to be seen alongside shifts discernible in the linkages between patterns of patronage and dominant emphases within the vernacular domain. Shivaji's policy of giving grants to holy and religious establishments was, in itself, not new.[37] Yet the stress on the close links between spiritual discipline, religious authority and political power in the best-known vernacular devotional text of the period, Ramdas' *Dasbodh*, tells of a religious and political pragmatism quite at variance with the inspiration of the bhakti poets. In making this point, my aim is not to reiterate the claims that brahmanical sources often make for the unique status of Ramdas or the *ramdasi mathas* during Shivaji's rule.[38] Rather, it is to emphasise visible mutations in vernacular devotional composition and shifts in the relation between religious expression and political power. That the rise of a Maratha polity coincided with a blunting of the subversive edge of Marathi bhakti verse suggests that new equations between political legitimation, modes of worship, and vernacular forms were being established.

Tracing the development of pre-colonial Marathi textual forms further, we see that, unlike within adjacent languages like Kannada and Telugu, the emergence of a courtly verse tradition in Marathi was most strongly visible only after the rise of Peshwa power, many years after Marathi was first used for devotional composition. These developments (analysed later) show that the inability of the pre-colonial vernacular sphere to shake off the normative influence of Sanskrit led to an impasse: the authority of Sanskrit was perpetuated, despite its stagnation. The

[37]See fn. 15 above.

[38]Apparently, Ramdas travelled extensively to preach his faith, and very soon the sect established an extensive network of *mathas* in many parts of the Maratha country, even in the Tanjore region. See G.S. Sardesai, *NHM*, p. 269. The *ramdasi mathas* trained disciples in the guru's preachings, copying of the central texts of the *sampradaya* was also undertaken; versions of the *Dasbodh* in Tamil and Thanjavuri Marathi were also produced. See Setu Madhavrao Pagdi, *Shri Samrath ani Samarth Sampradaya*, Bombay, 1985, p. 257.

rich archival resources available for the eighteenth-century Deccan show direct evidence allowing us to trace the circulation and exchange of manuscripts among Peshwa *sardars*. Their manuscript collections, their intercourse with religious and *puranic* texts (through a combination of reading and listening), as well as their familiarity with existing discourses on statecraft and other subjects of a less directly political nature— all these are available as data. This data needs to be placed along with data on new performative genres like *lavani,* and on shifts in older, popular oral narrative forms like *povadas* and *kirtans*—on account of the emerging structures of elite patronage and networks of dissemination for both these expressive forms. Collectively, these materials indicate an expansion in the repertoire and patronage of vernacular performative textual forms. Paradoxically, the evidence for the circulation and reproduction of texts in *written* form, suggests that Sanskrit texts comprises a large majority of the works commissioned for copying.

Literate and Literary Practices in the Peshwa Period

After Shivaji, under the Peshwas in the eighteenth century, Maratha power made substantial inroads into areas that had been under Mughal dominion. The reign of Shivaji's grandson, Shahu, marked a transition where effective control over the Maratha kingdom shifted into the hands of his chief minister, the Peshwa Balaji Vishwanath Bhat, and eventually to the latter's descendants. Balaji's son, Bajirao I, shifted the capital to Pune and ruled as Peshwa during the years 1720–40. These political shifts were accompanied by wider changes in economic activity. As Stewart Gordon has argued,[39] the displacement of Mughal influence over parts of central and western India saw a shift in the revenue and credit flows; these moved away from northern financial centres like Agra towards Pune, and even Bombay. The increased scale of military activity in the Peshwa period required an expanded resource base beyond what land revenue and predatory raids could mobilise. As Sumit Guha's work has shown, the evidence for the period 1740–

[39]Stewart Gordon, 'The Slow Conquest: Administrative Integration of Malwa into the Marathi Empire', in *Marathas, Marauders and State Formation*, p. 61.

1820 suggests that realising the political benefits from an increase in trading activity, the Maratha *sardars* and the Peshwas began to offer favourable incentives for merchants and craftsmen to set up *peths* in the areas under their dominion. These increases in commodity circulation and credit flows opened new reciprocal ties between village and urban centres.[40] The military and economic expansion saw 'Maharashtrian' brahmin families gain a prominent presence in all segments of the state structure, including the military and local administration, as well as in the commercial and banking professions. Simultaneously, Fukazawa's work[41] has shown the limited but decisive influence that the pre-colonial Maratha state was able to exert in the regulation of social rank, especially in the case of claims to a higher-caste status. Its influence on the prescription of social practices according to caste status, as well as in the extraction of forced labour within bounds of propriety ('*shisthapramanen*', as the officials records put it), has also been shown. Seen along with the evidence for the emergence of a limited but definite sphere of economic activity independent of the state,[42] this brahmanical consolidation in the eighteenth century contained tendencies towards a more centralised organisation of the resource base and power structure, which had important implications for structures of religious and cultural patronage.

The decline of the Mughal empire and the rise of smaller regional kingdoms perpetually seeking to expand their territorial and revenue bases created new problems of political legitimation at this time. One outcome of the expansion of commercial networks and the rise of new rulers was a heightened dependence of the political elite on blessed men and brahmins. Often the recipients of regular and substantial gifts in cash and kind, such figures established themselves as powerful

[40]Sumit Guha, 'Potentates, Traders and Peasants: Western India c.1700–1870', *Occasional Papers on History and Society*, Second Series Number LVIII, Nehru Memorial Museum and Library, New Delhi.

[41]H. Fukazawa, especially, 'The State and Caste System', *The Medieval Deccan*, pp. 91–113.

[42]See Sumit Guha, 'Potentates, Traders and Peasants' and Stewart Gordon, 'Burhanpore: Entrepot and Hinterland 1650–1750' in *Marathas, Marauders and State Formation*, pp. 162–81.

sources of influence who commanded the following of many members of the royal family and important *sardars*. In at least a few cases, this brought them opportunities to accumulate significant wealth. This was a long way from the image of religious and spiritual leadership that the makers of bhakti verse had aspired for. The Peshwa period bears out this development quite well. Wealthy religious figures with a personal stake in the fortunes of the ruling elite, and the regular practice of spending goodly amounts on charities to brahmins as part of the *shraavan dakshina*,[43] both exist. Comparable trends have been noted for other parts of the subcontinent: work on Rajasthan, Banaras and north India in the eighteenth century has documented the emergence of powerful monastic orders that combined impressive religious, trade and military prowess.[44] In Maharashtra, the career of Brahmendra Swami[45] corresponded most closely with these trends. He was consulted by many important personages, including King Shahu,[46] the

[43]For estimates of the expenditure on the annual *shraavan dakshina* for the years 1736–1801, see P.A. Gavli, *Peshvekalina Gulamgiri va Asprishyata*, 3rd edn., Kolhapur, 1990, pp. 64–5. During this period, the highest amount given away was an impressive 18,00,000 rupees in 1758. These charities were in addition to smaller amounts given away regularly at festivals and other auspicious occasions, as a way of increasing one's spiritual worth.

[44]See D.H.A Kolff, 'Sanyasi Trader-Soldiers', *IESHR*, Vol. 8, No. 2, 1971, pp. 213–18; C.A. Bayly, *Rulers, Townsmen and Bazaars: North Indian Society in the Age of British Expansion, 1770–1830*, Cambridge, 1983; and more recently, William Pinch, *Peasants and Monks in British India*, reprint, Delhi, 1996.

[45]Brahmendra apparently hailed from Konkan and came to live near Dhavadshi near Satara around 1727–28, not long after Balaji Vishwanath established himself as the Peshwa. For a biographical account, that sometimes borders on the disingenuous, see the introduction to an otherwise impressive selection of the Swami's correspondence, D.B. Parasnis, comp. and ed., *Shri Mahapurusha Brahmendraswami Yanche Patravyvahraa* (henceforth, *SMBP)*, Bombay, 1900. Additional primary sources about the Swami's activities are contained in V.K. Rajawade, comp. and ed., *Marathyanchya Itihasanchi Sadhanen*, Vol. 3, Kolhapur, 1901.

[46]See Introduction, D.B. Parasnis, *SMBP*, p. 93; also for Shahu's personal assurance to Brahmendra Swami that the latter would henceforth not be harassed for dues by state officials in Dhavadshi, see G.S. Sardesai, comp. and ed., *Selections from the Peshwa Daftar* (henceforth, *SPD*), Vol. 18, Bombay, 1931–4, pp. 12–13.

Peshwas,[47] important women linked to the ruling elite,[48] *sardars* and others ambitious to make their mark at court. The Swami had a reputation of being a demanding and hard-to-please guru, whose letters are replete with frequent requests for all manner of gifts, ranging from fine fabrics, cash, items of luxurious consumption, mount-horses, milch cows,[49] and even guns that he collected to give away as blessings to *sardars*.[50] An extremely wealthy man who was in a position to advance significant loans even to the Peshwa,[51] the Swami apparently followed a lifestyle reminiscent of contemporary Indian god-men.

This extension of economic activity and the shifts in the nature of the ties between the political elite and the religious establishment in the midst of political expansion coincided with important changes within the cultural sphere. Despite the support to holy men and Sanskrit scholars, Shivaji's reign was characterised by significant patronage for vernacular 'literary' composition. There do exist verse compositions with an explicitly public–political function such as the *prasastis*, which sing Shivaji's praises as a dutiful, righteous 'Hindu' king; and some historical ballads or *bakhars* dating back to this period.[52] However, it seems royal patronage was mostly extended to the composition of treatises on 'non-aesthetic' subjects like statecraft, administration and

[47]See letters from the Peshwa Bajirao Ballal to the Swami in D.B. Parasnis, *SMBP*, pp. 20–57; Balaji Bajirao, the next Peshwa, was far less amenable to Brahmendra's demands, see ibid., pp. 170–3.

[48]For letters from Shahu's queens, including one requesting total confidentiality and another from the important Virubai, see ibid., pp. 8–10.

[49]See Introduction, D.B. Parasnis, *SMBP*, p. 101; Brahmendra Swami's letter to Chimajiappa in G.S. Sardesai, *SPD*, Vol. 18, pp. 13–14; for another letter, see D.B. Parasnis, *SMBP*, p. 15.

[50]See Introduction, D.B. Parasnis, *SMBP*, p. 98; also in the same volume, one such request made by Yashwant Pawar for a cannon, ibid., p. 198.

[51]Brahmendra demanded back a sum of 3,500 rupees that the Peshwa had borrowed from him, see G.S. Sardesai, *SPD*, Vol. 18, p. 13; similarly, the Swami's name occurs twice, against sums of 5000 and 1,00,000 rupees, respectively, in the list of persons from whom the Peshwa government had borrowed in the year 1741–42, see G.C. Vad, comp. and ed., *Selections from the Satara Raja's and Peshwa Diaries* (henceforth, *SSRPD*), Bombay, Part 2, Vol. 2, 1906, pp. 171–2.

[52]G.S. Sardesai, *NHM*, p. 29.

ethics. Gagabhatta's *Kayastha Vyavhardeepika*, or his *Rajvyavaharkosh* mentioned above, or the *Ajnapatra* commissioned a little later, during the time of Sambhaji II, are the outstanding examples.

With the rise of Peshwa power, some clear shifts are visible. With the collection of revenue from far-flung areas being so crucial to the political structure of the Maratha state, it was difficult to sustain Shivaji's attempts at introducing a heavily Sanskritised idiom as the language of administration and official communication. Muzaffar Alam has shown[53] that the period of Mughal rule had seen the assiduous cultivation of Persian as a supra-regional language for maintaining records even at the village level throughout the empire, and even in places far from the imperial capital of Delhi. With brahmins and other literate castes readily taking to the study of Persian texts to make the most of these employment opportunities, firstly in the Sultanate and then in the Mughal bureaucracy, knowledge of Persian had become an important skill in the repertoire of both the cultivated classes and the political elite throughout central India and many parts of the Deccan. This affected the linguistic economy of the eighteenth-century Deccan in complex ways. The influence of Persian and Arabic on the language for important, non-esoteric activities like trade, land revenue and official communications increased. A Persianised Hindustani was the medium of formal exchange among the political elite, as seen in the conversation between Madhavrao and the v*akil* representing the English during Malet's first visit to the Peshwa court in March 1786.[54] Alongside, the

[53]Muzaffar Alam, 'The Pursuit of Persian: Language in Mughal Politics', *Modern Asian Studies*, Vol. 32, No.2, 1998, pp. 317–50.

[54]See account of the Malet–Madhavrao *darbar* quoted from D.B. Parasnis, *Itihaas Sangraha* in V.K. Bhave *Peshwekalin Maharashtra,* (henceforth, *PM*), Delhi, 1976, pp. 274–5. Also, Thomas Broughton, who spent considerable time as a Major in the Company Army in Bengal and was known as the author of a set of letters he wrote from a Mahratta camp, wrote that Hindustani was used in army life throughout the subcontinent. He observed 'With this language few of our Hindoo *sipahees* are conversant when they quit their native villages ... but throughout their lives, they generally acquire more of it.' See Thomas Broughton, 'Preface' to *Selections from the Popular Poetry of the Hindoos*, London, 1814.

The Bombay Regulations of 1827, passed under Elphinstone's governorship, changed the language to be used in the courts from Persian to Marathi and

expansion of Maratha power created a demand for the refinement of the regional vernacular, the mother tongue of the ruling elite. These pressures resulted in a greater internal differentiation within vernacular usage; for example, it seems that a less-Persianised vernacular idiom that was closer to *puneri* Marathi was in use for purposes of internal communication amongst members of the Peshwa household, or among the women.[55] By the end of the eighteenth century this variety of Marathi had gained considerable currency as the language of semi-official communication. Letters in the *puneri* idiom were being exchanged through a vast area extending from Banaras to Tanjore, including those addressed to Tipu Sultan and the Rajputs.[56] These adjustments in the relations between the high languages of Sanskrit and Persian, and the textualised varieties of Marathi, also had an impact on cultural forms and genres that found favour with the Maratha elite. Thus, there was a strong influence of North Indian cultural forms, especially in the styles of music, dance[57] and painting[58] that were fashionable in the courts of the eighteenth-century Maratha aristocracy. Alongside, there were sustained attempts to develop a classicised vernacular idiom, most visible

Gujarati, until court business, especially at the higher levels, was eventually made over to English.

[55]There is some evidence of letters from elders or guardians within the Peshwa household containing advice on matters pertaining to education and training of younger members, or the letters written on behalf of the women in the Peshwa family. While appropriate formal conventions were used, their language reveals the use of a less Persianised idiom closer to spoken Marathi. See V.K. Bhave, Chapters on '*Shikshanpadhati*' and '*Granthsangraha va Granthvaachan*' in *PM*, pp. 45–86.

[56]Deshpande, *Sociolinguistic Attitudes,* p. 81.

[57]See the letter informing that, in compliance with a previous order, two excellent troupes from Delhi had been procured at considerable expense, in G.S. Sardesai, *SPD*, Vol. 18, p. 37. Besides, dance and music being an essential part of celebrations and regular entertainment at the Maratha courts, several records allude to the demand for well-trained dancing girls.

[58]A letter dated 22 February 1783 from Nana Phadnis shows the taste for portrait painting in the Mughal style among the Peshwa elite. Nana himself seems to have been well aware of prominent portrait artists in Delhi, who had apparently moved away to Lucknow after the decline of Mughal power. See G.S. Sardesai, ed., *Aithihasik Patrabodh Marathshahitil Nivadak Patra 1596–1819*, Pune, 1939, pp. 111–12.

in the work of the *pandit kavis* patronised by elite families. The *peshwai* elite showed interest in the collection and reproduction of Sanskrit manuscripts, which no doubt encouraged the emergence of new genres and influenced tendencies towards the hierarchisation of vernacular forms.

There is some evidence enabling us to reconstruct the reading habits and modes of circulation of manuscripts and *pothis* among the political elite of the Peshwa period. These are mostly in the nature of letters exchanged between members of the ruling elite seeking a loan of certain *pothis*, or acknowledgements for the receipt of some previous request. It seems that the copying and collection of manuscript-books began to be encouraged during the time of Shivaji's grandson Shahumaharaj (1682–1749). Some of the Peshwas and their *sardars* took an interest in building up individual collections through commissioning copies of manuscripts. There are details of a scribal workshop (*pustakanchya kaarkhana*) maintained at one of the Peshwa palaces at Anandvalli, at a monthly cost of thirty-one rupees.[59] Other elite families frequently patronised the copying of manuscripts, either employing scribes or *lekhaks*, or buying books from copyists who worked independently. The prominent bankers, the Tulshibaagwale family of Pune, was one such; family records for the period 1760–1833 contain many references to patronage of literate practices.[60] Frequently, the copies commissioned were 'core' Hindu texts like the *Rigveda* or the *Gita*, other philosophical or exegetical commentaries like *Vijnaneshwargranth* or *Dnyanyoga*, or the popular epic *Mahabharat*—either in its entirety, or in parts.[61] In 1813 copies of the classical Sanskrit plays *Shakuntala* and *Mudrarakshas* were ordered;[62] occasionally, vernacular texts like the *Dnynaneshwari* or a *prakrit* text like the *Prabodhsudhakar* were requested. Although many of the texts copied were in Sanskrit, frequently, the names of the employed scribes identified them according to their linguistic background, suggesting that at least some importance was attached to regional linguistic identities.[63]

[59]See Bapu Purshottam Joshi, ed., *SSPRD*, Part 7, Vol. II, Pune, 1911, p. 327.

[60]N.G. Chapekar, ed., *Peshwaichya Sawleent*, Pune, 1877, pp. 176–80.

[61]Ibid., pp. 177–9.

[62]Ibid., p. 179.

[63]For instance, a Govindbhat Gujarati was commissioned to copy the

Ready *pothis* could be procured, but most often scribes were hired against fixed sums on an occasional basis, or sometimes on a more regular, monthly or, even, annual basis.[64] For instance, in 1760 Keshambhat Laturkar was paid 54 rupees for copying out an unnamed text that ran into 18000 verses; in 1765 Appanna bin Tammanna from Pandharpur was paid at an annual rate of 100 rupees towards his labour and the cost of paper; in 1772 a scribe, Krishna Joshi, was paid a sum of 515 rupees and fifteen annas.[65] Whatever the nature of the agreement, the rates were almost always fixed as charges per thousand verses, ranging from a little under two rupees to four rupees. An average price of two rupees and eight annas appears to have been quite common.[66] Sometimes the number of copied pages was also mentioned, but more as a way of checking the size of the manuscript lent out to the scribe. Records suggest that this activity would have followed a seasonal pattern, where the copying of some texts coincided with the timetable for recitation of religious narratives and prayers during certain 'holy' months of the Hindu calendar.

Interestingly, one of the families that gained prominence through their initiatives to establish a new *peth* on the family property in the Pune district, the Jadhavs,[67] also took an active interest in the procurement and collection of manuscripts. When Bajirao I wished to acquire parts of the *Ramayana*, the person he asked was Piloji Jadhav, who apparently supplied the requested manuscripts.[68] Then again, when Bajirao's mother Radhabai wanted manuscripts read out to her, Piloji's brother Sambhaji Jadhav was the person to whom she addressed

Yogavasistha and the *Dnyanyaogakhannd* in 1779; or in 1782, a Shankar Gujarati copied 8000 verses from the *Mahabharat*; see ibid.

[64]A copy of the *Panchprasar* was apparently bought for twenty-five rupees, see ibid.

[65]Ibid., pp. 177–8.

[66]3000 verses of the *Madhyasiddhanthkaumudi* were commissioned at the rate of one rupee and fourteen annas; 750 verses of *prakrit* text at a rate of two rupees; 10500 verses of the *Vijnaneshwar* at two rupees and eight annas; 140000 verses of the *Panchprasar* were copied at three rupees per thousand; 1700 verses of the *Rudrapaddhat* at the rate of four rupees. See ibid., pp. 177–80.

[67]See Sumit Guha, 'Potentates, Traders and Peasants', p. 4.

[68]See G.S. Sardesai, *SPD*, Vol. 19, p. 37.

her request. He obliged quite promptly.[69] Frequently, manuscripts could not be despatched in their entirety, both when lent for reading or when sent out to the scribal workshop to be copied.[70] In his reply to Radhabai, Sambhaji Jadhav acknowledged receipt of sections of the book (*adiparv pustak*) that were being returned, adding that he would be sending out the following sections in the next fortnight, which then ought to be returned only after they had been *listened* to at leisure. He also assured her that, should any further parts be required, her instructions would be heeded immediately. Rather than indicating the building of extensive private collections, these exchanges suggest attempts to share scarce resources. This is also borne out by instances of requests from even the Peshwa being turned down, as the manuscript asked for was not traceable on account of it being already on loan.[71] Equally, books could be procured from some distance, though most often copies were requested from scribes in one of the well-known centres for brahmanical learning such as Wai or Pandharpur. However, sometimes, richly crafted *pothis* were ordered from as far as Rajasthan.[72] Neither was it unusual to have requests for loans of *pothis* from *sardars* out on a military campaign, indicating that at least in elite circles the practice of performative reading and listening as an edifying and/or recreational activity was quite common. Often brahmins, *shastris*, *puraniks* and even *bhikshuks* travelled with the camp, with evenings and the intervals between battles devoted to the conduct of regular

[69]See ibid., Vol. 18, p. 45.

[70]A copy of the *Padmapurana* had been commissioned at Nanasaheb's behest but some confusion seems to have arisen about parts of the text and the exact number of pages lent out, whereupon one of the important clerks, Anataji Narayan, was asked to clarify, see ibid., p. 47.

[71]When Nanasaheb Peshwa wrote to one of his *sardars*, Naro Shankar stationed at Nasik, asking for a copy of the *Brahmavairvatpurana*, the latter replied saying that he had not been able to procure a whole copy and had only been able to come up with two sections, one of which had been borrowed by a brahmin in Trimbakeshwar, see ibid., p. 45.

[72]In 1747–8, copies of several Sanskrit texts, some encased in coverings of different kinds of silk or printed cotton fabric, were procured from Udaipur on behalf of Peshwa Balaji Bajirao, G.C. Vad, *SSRPD*, Part 2, Vol. II, Bombay, 1906, p. 199.

court business or simply to the recitation and listening of *puranas* and *kirtans*. Thus it seems that parts of the *Ganeshpurana* were being exchanged between the two parts of the Maratha camp headed by Gopalrao Patwardhan of Miraj and Naro Shankar Rajbahadur.[73] We learn from the same set of communications that the dramas of the Tanjore school also had a following among the Peshwa elite—especially the plays of a Jagannathkavi that depicted the love-life of the gods Vishnu and Shankar.[74]

Some of the Peshwas seemed to have been personally interested in reading and collecting manuscript-books. In 1754 Peshwa Raghunathrao, who maintained collections in both his residences at Anandvalli and Trimbakeshwar, advanced 147 rupees to Shankaru, an ink-maker, for the copying of 18 Sanskrit books,[75] followed by another 50 rupees for an additional 11 in the same year.[76] He is known to have asked for another 20 titles later.[77] The Peshwa might have had a significant collection of books and manuscripts, but the frequent requests for loans on his behalf suggest that even when a private collection was undertaken as a sign of cultural privilege, it was not fuelled by the wish to make it an exhaustive representation of the current 'store' of knowledge. Although there appears to have been a caretaker entrusted with

[73]With the two camps at some distance from each other, Naro Shankar requested for the second half of the *Ganeshpurana* while returning the first half, promising that it would be duly returned, see Bhave, *PM*, p. 85; see also a reference to a letter to Raghunathrao, when on a campaign, stating that certain *pothis* he had requested were being despatched, in G.S. Sardesai, *SPD*, Vol. 18, p. 46.

[74]Bhave, *PM*, p. 81, quoted from G.S. Sardesai, *SPD*, Vol. 45.

[75]Among the books listed with their prices and size are: *Apararakgranth (45 rupees-20000 verses), Madanparijaat (21rupees-10000 verses), Vijnaneshwar (22 rupees-12000 verses), Gitashankarbhasya and Adhyatmaramayana (9 rupees-4500 verses each), Sahastrachandividhan and Gayamahatmya (I rupee-1000 verses each), Shudrakamalakaar (4 rupees-4000 verses), Geetgovindsatik* (3 rupees-2000 verses). See G.S. Sardesai, *SPD*, Vol. 22, p. 94.

[76]Titles include texts like *Vrataark, Margasheershmahatmya, Shraddhamayukh, Brahmottarkhand, Ayodhyakand* etc. See G.S. Sardesai, *SPD*, Vol. 22, pp. 96–7.

[77]The list includes *Matsyapurana, Kavyaprakashtika, Manasollas, Eeshavasyabhasya, Hatpradeepika, Chandogyaupanishad, Ratnavali*, etc. See G.S. Sardesai, *SPD*, Vol. 22, p. 97.

the Peshwa's book collection, until 1750 there are few signs that the library was valorised as a specialised store-house of knowledge: it formed a part of the general *jaamdarkhana*, or treasury.[78] Native eyewitness accounts of the sack of Jhansi by British troops during the Great Rebellion tell of how the royal library, which had apparently housed an extensive, well-maintained collection of manuscripts produced in the surrounding regions, was ransacked and destroyed.[79] This suggests that the acquisition and collection of manuscripts was a fairly common activity patronised by powerful families in the Maratha empire, although it is unlikely that these collections were anything on a grand scale, especially as the copying process seemed to have remained a fairly slow and tedious one.[80] Given the general scarcity of books, these late medieval collections may have been prized cultural possessions, yet it seems quite plausible to argue that they would have hardly compared well with the libraries of manuscripts and books built up by aristocratic and merchant-princely families in post-Renaissance Europe.[81]

To conclude, a few remarks on the modes of reading and the distribution of literate skills in these elite circles would be in order. Some individuals among ruling families, e.g. Peshwa Raghunathrao, were adept at reading Sanskrit texts on their own,[82] and many others were

[78]In 1750, Nanasaheb Peshwa requested a complete copy of Vaman's commentary on the *Gita*, which was apparently available in the *jaamdarkhana* from the caretaker. See G.S. Sardesai, *SPD*, Vol. 18, p. 46.

[79]The account is from Vishnubhat Godse's '*Jhansi Varnan*', in *Majhe Pravaas athva San 1857chya Bandachi Hakikat*, probably written in 1884–5, first pub. 1907, reprinted, Bombay, 1992. Vishnubhat Godse hailed from a poor *puranik* family from Konkan, set out northwards to seek a living through gathering alms, and found himself in Jhansi at the time of the siege. See Vishnubhat Godse, *Majhe Pravaas*, Bombay, 1992, p. 95.

[80]For a letter from a pen-maker who, while despatching ten pens that were ordered, also complains of the quality of the reeds sent to him, see G.S. Sardesai, *SPD*, Vol. 32, p. 53. Another letter tells of the despatch of a small pot of ink, which the recipient is asked to use with the utmost care, for it could be replenished only after a week, see ibid., p. 58.

[81]See Lucien Febvre and Henri-Jean Martin, *The Coming of the Book: The Impact of Printing, 1450–1800.*

[82]Raghnunathrao had an extensive collection of Sanskrit texts and was known to have spent a great deal of time with his books. See Bhave, *PM*, p. 81.

well versed in vernacular texts. Some women in the Peshwa households seem to have been tolerably well-read: they were familiar with Sanskrit texts through repeated listening, even if not through their own reading skills. Likewise, some possessed their own modest collection of books,[83] their generally subordinate status notwithstanding, others like Anandibai appeared to have been fairly discerning reader-listeners, keenly interested in consulting standard, 'correct' versions of texts.[84] Yet it is important to recognise the significantly different meanings that reading would have had in a pre-print, scribal culture from our own understanding of it as a silent individualised activity. Pre-colonial 'readers' would have mostly acquired their familiarity with these texts through listening to them being read out,[85] or, depending on the type of text, through guidance by a *pandit* or *puranik* who would elaborate on its rhetorical, semantic, or moral significance. Writing and composition, whether of letters, records or business communication, were prized skills requiring a knowledge of set, formalised conventions, which were not generally distributed but remained limited to small circles outside of specially trained scribes. Committing the text to memory was an integral part of the reading exercise: thus, reading aloud was the norm even when people might have read alone. An individual attempting to read by herself was likely to have been doing this because of the unavailability of a *puranik* or other literate attendant.[86] The acquisition and possession of

[83]For a list of books in the possession of Sagunabai, wife of Peshwa Janaradhan Bajirao, prepared after her death in 1783, see G.S. Sardesai, *SPD,* Vol. 32, p. 24.

[84]A letter sought Nana Phadnis' permission about Anandibai's request for a loan of the corrected version of the *Mahabharat* that had been compiled; see G.S. Sardesai, *SPD,* Vol. 4, p. 19.

[85]For examples, see Bhave's chapters on '*Shikshanpadhati*' and '*Granthsangraha va Granthvaachan*' in *PM,* pp. 45–86. The *puraniks* in the employ of the royal household often hailed from distant places. For example, the services of a certain well-known *puranik*, Rajshri Bapubhat Jambhekar of Sawantwadi, were secured for the Gangapur residence of Madhavrao Peshwa's mother, Gopikabai. See the letters in G.S. Sardesai, *SPD*, Vol. 32 quoted in Bhave, *PM,* p. 84.

[86]See advice by Raghunathrao in a letter dated 22 February 1756, asking the recipient to persist with his reading of the *puranas* regularly even if a *puranik* was not at hand to help. The letter is quoted in Bhave, *PM*, pp. 82–3, from G.S. Sardesai, *SPD*, Vol. 16.

literate skills prior to print was predominantly a context-based matter and tended to be subject to many subtle gradations incommensurable with our own assumptions of standardised literate practices.

There is much to suggest that the Maratha political elite was interested in the cultivation of literacy. The availability of detailed and meticulously maintained records emphasises the point that the importance of writing had grown in many areas of life by the late medieval period. As the need to control political information and revenue shares exacerbated internal conflicts among the political elite, the administrative bureaucracy came to be perceived as a distinct locus of power and a potential threat that needed to be kept minutely in check. Frequent complaints that *karkuns* charged heavy fees were possibly one way of keeping up the pressure; detailed scrutiny and surveillance of all accounts and correspondence were also common in order to pre-empt these literate agents from advancing their independent interests.[87] The dominance of brahmin families among the political elite as well as in professions such as banking and trade under Peshwa rule would have made the importance of literate skills quite obvious to upwardly mobile Maratha families like the Jadhavs. Still, the practice of reading and writing remained confined to relatively small numbers within political elites, trading circles and brahmanical groups, and the primary mode of circulation of literary and learned texts, even in elite circles, remained oral, with writing reserved for specialist functions.

The political and economic expansion of Maratha power during the Peshwa period influenced literary composition in other ways too. New genres and the classicisation of some existing modes of vernacular expression came about. The earlier textual modes continued to inspire new efforts but in ways that showed perceptible shifts in aims and inspiration. The evolution of a new phase of the performative genre of the *kirtan* is a good illustration of these shifts. Combining devotional expression, religious narrative and commentary, in its earlier phase of the *varkari kirtan* this genre had predominantly expressed a subaltern sensibility. But influenced by the changing equations between the vernacular realm, religious authority and political power, the tradition

[87]Such measures became especially common under the autocratic regime of Nana Phadnis. See Sardesai, *SPD*, Vol. 39, pp. 74–5.

went through significant mutations: first, through its use by the *ramdasi sampradaya*, and then, in the eighteenth century, through its association with the *pant kavis*.[88] In marked contrast with the medieval *sant kavis,* these eighteenth-century literary practitioners, attached to elite courts, showed conspicuous fondness for a Sanskritic vocabulary, and classical forms and allusions, ostensibly in an attempt to evolve a 'learned' and self-consciously ornate vernacular idiom.

In its attempts to strike a new balance *vis-à-vis* popular religious sensibilities, the work of Sridhar (1658–1729) and Mahipati (1715–90) had links with the bhakti verse tradition. Both men were *kirtankaars* by vocation; but besides that, Sridhar's best-known compositions include his *Harivijay*, *Ramvijay* and *Pandavapratap*, while Mahipati was known for his verse biographies of the *sant kavis*. There were also discernible differences, seen in the nascent attempts, such as Mahipati's, to use the vernacular to document the biographical/social, as also in the evidence of increased patronage from the Maratha political elite towards forms with the potential to influence popular religious and cultural sensibilities and practice. Among the more fortunate of the *kirtankaars*, the grant of *inam* land to his family from Bajirao I helped Sridhar escape the life of an itinerant performer. He lived a relatively settled life, mostly in Pandharpur and Baramati.[89] Quite unlike the celebration of the spiritual that had pervaded the devotional idioms of bhakti, composed at a time when Maratha power was expanding, Sridhar's verse was cast in the heroic mould.

Moropant (1729–94) lived at the height of Peshwa glory and his work, more than any other, exemplified attempts to produce a high cultivated idiom in the vernacular. He too enjoyed steady patronage from the powerful family of Babuji Naik from Baramati, into which the Peshwa's daughter had married. Living in the Naik household as the family *puranik*, the learned Moropant, who was well versed in both *vedanta* and *alankaarshastra*, produced a voluminous output of courtly verse, much of which was in a highly stylised and Sanskritic diction

[88]Ashok Ranade, *On Music and Musicians of Hindoostan,* Delhi, 1984, p. 130. For an account of the history of the Marathi *kirtan* and its vernacular, see Yashwant Pathak's *Nachu Kirtanache Rangi*, Pune, n.d.

[89]See Bhave, *PM*, pp. 89–90.

intended to evoke sentiments of high drama and pathos.[90] His *Aryabharata* was an elaborate reworking of the well-known Mahabharata epic in a new metre called the *aryagati*, which he devised. Besides numerous versions of the *Ramayana* that he composed, his *Kekavali* (Cries of the Peacock) was also well received.

Although themes drawn from religious texts and the epics remained an important part of literary production, the Peshwa period saw the emergence of new varieties of eulogistic, heroic and erotic performative verse forms. The *povada* was a form of the heroic ballad meant to commemorate the exploits of Maratha warriors and their leaders on the battlefield through recitation and performance. The genesis of the form could be traced to earlier times, but it gained a new impetus in the work of *shahir* poets of the eighteenth century, the best known among them being Ramjoshi (1762–1812), Prabhakar (*c.* 1755–1843), Anant Phandi (1774–1819?), Parshuram (1754–1844), Honaji Bala, and Saganbhau. Another form that shared the commemorative function of the *povada* were the prose narratives or *bakhars*—like the *Sabhasadi bakhar*, based on the life of Shivaji and composed in 1697; or the *Panipatchi Bakhar* and the *Bhausahebanchi Kaifyat*, both accounts of the famous Maratha defeat at Panipat in 1761. The *bakhars* were intended either as a report of famous Maratha military expeditions or to provide a genealogical account of well-known Maratha heroes.

Many of the *shahir* poets, especially those attached to elite courts and households, led itinerant and colourful lives, performing at festivals and celebrations, frequently also travelling on military campaigns to entertain the court. The *shahir kavis* were often prolific practitioners of the *lavani* and the *tamasha*, the performative art-forms that combined music, song and narrative, and were mainly noted for their depiction of amorous themes, combined with a sharp commentary on social relations. Not only did these vernacular cultural-performative forms span themes ranging from the religious to the profane and erotic and from the heroic to the tragic, they were also remarkable for the diverse following that they had among different sections of pre-colonial Maratha society. They seem to have been enjoyed by elite and non-elite, rural and urban audiences.

[90]Ibid., p. 91.

Thus, there are clear signs of an expansion of the literary realm during the Peshwa period, seen both in the diversity of literary styles and increased patronage from the political and economic elite to practitioners. From its beginnings in the late thirteenth century to the end of the Peshwa period, the literarisation of Marathi exhibits a slowly expanding audience for vernacular texts, the emergence of secular tendencies within vernacular expression, a personalised and individuated authorial voice, and an increasing interpenetration between elite and non-elite literary idioms. There is also some evidence of attempts to compile definitive texts through comparing and collating different existing versions, as well as efforts to build up libraries and book collections, both by men in power and individuals. These changes parallel some of the shifts in literate and cultural practice crucial to the rise of modernity in the West. Alongside these shifts, and despite developments like the proliferation of vernacular genres that undermined Sanskrit, there was a clear and self-conscious tendency for elite patronage from the time of Shivaji to align itself with the reproduction of the esoteric 'high' realm represented by Sanskrit. Such attempts to renew the normative superiority of Sanskrit and its textual traditions meant that the emerging vernacular genres and expressive forms remained subordinated under the high, classical aesthetic tradition of Sanskrit. This had an essentially conservative impact on social and political structures. For, in a period of political flux, patronage for Sanskritic norms helped preserve caste and other social hierarchies and saved traditional structures from radical disruption. It was equally clear that continued privileging of the Sanskrit sphere was not simply an internal linguistic matter; it had much to do with containment, with the maintenance of cultural and political hierarchies.

The emergence of the new literary genres did not see an accompanying rise of alternative critical standards, especially in the vernacular. Some of the *shahir kavis* and *puraniks* were men of learning who also enjoyed prestigious and close links with the Peshwa and the other Maratha courts. But with the domain of cognitive or cultivated practices clearly still subject to particularistic social norms and oral modes of transmission, it was unlikely that these artists/*kavis*/scholars exercised any kind of general regulatory influence within the pre-colonial political sphere. It is important to assess the nature of the influence these men of learning/cultivation had on the affairs of the court, but in doing so one has to keep in mind that, despite the substantial use of vernacular varieties for official communication, record-keeping and literary expression, pre-colonial vernacularisation did not lead here to a development of alternative critical discourses in the domains of aesthetics or socio-political ethics. This left the normative status of Sanskrit and its high aesthetic and philosophical discourses unchallenged—and largely unpermeated by non-elite cultural values and practices.

Colonialism, Comparative Philology and Re-making the Politics of Language

Historians of the nineteenth century like Chris Bayly[91] have argued that social structures in South Asia towards the end of the eighteenth century contained signs of an emerging proto-modernity. Trends towards expansion and consolidation of the resource base discussed earlier would seem to bear out the view. The plausibility of such a view, is not centrally my concern here; the valid point made by Sumit Guha[92] is that, at least, for the eighteenth-century Deccan, there is little evidence for the emergence of a Western-type early-modern, absolutist state capable of a spectacular and sustained display of its monopoly to exercise coercion. Implicit in this debate are standpoints about the nature of cultural impact in the colonial encounter, especially the extent to which the changes that occurred with colonialism were unprecedented. Following the approach adopted here of plotting convergences between linguistic/textual hierarchies and political structures, I will attempt to put in perspective some of the *differences* between state–society relations prevailing in South Asia and Western Europe in the period immediately before the colonial encounter. Any attempt to discuss the difference

[91]Chris Bayly, *Empire and Information 1780–1870,* Cambridge, 1996; also his *Rulers, Townsmen and Bazaars: North Indian Society in the Age of British Expansion, 1770–1870,* first pub. 1983, reprint, Delhi, 1992.

[92]Sumit Guha, 'An Indian Penal Regime: Maharashtra in the Eighteenth Century', *Past and Present,* No. 147, May 1995, p. 125.

between the West and South Asia has to grapple with the complicated legacy of such representations within colonial discourse, a task made difficult by the fact that the construction of difference between the modern West and the rest of the world was so central to the construction of colonial ideology. A major task for post-colonial studies is to devise comparative frameworks that can recover the divergent cultural logics of non-Western societies from their essentialised assimilation into Eurocentric narrative frameworks. With this in mind, I will highlight some inferences that can be made about the discrepancies between prevailing assumptions about linguistic hierarchies and the distribution of power in eighteenth-century South Asia and pre-/early-modern Europe. Major cultural shifts introduced through colonial rule, especially through its interventions in linguistic functions, textual hierarchies, and literate skills—via the discipline of philology and the more pragmatic agency of education policy—will also be noted.

Difference and Trajectories of Vernacularisation

An important difference between the processes of vernacularisation as they unfolded in Western Europe and South Asia is the relation that emerged between the vernaculars and the 'high' languages, Latin and Sanskrit, respectively. A foundational element in the Western context was the production of vernacular versions of the Christian scriptures.[93] But in South Asia, despite several attempts from the Marathi *Dnyaneshwari* onwards, through instances in other languages like the compositions of poets like Tulsidas to retell the sacred texts, it may be justifiably argued that the corpus of scriptural texts did not get translated out of Sanskrit and into the South Asian vernacular idioms[94] quite in the same way as

[93]The aim here is not to over-generalise the West European case. This was truer of the countries where the Reformation had a strong influence. Thus Italian, for example, saw the vernacularisation of poetry and imaginative writing, but sermons and religious treatises continued to be composed in Latin long after the Reformation. Also, as is well known, Latin continued to serve its 'high' intellectual function until as late as the time of Newton and Hobbes in the seventeenth century. I thank David Taylor and Francesca Orisini for these clarifications.

[94]Here, thanks are due to an anonymous referee who pointed out the need to qualify the generalisation about scriptural translations in South Asia, because within

happened in Europe. The translation of Christian scriptures into the West European vernaculars may have been an early instance of the tendency towards linguistic objectification discernible in Western epistemology or, alternatively, it could be seen as an outcome of the religious homogeneity that characterised Europe from the early-modern period. Whatever the case, in effect the processes of religious vernacularisation formed a very important aspect of the textualisation of the West European vernaculars and the rise of early-modern Europe from medieval Christendom.[95] Paradoxically, on the one hand the decomposition of the realm of the Holy Christian Empire into contesting breakaway faiths led to structures of centralised authority and a consolidation of the institutional power of the main branches of the Christian Church; and on the other, to regionalised polities and a potent space for the articulation of a secular wordview. These seemingly contrary developments resulted in the displacement of Latin's monopolistic claims as a sacral language and the medium of cultivated exchange, and the simultaneous appropriation of the range of its high functions by the European vernaculars. But the close homology that developed between the functions of the high domain of Latin, and which were deemed 'permissible' through the vernaculars from the Renaissance onwards, was crucial not only to the emergence of absolutist structures of control in early modern Europe but also to the very emergence of the discourses of modernity.

It is well known that besides the translation of the Bible during the Reformation, the literarisation of the European vernaculars was greatly serviced by 'direct' inputs through translation from Greek and Latin texts. The idea of translation as it has developed in the West since the European Renaissance did not imply mere *retelling*; the practice amounted to a more or less direct transaction of transfer from one language into another. The levels of standardisation supported by print

---

the Islamic tradition the Quran was rendered into the vernacular by Shah Waliullah and his successors in the eighteenth and nineteenth centuries.

[95]Sheldon Pollock describes these overlapping processes in the West European case as 'an overdetermination of literary vernacularisation with religious vernacularisation': see 'India in the Vernacular Millennium: Literature, Culture and Polity 1000–1500'.

no doubt facilitated the close articulation of functions that developed between the classical and vernacular languages in Europe. Arguably, the widespread concern of modern European culture and linguistics with origins and genealogical purity may be seen as a legacy of the rhetorical strategies through which the Western vernaculars played out their close rivalry with Latin, which subsequently came to be embedded as a constitutive feature of the emerging European vernacular cultures. The close affinity of possibilities that thus emerged between the classical and vernacular cultures of Europe endowed the latter with a more effective potential to produce homogenised polities and centralised structures of authority than were generated by pre-colonial vernacularisation in South Asia. As a result, despite some analogous trends, post-Renaissance European literary traditions were characterised by a greater degree of cultural and political instrumentality than was the case in pre-modern South Asia.

On the subcontinent, the processes of vernacularisation showed a divergent trajectory. Long after its disintegration of the Sanskrit cosmopolis and its supercession, it was able to retain its aura of exclusivity and status not only as the language of ritual worship, but also as the medium of high intellectual discourse—in the Hindu tradition and, significantly, even within the dissenting systems of Buddhist and Jain thought. The subversive potential of the South Asian vernaculars was inherently constrained by their inability to displace the overarching, normative influence of Sanskrit. The literarisation of the vernaculars here did not lead to a redefinition of aesthetic norms and ideas of cultivation or notions of collectivity, as happened through the Renaissance in Europe. In the absence of alternative conceptions of the aesthetic and political community, the emerging traditions of vernacular textuality in South Asia, including the corpus of bhakti verse, remained subject to the critical norms within the Sanskritic discourses on *kavya, sahitya* and *shastra.* The sphere of Sanskrit discourse was able to respond to the tendencies towards laicisation within bhakti and, more generally, to the subversive potential within vernacular textuality in an incredibly disdainful way. It simply refused to take serious note of what were, without doubt, fundamental and irrevocable cultural and political shifts. Even when Sanskrit drew upon the 'lesser' Prakrits to enrich its literary and metrical repertoires, the South Asian high traditions successfully preserved their dominance by maintaining a lofty distance from the emerging vernacular forms. The discourses of Sanskrit asserted their power by a supreme act of snobbery; they categorically refused to even acknowledge the presence of the hierarchically 'inferior' vernacular literary idioms.[96] If the appropriation of high cognitive functions by the Western vernaculars was crucial to the definition of collective identities and the emergence of discourses of modern social rationality in the West, it would be logical to consider the social, political and epistemological differences and disparities in the analogous processes of pre-colonial South Asia.

Although vernacular textualities emerged from fissures in the Sanskrit cosmopolis, the relation between vernacular literarisation and the intellectual traditions represented by Sanskrit remained largely undiscussed. Pre-colonial literary vernacular forms, especially devotional verse, abound with allusions to asymmetrical relations in the status that these non-elite idioms could claim in comparison with Sanskrit. This meant that the pre-colonial South Asian ideological universe remained riven by crucial ruptures. However much the pre-colonial economic and political spheres may have embodied signs of an incipient modernity, it is more difficult to apprehend similar effects in the sphere of cultural production. The effort of ruling elites notwithstanding, the pre-colonial South Asian cultural universe was characterised by a low degree of integration between elite intellectual discourse on the one hand, and 'ordinary' textual and cultural forms and 'popular' religious practice on the other. This lack of cultural cohesion surely stemmed from a severely segmented social structure. The absence of a shared, core set of beliefs and practices across the pre-colonial South Asian social hierarchy was often identified as a major 'flaw' in the Hindu belief system by nineteenth-century native intellectuals. Arguably,

[96]There were, of course, exceptions; poets who composed in both Sanskrit and vernacular idioms like Vidyapati, or those who, like the seventeenth-century poet Jagannatha at the Mughal court, drew upon vernacular poetry in their use of Sanskrit so as to reflect the new literary sensibility. However, such instances do not alter the general point about the reluctance of the 'high' Sanskritic tradition to engage meaningfully with the capabilities of vernacular idioms.

such sharp gaps between the realm of 'high' and 'ordinary' culture would be antithetical to the fundamentals of a 'modern' culture. However, as I will show, possibilities of homogeneous cultural distribution were first introduced into the South Asian social world through the frameworks of colonial philology.

Colonialism, Modernity, Linguistic Hierarchy

The structural discontinuity between the worlds of high discourse and the vernacular were altered by colonialism. Colonial rule brought about structures of authority based on cultural premises very different from those that had long prevailed. In the face of the new conceptual, cultural and political asymmetries, establishing a common ideological space between the new rulers and their subjects assumed the utmost significance. Therefore colonial ideology foregrounded language, communication and authority in an unprecedented way. Colonial power required English, but the ground had to be cleared before English displaced Sanskrit and Persian from their high status and established its own relation with vernacular idioms. Cohn[97] has highlighted the ability of the colonial imagination to secure its interests through its command of language. But the colonial ideological project was not confined to selectively appropriating material from indigenous cultural and cognitive traditions; it also established relations between English and the native vernaculars so that the latter could be rapidly 'reformed' under the new influences. Colonial power may not have arrived with a premeditated approach towards native intellectual and cultural systems, yet the sustained application of an instrumental rationality gave it a consistent and radical deliberateness. For this reason one can speak of discernible continuities between early orientalist and missionary efforts to study native classical and 'vulgar' tongues—the assumptions of comparative philology, and later colonial policy on education and language. The imperial imagination was assisted by cultural memories of the ways in which the European vernaculars had derived their modernised forms through direct translations of Greek and Latin. If the European vernacular textual repertoires were renewed through

[97]Bernard Cohn, 'The Command of Language and the Language of Command' in *Subaltern Studies IV: Writings on South Asian History*, Delhi, 1994.

linguistic 'transfers', surely the philosophical and cultural discontinuities between eighteenth-century Europe and South Asia too could partially be resolved if viewed as a 'mere' linguistic problem. The huge cultural unfamiliarity could be pragmatically ironed out through the potent technique of translation. This would place English as the new normative classical language against which the native vernaculars could be redefined and modernised.

Colonial policy envisaged English as a high language within the South Asian cultural world in ways that would eventually reinscribe vernacular textuality, speech and social practice. Initially, the objective was not for English to supplant Sanskrit and Persian completely, especially as much of the valuable information about native legal, political and religious codes was contained in texts in these two languages. The desire to open up indigenous judicial and moral codes to frameworks of Western reason had impelled an interest in the South Asian high languages, but ultimately the goals of colonial ideology could be met only by refashioning the vernaculars. However, despite these differences in motive, colonial study of the classical languages and its engagement with 'vulgar' tongues were both marked by overriding concerns with fixity of meaning and purity of origin. The paramount need was to cultivate a language that would serve as the medium of intercourse between a small number of governing Europeans and a vast and diversely stratified social world. The scale of expansionist ambitions presented further problems, for these ideological designs had to be carried out in an amazingly polyglot setting. Committed to a simultaneous cultivation of several regional languages, the British seemed trapped in a classic situation which reinforced the cognitive predilection that the European mind had developed for responding to the unfamiliar, i.e. with questions about origins and descent. Such questions were to be resolved through the construction of elaborate classificatory models. Beginning with samples of each identifiably 'distinct' linguistic variety, the colonial study of the South Asian languages produced formal descriptions of morphological, syntactical, lexical and phonological structures derived from spoken forms. These accounts were backed by apparently definitive observations about the origins, territorial spread and estimated number of users for each language, and speculations about the interrelations between Indian classical languages and the plethora of spoken forms. Assumptions such as the following, made in this case by Rev. Stevenson—one of the earliest modern scholars of Marathi—were typical of the methods of the colonial linguistic project, better known as the discipline of philology: 'The assertion that no language can be thoroughly understood till it has been compared with others, belonging to the same family, is nowhere more true than in relation to the vernacular languages of India.'[98]

Relying on techniques of objectification, enumeration, measurement and classification, the emerging fields of philology, geography and ethnology aimed to create a cognitive order that was a systematic empirical reconstruction of native ways. Actually, this process invented seemingly authoritative discourses on cultures that Western modernity took as its Other. Philology and ethnology had comparable concerns, made explicit in another article by Stevenson around the same time: 'Philology and ethnology ... though seemingly independent are yet intimately connected, and throw mutual light on one another ... It is usually found that difference of language characterise difference of race.'[99] Undoubtedly, a critical tenet of the Western colonial imagination was its self-perception as the teleological agent of a universal history. However, the emergence of such globalising narratives of historical consciousness presumed a magisterial knowledge of the geographical and cultural spaces that European civilisation regarded as its Other. The comparative frameworks of ethnology and philology seemed designed to fulfil such needs. The application of these cognitive technologies sought to impose a semblance of order on what appeared to the colonial mind as a proliferation of 'peculiar' languages and dialects, all seemingly related to each other, albeit in unknown ways. In attempting to classify the linguistic diversity on the subcontinent, philology aimed to control this apparently perplexing scenario by positing a theory of original languages with which to map the interrelations

[98]Rev. Stevenson, 'Observations on the Grammatical Structure of Vernacular Languages of India', *Journal of the Bombay Royal Asiatic Society* (henceforth, *JBRAS*), Vol. III, 1849–51, p. 71.

[99]Rev. Stevenson, 'A Comparative Vocabulary on non-Sanskrit Vocables in the Vernacular Languages of India', *JBRAS*, Vol. IV, 1853, p. 117.

and genealogies of the vernacular forms, including their 'origins' in 'pure' classical tongues. The discourse of philology thus effectively displaced and rewrote what had been an essentially discontinuous and largely unarticulated relation between Sanskrit and the vernaculars. Although colonial suspicions of 'impurity' and 'mixture' coincided with analogous anxieties in the brahmanical roots of most native informants, the resultant discourse of philology articulated the links between classical and vernacular according to European categories. For instance, working with such assumptions, the influential introduction to Halhed's *Bengali Grammar* typically tried to expunge all words from Persian and Hindustani so as to categorically fix the 'direct' descent of the vernacular from Sanskrit: 'The following work presents the Bengali language merely as derived from its parent Shanscrit [*sic*].'[100]

However, it soon became clear that the hope of constructing a comprehensive taxonomic philological grid that showed the diversity of spoken varieties on the subcontinent as deriving from an unique and originary past language was going to prove elusive. Following the underlying rationale of philology, but unable to reconcile the variety of linguistic forms into a single all-inclusive genealogy, each of the three groups of British orientalists working at the Fort William, Fort St George and Bombay establishments[101] produced arguments that posited at least three separate language families, each going further back to an elusive point of origin. Not surprisingly, such attempts to recover the story of linguistic displacement and accretion into a linear narrative—constructed upon an opposition between a serialised past and a continuous present—yielded more complexities than clarifications. Philological scholarship had its explanatory limits and the following observations by Rev. Stevenson suggest its unresolved methodological dilemmas:

> 1. The languages spoken North of the Krishna all have a strong family resemblance, and all draw largely from the Sanskrit, which is the prevailing element in their composition.

[100]Nathaniel Halhed, *A Grammar of the Bengali Language,* Hoogly, 1778, reprint, Menston, U.K., 1969, p. xxi.

[101]For an account of the differences between these various groups of Orientalist scholars, see Tom Trautman, *Aryans and British India,* Berkeley, 1995.

2. That the languages to the South of the Krishna also have a strong family likeness, while the prevailing element is not Sanskrit.[102]

Delving further into the recesses of an indefinite past, philologists encountered traces of 'more' primitive classes of languages that were apparently even 'more ancient' than the northern and southern linguistic groups. Confronted with discontinuities between the 'Aryan' and the 'Dravidian' linguistic families, Rev. Stevenson advanced the idea of an underlying 'aboriginal' layer from which all vernaculars derived the non-Sanskritic part of their lexicon.[103] Such explanatory schemes were never more than rough hypotheses. Nevertheless, they produced an influential and rationalised account of linguistic contestation and change which naturalised the role of writing in pre-colonial hierarchies. Colonial power proceeded simultaneously on its attempts to reinscribe relations between social and textual order and authority.

Philology, Colonial Policy, Hegemony

Even if flawed, these theories did not stay at the level of 'pure' discourse. They had direct pragmatic implications, as illustrated by an article that followed Rev. Stevenson's philological pieces in the same journal. Entitled 'On the Geographical Distribution of India, and the Feasibility of Introducing English as a Lingua Franca',[104] this article was by Sir Erskine Perry,[105] President of the Board of Education and a great enthusiast for the introduction of English in India. Troubled by the 'many distinct and peculiar language groups'[106] that the native

[102]Stevenson, 'Observations on the Grammatical Structure of Vernacular Languages of India', *JBRAS*, Vol. III, 1849–51, p. 72.

[103]Ibid., pp. 71–2.

[104]Erskine Perry, *JBRAS*, Vol. 4, 1853, pp. 289–317.

[105]Erskine Perry played an important role in restructuring education policy in Western India. His tenure as President of Board of Education between 1848 and 1852 saw a series of crucial moves away from the policy followed since 1818. Until Perry's time, an emphasis upon instruction through the vernacular had been an important part of the policy in the Bombay Presidency. But from the late 1840s, increasingly, instruction through English found greater favour with the authorities.

[106]E. Perry, *JBRAS*, p. 309.

population was presently immured in, Perry admitted that his connection with the Board of Education had made him aware of the need to develop a common medium between the British and their Indian subjects. Revealing the overlap between colonial education, philology and statistics, his article proposed that the 'language of the new governing authority', English, replace Persian, the erstwhile official and business language, this being essential if the 'interests of 140 millions of mankind' were to be 'justly realised'.[107] Perry was candid that in such matters the interests of literature were so irrevocably blended with political considerations that 'it was impossible to sever them'.[108] The course of colonial policy, especially in the field of education, showed how the mapping and regulation of 'native dialects' was a necessary prelude to their 'rebirth' as the languages of a colonial modernity under the normative authority of English.

The exercise of mapping the linguistic past through philological frameworks conferred distinct possibilities of control in the present. If awareness of these advantages informed the rationale of colonial policy on education, the same was not lost on colonial-educated intellectuals either. Philology cleared the ground for the redefinition of linguistic identities mainly by setting up normalising mechanisms through which the vernaculars acquired their modern forms. But even more importantly, the links between philology and colonial education ensured that such theories of linguistic kinship entered the discourse of the emerging intelligentsia to suggest the possibilities for a greater hegemonic discourse with impressive spatial and temporal dimensions. Once the norms of standardised vernacular usage had been put in place through the first few decades of colonial rule, the 'insights' of comparative philology were used by colonial-educated intellectuals to lend 'scientific' and moral weight to their aspirations of extending their dominance. The philological valorisation of claims of purity and noble descent enabled their claims to cultivation and moral superiority in the present to be grounded in their now 'proven' record as custodians of 'correct' linguistic and moral practice in the past. By the later decades of the nineteenth century, drawing on philological beliefs about the

[107]Ibid., pp. 314–17.
[108]Ibid., p. 317.

essentially interrelated genealogy of the Indian vernaculars and their common descent from the immaculate purity of the great and ancient Sanskrit language, English-educated intellectuals in different parts of the subcontinent could claim to constitute a transregional kinship with an immaculate 'high' cultural pedigree. An important part of this elite self-image was their shared status as custodians of 'correct' cultural practices. Thus, when giving the Wilson philological lectures in 1877, claiming descent from the noble brahmins of the 'ancient *aryavarta*' was, for the well-known orientalist scholar Bhandarkar,[109] clearly, a way of enlarging the cultural capital which the native intelligentsia had already established through their dominance over the regional vernacular spheres. And yet the act of specifying the social and spatial boundaries of the 'cultivated' elite in present times was also simultaneously to assert control over the claims of collective memory, of extending themselves all the way into the ancient past in ways that could now claim the status of 'historical' truth:

> We have the clearest possible evidence that Sanskrit was the vernacular of holy or respectable Brahmins of Aryavarta or North India, and who could speak the language without the study of grammar. ... Who is it that speaks good or correct Marathi? Of course brahmins of culture. The language of the other classes is not correct Marathi. The word 'sistha' may be translated as 'a man of culture or education', and this education or culture has since remote times been almost confined to brahmins. Thus the dialects of the inscriptions of Asoka and Pali were the vernaculars of the non-Brahmanic classes; but a greater importance must evidently have been attached to them in the times of Asoka than is now assigned to the Marathi of the non-Brahmanic classes, since they are used in the inscriptions. They are, however, not recognised as

[109]Born in Ratnagiri, Bhandarkar (1837–1925) studied at the English school there before coming to Elphinstone College, Bombay. Graduating with a Major in Sanskrit along with Ranade in 1864, Bhandarkar served as the headmaster of the Ratnagiri School and was an important member of the Prarthana Samaj. His appointment as professor of Sanskrit at Deccan College in 1882 was hailed by the native press as a major triumph for the campaign for senior appointments in government establishments. He became the vice-chancellor of Bombay University in 1894.

independent languages by our grammarians who treated them as we treat the Marathi of the lower classes; but they were in use and bore the same relation to Sanskrit that low Marathi does to high Marathi. ...[110]

Such connections between notions of noble descent, Aryan 'racial' purity, and moral superiority across space and time were an intrinsic part of European attempts to produce a discourse of extensive affinity and difference that simultaneously maintained hierarchical boundaries between 'primitive' and 'advanced' levels of civilisation.[111] With their ability to authorise powerful narratives about the unremitting advance of ascendant elites through a serialised past, the value of orientalist ethnography and philology was affirmed by the emerging nationalist imagination. This affirmation not only endorsed constructions of the past that would 'historically' substantiate current claims, it also helped extend and consolidate hegemony over cultural hierarchies and social relations that had been previously characterised by considerable discontinuity.

Philology and Narratives of Subalternity

If the extensive horizons of Western philology and ethnology could be harnessed to reinforce the hegemonic claims of an emerging nationalist consciousness, the universal compass of these discourses could also be appropriated by subordinated groups to produce 'historical' narratives of humiliation and injustice. Uniquely for that juncture in the colonial period, Phule's[112] writings enunciated a powerful discourse

[110]R.G. Bhandarkar, *Relations between Sanskrit, Pali, the Prakrits and the Modern Vernaculars*, Bombay, 1914, p. 296.

[111]Given their sweeping normalising ambitions, the discourses of race and philology were prone to several ambivalences: it has been argued that in its strongest form, the racial theory of civilisation could be turned against the comparative frameworks of philology and the study of Sanskrit. For an account of the tensions between philology and race science in mid-nineteenth century, see Tom Trautman, *Aryans and British India*.

[112]Phule (1827–90) was born into the *phulmali* community. He went to the school managed by the Scottish Mission in Pune, where he learnt English and became familiar with Western rationalist ideas, especially the writings of Tom Paine, as well as the emerging discourse of philology. Phule remains a unique figure among colonial intellectuals, with his bold initiatives in establishing a

that sought to amplify the grievances of marginalised, lower-caste communities beyond their immediate local significance. His texts sought to establish links between marginalised low-caste groups in the present and their 'original' displacement in ancient times by the invading Aryans on the one hand, and, on the other, spoke of correspondences between such subaltern groups in South Asia and the saga of American slaves. In doing this, Phule was drawing upon prominent methodological elements within philological discourse which he had encountered through his contact with the Scottish missionaries at Pune.[113] This is best illustrated through his important text, *Slavery*, which was published in 1873 with the subtitle, 'In this civilised British Government under the cloak of Brahmanism'. Dedicating the book to 'the Good People of the United States' as a token of his admiration for 'their sublime disinterested and self-sacrificing devotion in the cause of Negro Slavery', Phule expressed his earnest desire that his countrymen would use the latter 'noble example as their guide in the emancipation of their Sudra brethren from the trammells of *brahmin*

school for girls as well as schools for lower-caste boys in Pune in 1852–3. He established the Satyashodak Samaj in 1873, which aimed to promote the interests of the lower castes and challenge brahmanical dominance. In the 1840s and 1850s, Phule had close links with some upper-caste intellectuals like Gopal Hari Deshmukh, Bhavalkar and Ramchandra Balkrishna who were important members of the anti-caste Paramhansa Mandali. Some of them also taught in the lower-caste schools that Phule opened in Pune. However, the upper-caste intelligentsia's reluctance to address the question of caste hierarchy eventually led to a bitter parting of ways. Phule's writings represent a powerful counter-discourse that contests the emerging dominant upper-caste view of the political possibilities within colonial modernity. Phule published frequently in the missionary paper, *Satyadeepika*. Among his other works are *Chatrapati Shivaji Raje Bhosleyanche Povada* (1869), *Brahmanache Kasab* (1869), *Gulamgiri* (1873) and *Shetkaryanche Asud* (1883). For a detailed account of Phule's life and position within the low-caste movement in Western India see Rosalind O'Hanlon, *Caste, Conflict and Ideology: Mahatma Jyotirao Phule and Low-caste Protest in Nineteenth-century Western India*, Cambridge, 1995. See also Y.D. Phadke, Dhananjay Keer and S.G. Malshe, eds, *Mahatma Phule Samagra Vangmaya* (henceforth, *MPSV*), fifth edition, Bombay, 1991.

[113]Phule, 'Preface to Slavery' in Phadke *et al*, eds, *MPSV*, Bombay, 1991, pp. 117–28.

thraldom'.[114] Strategically choosing as his premise the philological 'belief' that the Indo-Aryan family of languages supplanted and appropriated an earlier family of 'aboriginal' languages, Phule linked it with his principal claim that Aryan ascendancy had been mainly established through the textual control that brahmins had exercised down the ages in order to make 'pernicious legends and laws' through which they had successfully deluded and subjugated 'ignorant masses'. In this way, Phule cleverly attempted to insert lower-caste subordination into a global discourse of marginality by asserting equivalence between the subjugation of non-literate, labouring communities—across space and time—at the hands of groups who controlled inscription. In establishing a correspondence between the sufferings of the lower castes under brahmanical rule, especially during the Peshwa period, and the condition of slaves in America, Phule was aspiring to create a narrative with quasi-historical claims. By virtue of representing a 'higher' order of rationality than the unjust myths and legends that had legitimised brahmanical dominance, these 'truths' helped Phule to ally his narrative with emerging international idioms in which subalternity was being newly based on notions of human dignity and entitlement.

In portraying lower-caste selves condemned to a degrading subhuman existence, Phule ignored indigenous traditions of dissent available in bhakti compositions. His refusal to draw upon medieval vernacular bhakti could have been the outcome of several factors. Despite their remonstrance against a dominant ritualistic order, the fact that

[114]Thus ran the English part of the bilingual dedication that Phule inscribed on the opening pages of the 1873 edition of *Gulamgiri*. The opposite page carried the corresponding Marathi version. However, interestingly, the main text was entirely in Marathi. But Phule prefaced it with a long introduction in English which acknowledged his debt to recent ethnological researches, especially the work of Dr. Pritchard, that had 'proved' that the Aryans were not the 'original' inhabitants of Hindustan. In *Gulamgiri*, Phule interprets the mythological accounts of Vishnu's incarnations as an allegory for brahmanical attempts to establish their dominance over the 'aborigines' who had been the 'original' inhabitants. See Phadke *et al*, eds, *MPSV*, pp. 109–92. For a discussion of Phule's negotiation of the bilingual relation between English and Marathi that critically structured colonial politics, see chapter two.

bhakti compositions had remained intimately tied with the tenets of Hindu religious practice must surely have been crucial to Phule's reluctance to deploy this tradition. As someone who had internalised the rationalistic critique of religion and the writings of Tom Paine, Phule perceived a greater radical potential in the language of rights than in the invocation of pre-modern idioms of bhakti. Aiming to articulate a discourse that not only thematised displacement and marginality, but which made a radical break with the past, Phule was less likely to be attracted by the language of bhakti. As already discussed, bhakti texts held a strong ideological fascination for upper-caste intellectuals intent on appropriating pre-colonial vernacular textual forms into the new linear narratives of literary history. For his part, Phule was quite convinced that neither in their role as custodians of traditional learning, nor as the recipients of the new knowledges, had brahmins shown any great proclivity to share their knowledge with their fellow beings. He believed that this persistent brahmanical tendency to regard their 'knowledge as a personal gift, not to be soiled by contact with the ignorant vulgar'[115] could only be opposed by the 'wondrous changes brought about in the Western world, purely by the agency of popular knowledge'. However, if such a transformation was to occur in India, it was not likely to be encouraged through the government's policy of using the taxes collected from the labouring ryots to give 'a superior education to the superior classes.'[116]

Conclusion

We have noted some of the major cultural and political shifts that occurred through colonial interventions that reordered linguistic functions, textual hierarchies and the content and distribution of literate skills in South Asia. Colonialism accomplished these vast changes philosophically and epistemically via the discipline of philology and then via the more pragmatic agency of education policy. Given that language is foundational to all forms of cultural practice, the importance

[115]Phule's Preface to 'Slavery' in Phadke *et al*, eds., *MPSV*, Bombay, 1991, p. 127.

[116]Ibid., p.126.

of focusing on language while mapping major shifts seems almost commonsensical.

Primary to any consideration of the cultural impact of colonialism are questions about the nature and development of modernity in non-Western societies and the extent to which the 'transfer' of modern discourses in these contexts overlapped with the ambitions of colonial rule. Some historians have argued that traces of processes that we call 'modern' are discernible in pre-colonial polity and economy, especially in the northern parts of the subcontinent. I am not persuaded by this view. Therefore, I have argued for distinct cultural processes prior to colonial rule and delineated some of the changes that occurred through colonial intervention as unprecedented. In doing this I have sought to establish a framework for my argument that the coming of colonialism made for decisive shifts in the structure of cultural production, as well as in the norms for articulating the possibilities of contestation and containment.

2

Colonial Education and the Laicisation of Knowledge

Remaking Cultural Hierarchies and Modes of Contestation

Introduction

The ideological role of colonial education and the changes effected by education policy played a unique role in legitimising the superior claims of colonial power. On its own admission, education policy represented nothing less than a desire to restructure native ways of thinking, especially the way colonial subjects would receive and interact with state power. It intended to do this by redefining existing cultural and political norms and simultaneously exercising a monopolistic authority over such matters. In effect, the education project was a body of proposals to bring about discursive and institutional shifts that would alter the norms and modes of cultural and political contestation.

Two main radical consequences are attributed to colonial education. First, the Indian vernaculars are recognised as having attained their modern forms because of education policy. Simultaneously, colonial designs to educate natives meant the introduction of general literacy into a social world where, previously, social and ritual status determined access to such skills. That said, these changes are seldom linked; nor are their combined implications for the emerging social structure properly examined. The existing scholarship does not address the central tension of the education project, namely that while this was the main channel for modern liberal ideas reaching the subcontinent, it was simultaneously the primary instrument of colonial ideological domination. Arguments on colonial education tend to stress only one or the other of these aspects. This is most common in nationalist accounts of the emergence of the modern intelligentsia, where little explanation is offered for the miraculous transition of colonised subjects into modern, liberal individuals capable of resisting colonial domination. Some historians,[1] and more recently political scientists,[2] have addressed the complex questions posed by the transfer of liberal ideology through colonial rule; yet few attempts,[3] have been made to extend these insights to explicate tensions underlying the education project. Similarly, the processes through which education policy actually worked await close study, especially how policy was able to hold together and intiate radical cognitive, social and political shifts.

How were liberal, universalist principles and the elitist designs of colonial ideology worked into education policy? In what ways did colonial education policy enunciate the principles of universal access? Given its ideological moorings, the education project was unlikely to enunciate the idea of universal access to literacy unequivocally. This raises questions about the means and extent to which colonial education was able to open a distribution of laicised knowledge.[4] Nor can we regard the linguistic shifts resulting from education policy as

[1]Ranajit Guha, *A Rule of Property for Bengal: An Essay on the Idea of a Permanent Settlement*, Paris, 1963; Ranajit Guha, 'Dominance without Hegemony and its Historiography', *Subaltern Studies VI*, Delhi, 1989, pp. 210–309; Dipesh Chakrabarty, *Re-thinking Working Class History*, Princeton, 1989.

[2]Partha Chatterjee, *Nation and its Fragments.*

[3]One of them is Krishna Kumar's excellent study of the politics of Indian education. See Krishna Kumar, *The Political Agenda of Education: A Study of Colonialist and Nationalist Ideas*, New Delhi, 1991.

[4]The term laicisation is used to denote the conditions within modern political structures whereby the distribution of knowledge and power are premised not on ideas of exclusivity, but rather on ideas of general circulation. Such processes of laicisation would necessarily be intimately linked with shifts in linguistic practices, leading to what may be termed the vernacularisation of dominant ideologies.

discontinuous with its overall ideological mission and influence. Political constraints on the articulation of universalist principles within colonial discourse meant that these could be enunciated only in oblique ways. Colonial policy was, I argue, mainly able to suggest the possibility of a diffused laicised knowledge through its abilities to restructure linguistic exchanges and redefine the vernacular realm.

Colonial Education, Disseminating Modernity and the Possibility of a Public Sphere

Existing histories of modern Indian education[5] have been satisfied with tracing the chronology of various educational institutions and outlining the contributions of modern education to the emergence of nationalist consciousness. More recently, scholars trained in the discipline of English[6] have taken critical note of connections between colonial literacy and its ideological underpinnings. We now need to see the links between the education project, linguistic shifts, and hierarchical patterns that emerged through the colonial period.

In speaking of colonial education as the 'steel frame' that held the British raj, nationalist historiography hinted at the role of education in institutional changes, while left-minded sociological analyses have branded the colonial/modern Indian intelligentsia as predominantly 'collaborationist'. More recently, post-colonial theorists have focussed on the impact of colonial ideology in order to uncover the discursive strategies through which colonial power exercised its domination. Yet

[5]S. Nurullah and J.P. Naik, *A History of Education in India During the British Period*, Bombay, 1951; Boman Behram, *Educational Controversies of India: The Cultural Conquest of India under Imperialism,* Bombay, 1946; Bruce McCully, *English Education and the Origins of Indian Nationalism*, New York, 1940; Aparna Basu, *The Growth of Education and Political Development in India, 1888–1920*, Delhi, 1974.

[6]Gauri Vishwanathan, *Masks of Conquest: Literary Study and British Rule in India*, London, 1994; Rajeswari Sunder Rajan, *The Lie of the Land: English Literary Studies in India*, New Delhi, 1992; Svati Joshi, *Re-thinking English: Essays in Literature, Language, History*, New Delhi, 1991; Gayatri Spivak, *In Other Worlds*, London, 1988; Gayatri Spivak, 'Can the Subaltern Speak?' in Cary Nelson and Lawrence Grossberg, eds, *Marxism and the Interpretation of Culture*, London, 1988.

these conceptualisations remain inadequate. For, the most crucial fact about colonial education is that it was the stimulus to native empowerment even as it managed an internalisation of adverse judgements against indigenous intellectual traditions and social practices. Colonial education could not have introduced modern social and political categories without altering pre-existing notions of self and the social, and assumptions and modes of native knowledges and languages.[7] If colonial power aimed at a standardised cultural order, these shifts had to be reproduced throughout the subcontinent. The dissemination of modern ideas and the restructuring of vernacular languages were thus concomitant processes, and any attempt to analyse the one will inevitably consider the implications of the other. By remaking the linguistic hierarchy and vernacular forms, and by remodelling cultural and political codes, colonial education transformed both the universe of ideas and the structures of cultural exchange and social communication. Clearly, then, we need a more nuanced understanding of the links between colonial education, articulations of the modern self, and shifts in the linguistic field as well as in the norms of social communication.

Krishna Kumar's work on colonial education has been exceptional in examining structural changes[8] and arguing that the agenda of control within the education project was far more sophisticated than is

[7]The appropriation of indigenous languages and knowledges into frameworks of Western rationality and the subsequent introduction of English and colonial education were chronologically related within the transformative designs of colonial power. However, these shifts did not follow a uniform, set pattern throughout the subcontinent. There were significant differences in the duration and the sequence of these two phases in Bengal and Western India. Whereas in Bengal, the orientalist phase preceded official education initiatives by at least a few decades, the establishment of British power at a relatively later date in Western India meant that the timing of the orientalist and education projects overlapped to significant extent in the Bombay Presidency. The different trajectories of education policy in the Bengal and Bombay Presidencies, especially regarding decisions about the medium of instruction, had long-term implications as it affected the communicative capabilities and choices before intelligentsias that emerged in the two regions. For a discussion on bilingualism and political hierarchy in Western India, see chapters three and five. See also fn. 19 below.

[8]Krishna Kumar, *The Political Agenda of Education*.

understood in functionalist terms. It was not merely aimed at producing subordinate clerks for the colonial bureaucracy. It elaborated bourgeois principles of social order, economic distribution and political entitlement in ways that 'adjusted' these with the requirements of colonial difference. His analysis reveals the profound tensions created by attempts to import modern notions of political subjectivity through the system of colonial schools. Kumar stresses that education policy was unmindful of the possible consequences of these attempts to reproduce a version of Western modernity. In its attempts to selectively reorder native social structures, education policy seemed oblivious to the possible repercussions of its elitist orientation and vision of a severely hierarchical and divided social order.[9]

Sudipta Kaviraj's writings provide additional insights into the political divisions that colonial discourse created within native society. Observing that the transfer of liberal ideology through colonial education was a mode of address which colonial power reserved for a numerically small but ideologically congenial intelligentsia that it required for its legitimation, Kaviraj argues[10] that the distinct methods through which colonial power presented itself to different strata ruptured existing social 'commonsense' into two incommensurable parts. But the ideological and political divides resulting from colonial discourse and education were more complicated than Kaviraj's account suggests. His insights could be fruitfully extended into an analysis of how tiers within education policy shaped the emerging political structure. His work has alerted us to the importance of linguistic shifts during the colonial period; the implications of the standardisation of the vernaculars as part of the plan to extend colonial ideology can be more clearly demonstrated.

Language and the Colonial Public Sphere

The importance of the language question had become apparent even before the British gained formal political command. Bernard Cohn's

[9]See especially 'Colonial Education as an Educational Ideal' in Krishna Kumar, *The Political Agenda of Education*, pp. 23–46

[10]Sudipta Kaviraj, 'On the Construction of Colonial Power: State, Discourse, Hegemony', in Engels and Marks, eds., *Contesting Colonial Hegemony*, London, 1994, pp. 19–54.

seminal essay[11] showed how the cultivation of native languages and the foundation of colonial rule went hand in hand, and how this transformed the ways in which these languages were spoken, read, written and studied. Colonial authority also needed to foreground English as the paramount symbol of the ideal order, though officials were quick to realise the limits of political influence if colonial power was expressed solely through English. Paradoxically, the power of English would be secured through its potential to redefine the vernacular domain. The remaking of language, the extension of colonial ideology, and the definition of new social norms were inter-related objectives built into the design of the education project, and the emerging bilingual relations had important political implications. Here, the concept of the public sphere within our analysis of colonial modernity, and the reasons why language was such a critical factor within the discursive arenas, become important.

The concepts of 'civil society' and a 'public sphere', as derived from the history of the modern West, subsume several large and overlapping social processes. These would include the formation of the intimate sphere of the bourgeois nuclear family, the extended networks of literacy through the rise of vernacular reading publics, and the creation of large-scale, impersonal, collaborative social structures through the growth of the market. Aiming to transplant the social and historical processes that had formed part of the rise of modernity in the West, the colonial education project served as a proxy tool to stimulate several of these results into subcontinental society through a grand bureaucratic scheme. Of course, care needs to be exercised in presuming that these processes were engendered *primarily* through the educational project. Gauri Vishwanathan's work[12] has shown that the colonial state undertook the responsibility of educating its native subjects even before similar mass-education initiatives were directed towards 'home' populations in Western societies. This has sensitised us to the varying chronology of events leading up to the emergence of modern education systems in nineteenth-century Britain and colonial India. However, the 'prema-

[11]See Bernard Cohn's essay cited in chapter one.

[12]Gauri Vishwanathan, *Masks of Conquest.*

ture' intervention by the colonial state in native education indicates the complexity of the education project. Given the general ambition to govern native society through a selective conferment of modernity, it was not enough for colonial policy to cull together an appropriate subset of modern ideas and practices. To be fully effective, ways had to be devised for these discourses to be disseminated as a hegemonic programme of 'useful' learning among the natives. And if colonial discourse was to acquire a hegemonic influence, it needed to render itself more generally accessible: and this then brought up the question of its translation into the vernacular. Such an ambitious programme of dissemination presumed standardised, normalised forms of the vernaculars, whereas these were not among the features of pre-colonial social reality. Yet what lent an air of feasibility to colonial ambitions of producing a uniform commonsense within native society was the ability of the colonial imagination to conceive of a standardised educational programme throughout the subcontinent, backed by print. The task of producing extended literate networks was displaced and subsumed into official schemes to monopolise cultural authority under a standardised educational project. Consequently, a dominant concern of the discourses in colonial public arenas was the superiority of Western 'useful' learning and the possibility of its vernacularisation in order to effect a 'general improvement' of native society.

However, there were limits to extending liberal discourses for 'native benefit' in this way. One of the primary contradictions within colonial modernities has been the fact that the use of liberal ideology in the design of colonial governance precluded any earnest application of market principles towards the expansion of native economies. Thus, despite the importance of vernacular forms to colonial ideology, the rule of difference allowed little room for the replication of large-scale vernacular reading publics—which had been crucial to the emergence of Western modernity. With the basic conditions for the emergence of 'print capitalism'[13] unavailable in the colonial context, the education project was ambitiously entrusted with performing more than one

[13]Benedict Anderson, *Imagined Communities: Reflections on the Origin and Spread of Nationalism.*

'surrogate' function. It had to rationalise liberal ideas about private property, but it had to do this within a context that afforded minimal scope for the growth of processes of individuation and structures of impersonal collaboration.[14] As a result, the telescoping of liberal principles through colonial pedagogy did not allow the emergence of individuated selves, which formed the basis of modern collectivities. When analysing modern ideas on the subcontinent, therefore, scholars have argued that the displacement of liberalism as colonial ideology saw the modern idiom of universal and equal rights being appropriated by communities rather than by individuals.[15] Even when colonial discourse and its pedagogic elaboration as the ideology of improvement aimed to produce individual subjects, its benefits were appropriated not by *all individuals* but, at best, by representatives drawn from *all native communities*. The appropriation of liberal vocabularies in these ways could be partly attributed to the uneven access to these new cognitive and political discourses. The reification of group boundaries under colonial influence counteracted the transfer of modern egalitarian possibilities through pedagogy. Yet these shifts in identities were occurring within new public arenas defined by official initiatives to introduce intellectual, cultural and political practices based on bourgeois liberal norms.

In light of these constitutive factors, it would appear that the Habermasian public sphere, rather than the idea of civil society, is

[14]Krishna Kumar has rightly argued that the education project was intended to overcome what were perceived as the fundamental 'deficiencies' of indigenous knowledge and culture. He suggests that the ideological agenda of colonial education was linked to the problems of transferring bourgeois ideas of private property and economic order into the colonial situation. However, to read this telescoping of functions into the education project as a 'mask' for the drain of the indigenous economy by the metropolitan bourgeoisie, as Gauri Vishwanathan's work tends to, is to elide over the complex contradictions underlying the making of colonial modernity. See Krishna Kumar, *The Political Agenda of Education*, pp. 14–15.

[15]Sudipta Kaviraj, 'Religion and Modernity in India', paper at the conference on *Identity, Modernity, Politics*, School of Oriental and African Studies, London, 14–15 September 1994; Rajeev Bhargava, 'The Right to Culture', *Social Scientist*, Vol. 18, No. 10, October 1990, pp. 50–7.

appropriate in analysing the specific formative trajectory of colonial modernity. Evidence on aspects of Western modernity that colonial intellectuals were most impressed with also backs this approach. Early native assessments of British rule were driven by the need to appropriate the cognitive 'riches' of the West, and these will be discussed. We note here that early native discourse contained many enthusiastic responses about the communicative possibilities opened up between native society and the West, specifically the scope for publicity under the new regime. Indeed, native elites participated in collaborative discursive arenas such as the Native Education Society, impelled by the political advantages of proximity with the new rulers. Such support was not always given with the hope of securing immediate, pragmatic rewards. When committing resources towards colonial education, native responses revealed keen awareness of the serious challenge that the new cognitive and communicative networks posed to the indigenous social order.[16]

Centralised Regulation, Colonial Ideology, General Access

The new intellectual elite acquired their notions of modern universal principles only partially through readings of Western history, for modern ideas were not always absorbed through direct instruction in the classroom. The underlying design of the education project more potently suggested modern political principles than the fare directly on offer in colonial schools. Representing an overall plan to school a

[16]See chapter four for a discussion on print and the making of a modern vernacular discourse in Marathi. However, we need to note that wealthy, Marathi-speaking Hindu *seths* were much more forthcoming in their support to the new schools and the Education Society than to invest in Marathi printing presses. Interestingly, the story of the negotiation of the new literary norms by the Gujarati-speaking Parsi community in Bombay followed a different trajectory. The extensive involvement of the Parsi community in the China trade as well as their investment in colonial trading companies created a market for commercial information about the movement of goods. This provided inducement for native investment in the first presses for Gujarati newspapers. In comparison, *seths* from Marathi-speaking communities participated in the colonial trade only minimally and, therefore, the emergence of the Marathi newspaper press had to await the rise of the first generation of colonial-educated intellectuals.

small sub-set of the native population into an 'abridged' version of liberalism, education policy statements were characteristically reluctant to elaborate upon the idea of universal and general entitlement.[17] Indeed there is ample evidence to bear out Kumar's assertion[18] that colonial education policy used its resources to author an elitist discourse accommodating the principles of bourgeois universalism into an agenda of ideological control and management. Elphinstone's 'Minute on Education' of March 1824, a significant policy document in the Bombay Presidency, made only a token gesture towards encouraging the 'lower order of natives to avail themselves of the means of instruction' as part of its general plan to improve the state of the native schools.[19] The allocation of actual resources was even less likely to be guided by any eagerness to extend the scope of liberal temper in native society; rather, it tended to depend on calculations of potential political benefits

[17]It would be problematic to apply the term 'rights' for the emerging space for possibilities of empowerment according to universalistic within colonial modernity. Therefore, the deliberate use here of the weaker term 'entitlement'.

[18]Krishna Kumar, *The Political Agenda of Education*, pp. 30–7.

[19]Early education policy documents always argued for the need to *alter* and *improve* the *existing* arrangements in the native schools. This kind of adaptive language camouflaged the extent of the radical transformative ambitions that colonial policy harboured. However, it also showed that colonial policy was alert to the need of taking into account regional circumstances. It would be important not to lose sight of the regional variations in colonial policy, especially as the circumstances and the time-span over which the British established control in Western India were quite different from the story in Bengal. The seemingly tentative attitude in Elphinstone's plan for Bombay was surely linked to the realisation that education policy in Western India could not afford an aggressively Anglicist stance like the Bengal situation allowed by that time. See Mountstuart Elphinstone, 'Minute on Education' dated March 1824', in G.W. Forrest, ed., *Selections from the Minutes and Other Official Writings of the Hon. Mountstuart Elphinstone*, London, 1884, pp. 80–1.

For instance, the emphasis on vernacular education in the early colonial period in Western India is strikingly different from the story in Bengal where the debate was cast mainly in terms of the 'Orientalist' or the 'Anglicist' 'options'. The latter prevailed with few resources allocated for vernacular education. These regional divergences in policy diminished with the increasingly centralised administration after 1857 and the establishment of the universities around the same time. See also fns. 7 and 39.

or risks. Elphinstone's 'Minute' is hardly exceptional in admitting the exclusive designs of the education project:

> It is observed that the missionaries find the lowest castes the best pupils; but we must be careful how we offer any special encouragement to men of that description; they are not only the most despised, but among the least numerous of the great division of society; and it is to be feared that if our system of education first took root among them, it would never spread further, and in that case we might find ourselves at the head of a new class superior to the rest in useful knowledge but hated and despised by the castes to who these new attainments would always induce us to prefer them. Such a state of things would be desirable if we were contented to rest our favour on our army or on detachment of a part of our population, but inconsistent with every attempt to found it on a more extended basis.[20]

Furthermore, policy statements[21] and the historical record[22] contain several cases which show that the colonial government acceded to pressure from the higher castes to prevent lower-caste students from attending government schools. This is not merely to draw attention to the 'duplicity' or 'illiberalism' underlying colonial policy. Rather, it is important to understand how, such instances notwithstanding, subaltern groups and their leaders repeatedly petitioned the 'benevolent' colonial government for redressal against the 'unjust' upper-caste monopolisation of opportunities intended for all subjects. I will elaborate on the conditions under which a low-caste counter-discourse emerged within the colonial public domain in Western India: here it

[20]'Extract Minute by the Hon. Mountstuart Elphinstone, Governor of Bombay, dated 13 December 1823' in Aparna Basu, ed., *Indian Education in Parliament Papers, Part I* (henceforth, *IEPP*), Bombay, 1952, pp. 211.

[21]See ibid., pp. 205–6.

[22]Dadoba Pandurang's autobiographical account reveals how, around 1828, Dadajee Dhackjee, one of the wealthy native patrons of the Bombay Education Society, prevailed upon the British Government to prohibit lower-caste students from attending the Society School. Because of this pressure, *koli, bhandari, kunbi* and *marathe* boys were temporarily, but immediately, struck off the rolls. See A.K. Priyolkar, ed., *Dadoba Pandurangyanche Atmacharitra Va Charitra*, (henceforth DPA), Bombay, 1947, pp. 45–7.

is important to note that these shifts can hardly be traced to the articulation of egalitarian, non-hierarchical social principles within the new educational discourse. Rather the 'liberalising' stimulus came from the altered structures of cultural production and the relations of bilingual literacy. In introducing these changes the colonial government wrested complete authority not just to sanction and regulate the content and distribution of literate skills but also to arbitrate upon what, in fact, did or did not constitute 'knowledge'. This centralisation of authority over the sphere of cultural production carried potentially radical implications. Educational discourse was able to suggest the possibilities of equal access not through any purposive commitment in financial outlays or actual pedagogic practice, but by altering the structure of state–society relations, especially by opening a minimal collaborative space for the construction of colonial ideology. These collaborative channels between the administration and native elites took the form of Native Education Societies set up in each of the three Presidencies.

Education policy thus worked as a paradigmatic influence in defining spaces and establishing channels of cultural and political negotiation between the new rulers and their subjects. Meant to structure ideological relations between the colonial state and native elites, the Education Societies formed in the three Presidencies became fora through which were initiated normative and cultural shifts necessary to colonial power. Regional differences notwithstanding, these Education Societies were entrusted with the responsibility of setting up schools that would be managed according to standardised principles, and of preparing appropriate reading material and books to be used in these 'reformed' schools. The Bombay Native School Book and School Society,[23] as it came to be called from 1823 under

[23]A Christian organisation called the Bombay Education Society was set up in 1816 to provide education for destitute children, especially the offspring of Englishmen. In effect, it was the first initiative towards native education, as it was also open to local children. This Society introduced the teaching of the native languages in 1820, but found that the main obstacle was the great 'deficiency of school books'. In 1821, the Native School and School Book Committee was formed as a branch of the Bombay Education Society with Mountstuart Elphinstone as its President, and provisions were made for a joint fund of subscriptions from both

Elphinstone's stewardship, had a clear two-fold structure reflecting the official view of the native world. It was presided over by the governor, with four European officials as vice-presidents. With an equal number of Europeans and native members in the managing committee of twenty-four members,[24] the native section of the Bombay Committee had an 'equal' community-wise representation of Parsees, Hindus and Muslims.[25] These Education Societies were the first of their kind to be set up in the colonial world and played a crucial role in establishing structures of ideological mediation. The Native Education Society also performed a more indirect and, perhaps, unintended purpose by functioning as a concrete demonstration of the modalities of colonial power and of how it was to be approached. All members of the society were nominated by the administration. Nevertheless, in adopting operational procedures based on principles of voluntary association, these societies proved a valuable first-hand lesson in the way colonial

---

Europeans and wealthy or interested natives. The Society was restructured in January 1827, when it began to be called by the more general name of Bombay Native Education Society. As the scale of its operations expanded, this Society was reconstituted, first, into the Board of Education and later, in the early 1850s, into the Department of Public Instruction. This summary is drawn from R.V. Parulekar, ed., *Selections from Educational Records (Bombay) (1815–1840)* (henceforth, *SERB*), Part II, Bombay, 1955.

[24]The ideological initiatives of the education project were to be mediated through a small number of influential natives. An official document issued in 1845 described the special nature of the colonial ideological mission as follows: 'The main principle on which the Board seek to diffuse the benefits of national education is to endeavour to obtain the co-operation of influential Natives in the efforts made by Government to improve the moral condition of the people.' See 'Rules and Regulations of the Educational Establishments under the Board of Education, 1845' in J.A. Richey, ed., *Selections from Educational Records 1840–59* (henceforth, *SER*), Part II, Calcutta, 1921, p. 159.

[25]The composition of the Education Society reflected the colonial view of the South Asian social structure. Historians of the later colonial period have pointed out how colonial categories resulted in the thickening of boundaries between major religious groupings. The implications of such a colonial sociology were not confined to the level of discursive representation; these perceptions acquired institutional significance and were powerfully reproduced through policy measures, especially in the field of education.

power legitimated and reproduced itself. Hence, the Education Society can be regarded as a crucial dialogic arena which inaugurated and instituted in abbreviated version a quasi-civil-society type of political order in the colonial context. As a mediating channel, its procedures became models for similar arenas that the new intelligentsia would soon establish to articulate native interests. These attempts to negotiate with native interests and involve local elites and literate personnel through the Bombay Native Education Society mirrored the operational principles of liberal politics. The institution of the Native Education Society was a limited and, for some time to come, the only discursive forum for the negotiation of interests between a sovereign, modern governmental apparatus and native, private initiative.

English as the New High Language of Colonial Modernity

It was true that educational policy documents were always in English. But given the complexity of its ambitions, colonial education could not speak either in a unitary voice or in a single language. As an exercise in bridging the seemingly irreconcilable gaps between disparate conceptual orders, colonial education had to take on complex levels of translation if it was to span the cultural and linguistic divisions of local society. Because the gap between English and the vernaculars symbolised the divide between the state and its subjects, one of the primary decisions that policy had to make concerned the appropriate language for the communication of colonial ideology. English was the most convenient choice from the official point of view, but it would hardly assure a wide reach for the 'lessons' that it had to transmit. The use of the vernaculars, on the other hand, promised a more successful extension of this ideological burden and, by implication, of the circulation of liberal discourses. But this dependence on the vernaculars meant that the asymmetries coded into the bilingual relation would be reproduced on an extensive basis through the education system. Not only did the bilingual hierarchy reinforce the elitist scope of educational discourse, it implied that the reception of modern discourses would be contingent upon access to English and the new, officially recognised forms of the vernaculars. The bilingual divide meant that liberal ideas would be received and read differently according to the opportunities or competence that individuals or communities had to English and/or the vernacular. Political modernity in the colonial context thus rewrote not just the lives of those with access to colonial schools and an English education: the majority encountered English as a condition that denied them knowledge and power.

The emerging democratic *imaginaire* was thus internally differentiated into potentially conflicting segments whose conceptions of liberalism and colonial-modern power were defined by the extent of literate skills they could claim *vis-à-vis* English and the vernacular. These processes of ideological transfer—perhaps best described as multiple levels of the vernacularisation of liberal discourses—were based on norms consistent with a laicised cultural and political order. Yet with textual expositions on liberalism largely limited to a privileged few, the design of educational policy was also a blueprint for a hierarchy based on the control that groups could assert over these processes of vernacularisation. Conceived as a pedagogic project, Indian modernity internalised the tensions between liberal egalitarian norms and the divisive and hierarchical effects of a bilingual educational policy.

As has been remarked, English represented much more than a scheme to produce a subordinate bureaucracy. English hoped to displace Persian and Arabic as the language of official business and record-keeping. The status of English as official symbol derived not just from its political superiority. Its 'high' position *vis-à-vis* local languages stemmed equally from its standing as the language of the imperious discourses of modernity. This therefore brought about a radical reassessment of the capacities of the vernaculars, especially since colonial power depended on its abilities to create dependence between English and local languages. The latter were now evaluated not so much in comparison with the 'indigenous' high languages of Persian and Sanskrit, but through their competence to extend the discursive frameworks of English. What counted against them most was their 'unpreparedness', which was judged as the absence of resources to articulate concepts and thought-processes germane to modernity. This sufficed to create a judgmental discourse about their 'underdeveloped' and 'primitive' condition. If the indigenous languages hoped to retain their cultural legitimacy, they would have to demonstrate their potential to emerge out of such 'backwardness'.

The discursive domain represented by English constituted the apex of the colonial public sphere and was mirrored by the structure of command within the Native Education Society. Reflecting the political asymmetries of colonial society, its linguistic hierarchy hinged crucially upon the 'low' vernaculars developing their standard forms with English as their exemplar. Fundamentally dependant on large-scale translations, colonial literacy altered the prevailing structures of linguistic subordination and dependence between the pre-colonial high languages and the pre-print forms of local languages. The association between English and the vernaculars was subject to financial and political considerations determining educational policy. As a result, the emerging linguistic economy did not represent a straight division between English and the vernacular spheres, especially since vernacular standardisation set up pressures determining privilege and disadvantage within each linguistic cluster. The distance or proximity of linguistic communities from the ones that eventually gained currency as the standard varieties determined access to a range of symbolic, cognitive, social and economic benefits. If such processes qualified access to the new literate regime and, by implication, to the emerging arena of colonial-modern politics, any account of the liberalising influence of the education project has to consider the asymmetrical effects of colonial bilingualism in defining social marginality and mobility.

Colonial Policy, Bilingualism and General Access

Soon after the takeover of power in 1818, Mountstuart Elphinstone was quick to realise the importance of a colonial ideological apparatus. Well acquainted with circumstances in Western India through his role in the military campaign against the Peshwa, Elphinstone believed that education was crucial to plans for 'native improvement'. These initiatives would need to contend with memories of state patronage to brahmins and brahmanical learning through the annual ceremonial awards of the *dakshina*[26] instituted under Peshwa rule. Moreover,

[26]The *dakshina* was established by the Peshwas as part of their policy to encourage brahmanical learning. It was the annual ceremonial award made during the auspicious month of *shraavan* as donations and gifts to various categories of brahmins. *Shastris* and *vydicks* were honoured at the Peshwa's court, after being

considering that British rule was attempting to replace a brahmin government, he felt it would be unwise to allow missionaries the same measure of liberty they had been allowed in Bengal. Considering this, the government needed to put in place a well co-ordinated and prudent plan to provide the necessary ideological reorientations. Elphinstone's Minutes on Education are among the earliest full statements of the intentions of the colonial imagination to forge a 'commonsense' that would ideologically unite the new rulers with at least a section of the native population:

> the dangers to which we are exposed from the sensitive character of the religion of the natives, and the slippery foundations of our government, owing to the total separation between us and our subjects, require the adoption of some measures to counteract them; and the only one is, to remove their prejudice, and to communicate our own principles and opinions by the diffusion of a rational education.[27]

Once the overall imperative for these operations was admitted, the next consideration was to lay down steps through which the government could secure these results at minimal expense: 'It is probably, some considerations like these that have induced the Legislature to render it imperative on the Indian Government to spend a portion of its revenue in the promotion of education ... It may be urged that expense, however well applied, ought not to fall on the government; that those who are to benefit by education ought to pay for it themselves ...'[28]

Yet it was not enough merely to evoke native interest; it seemed fitting to the colonial imagination that this native curiosity would be most effective if backed by a willingness to pay for these intellectual

---

examined on their learning; the 'lower' brahmanical orders of the *bhats* and *bhikshuks*, many of whom travelled considerable distances, had to queue outside a large ceremonial *pandala* erected near the famous Parvati temple outside the capital city, to receive their donations. At the time of the take-over, the total donations made through the *dakshina* apparently amounted to about five lakh rupees. For estimates of the *dakshina* expenditure during the Peshwa period, see chapter one, fn. 43.

[27]'Extract Minute by the Hon. Mountstuart Elphinstone dated 13 December 1823' in A. Basu, ed., *IEPP*, p. 209.

[28]Ibid.

and cultural 'benefits'. As colonial officials admitted, the 'greatest difficulty [was] to create the *demand* for knowledge.[29] In approaching this difficulty, policy-makers took recourse to the well-developed bourgeois ability to briskly break down a radically ambitious scheme into a series of pragmatic measures that could normalise, if not overcome, conflicting circumstances and interests. Accordingly, the discourse on native education cleared a space by audaciously casting its intended addressees as 'wanting' and 'inferior'. They could be redeemed through zealous intervention. Adopting a strategy that was quickly internalised by native reformist discourse, educational policy spoke of the '*want of preparation among those for whose benefit it* [*was*] *intended*'.[30] In thus representing itself as fulfilling native demand for a knowledge that was morally superior and irrefutably true, the discourse of colonial education betrayed similarities with capitalist rationality and Christian missionary rhetoric. Logically speaking, the optimum way for native elites to obtain the cognitive value on offer would be through investments in the government proposals. It was not just a matter of expediency that the colonial government did not assume direct financial responsibility. Colonial ideology strategically represented the administration as authorising the discourse on native education, but subsequently participating only as one among many actors, chiefly to co-ordinate the 'common' arena of the Education Society:

> If it be admitted that the assistance of Government is necessary, the next question is, how best can it be afforded, and there are two which present themselves for consideration. The Government may take the education of the natives entirely on itself, or it may increase the means and stimulate the exertions of the Society already formed for the purpose. The best result will probably be produced by a combination of these two modes of proceeding. Many of the measures necessary for the diffusion of education must depend on the spontaneous zeal of individuals, and can not be effected by any resolutions of the government. The promotion of those measures, therefore, should be committed to the Society; but there are others which require an organised system and

[29]Ibid.
[30]Ibid.

a greater degree of regularity and permanence than can be expected from any plan, the success of which is to depend upon personal character. This last branch therefore must be undertaken by the Government.[31]

It was evident from these space-clearing efforts that such attempts to institute a system for the diffusion of 'useful' knowledge among natives would also involve shifts in the prevailing principles of social organisation. Although colonial officials were unanimous about the basic need for such a project, there were disagreements on the actual method to be adopted, especially the extent of responsibility that the colonial administration should take. In the Bombay Presidency this debate was played out as the conflict between the 'conservative' and the 'enlightened' positions represented by Francis Warden and Mountstuart Elphinstone. Francis Warden argued from a more orthodox *laissez-faire* position which maintained that government initiatives towards education ought to be minimal and should mainly proceed through setting the rules for natives to compete 'openly' for official positions. He conceded that 'Of the necessity that exists for the diffusion of an improved system of education among natives, no difference of opinion can well exist, but the best means of doing so involves a difficult and delicate problem'.[32] According to Warden, the colonial government only needed to provide the appropriate circumstances by 'stimulating' the market for native labour schooled in the English language and European knowledge to create the necessary ideological links with its subject population. It was sufficient for policy to create the conditions for a surplus supply of such skills by 'exciting the zeal of individuals', 'by holding out a preference to official employment to those who may qualify themselves by a particular course of study, rather than be too forward in incurring the greater portion of the expense in diffusing education'.[33]

The extensive use of local skills in subordinate bureaucratic positions would help cultivate the necessary links with native society, besides

[31]Ibid., p. 197.

[32]Minute by Francis Warden, Member of Council at Bombay, dated 29 December 1823, in ibid., p. 212.

[33]Ibid.

altering the prevailing custom of hereditary employment.[34] Warden had little patience with Elphinstone's argument for the elaboration of discursive links between the administration and native society for the dissemination of colonial ideology.[35] Elphinstone's views, which eventually prevailed, emphasised the need for a comprehensive plan to extend the colonial ideological project using the vernaculars. This did not imply concern for the universal spread of literacy among the native population. Rather, both Elphinstone and his successor John Malcolm realised it would be difficult to achieve the ideological objectives of the education project without simultaneously advancing plans to create a standardised cultural order within native society. The latter task was, clearly, inconceivable without the use of the local languages. Accordingly, Elphinstone's 'Minute' of 1823 contained a series of exhaustive proposals that impressively enunciated the full scope of appropriative intentions:

> The following are the principal measures required for the diffusion of knowledge among the natives: 1st to improve the mode of teaching at the native schools, and to increase the number of schools; 2nd, to supply them with school books; 3rd, to hold out some encouragement to the lower orders of natives; 4th, to establish schools for teaching the European sciences and improvements in the higher branches of education; 5th, to provide for the preparation and publication of books of moral and physical science in native languages; 6th, to establish schools for the purpose of teaching English to those disposed to pursue it as a classical language, and as a means of acquiring a knowledge of European discoveries; 7th, to hold forth encouragement to the natives in the pursuit of those last branches of knowledge.[36]

Elphinstone's Minute demonstrates the ability of the colonial administration to translate its vision into a coherent set of pragmatic measures. It contained clear hints of the hierarchical asymmetries in the

[34]Ibid., p. 213.

[35]The above Minute by Francis Warden shows his strong opposition to publishing 'useful' reading material in the vernaculars at government expense. He also had reservations about letting natives learn printing techniques.

[36]'Extract Minute by Elphinstone', in ibid., p. 197.

bilingual relation between English and the vernacular. As the following extract from an earlier report of the Bombay Education Society's Report shows, the 1823 Minute only formalised what had already been implicitly recognised:

> In imparting to the Natives useful knowledge to any extent, and with the hope of any good and permanent effect, it is evident the language of the country must be the chief and proper vehicle ... it is impossible to look with any hopes of success, to imparting knowledge generally and usefully in a language which must remain to the greater portion a foreign one.[37]

Given its intentions, an important measure of the success of Elphinstone's scheme was the extent of native support that his proposals would elicit. On this count, his record was impressive, for he was able to secure the collaboration of 'representatives' drawn from native elites, including handsome financial commitments for a series of subscriptions to fund the appointment of suitable Englishmen to prestigious professorships in Bombay. The terms on which these funds were committed testified to the force of colonial ideology; but equally they indicated the nature of native interest in the education project:

> Your Society will be pleased to bear in mind, what the Natives have desired us particularly to express, that by the study of the English language, they do not contemplate the supercession of the Vernacular dialects of the country, in the promotion of Native Education; but that they regard it merely as a help to the diffusion of the European Arts and Sciences among them, by means of translations by those who have acquired a thorough acquaintance with it; and as a branch of classical education to be esteemed and cultivated in this country as the classical languages of Greece and Rome are in the universities of Europe.[38]

[37]'Extract from Sixth Annual Report of the Bombay Education Society for 1821', pp. 20–6, R.V. Parulekar, ed., *SERB*, Part II, p. 27.

[38]Letter dated 1 December 1827 from the Committee representing the native community to the secretary of the Bombay Native Education Society, excerpted in 'Extract from the Fourth Report for 1827 of the Bombay Native Education Society', pp. 39–47 in ibid., p. 109.

It would be interesting to compare this petition with Raja Rammohan's

The interest native elites showed in the official educational initiatives signalled its importance to the emerging political structure. Not surprisingly, the articulation of native interest emphasised translations into the vernacular, indicating that the project of education tended to converge upon considerations of language. Although the 'minimalist' position advocated by Warden was superseded by the argument for greater state intervention, the differences between these two perspectives were hardly likely to be finally resolved at this point and were to re-emerge soon. For, once the idea of using the vernaculars[39] had been

famous letter of 1823 to the Calcutta Government protesting against the decision to support traditional 'Oriental' learning at the Calcutta Sanskrit College and, instead, asking them to make European learning, especially science, available to native society. Although official policy in Bombay contained moves to 'preserve' traditional indigenous scholarship at the Poona Sanskrit College, interestingly, the native responses from Bombay took little note of that aspect of the government's provisions.

[39]For details of the divergence in the early directions followed by educational policy in the Bengal and Bombay Presidencies, see Parulekar's essay, 'The Medium of Instruction' in J.P. Naik, ed., *The Educational Writings of R.V. Parulekar*, Bombay, 1957, pp. 1–40.

These differences were also the subject of comment in the contemporary press. An account in a Bengal missionary paper in 1837 observed: 'We have been favoured with copies of the reports of the Bombay (Native) Education Society and are most happy to find that the attention of that body has been directed from its institution in 1822 to the instruction of the Natives in their own tongue, to the preparation of Native Schoolmasters, and the translation and printing of a body of works in the language of the country. ... The General Committee of Public Instruction at this Presidency declare in their report that Vernacular Education is the ultimate object of all their labours, but years pass by after years without any attempt whatsoever to bring us any nearer to its accomplishment. ... The Bombay Society patronise to the full extent of its importance the diffusion of English. ... The number of valuable works published by the Society in the Native languages on some of the most abstruse subjects, fully demonstrates the fallacy of the notion that the Native language are not at present fitted for the conveyance of knowledge', report in the *Friend of India*, 26 January 1837, Serampore, quoted in Parulekar, 'The Medium of Instruction', in Naik, ed., *The Educational Writings of R.V. Parulekar*, p. 8. Parulekar also quotes a similar point made by Colonel Sykes, 'The vernacular schoolbooks in use in Bombay are objects of praise by the Bengal Government. They consist of translations into Maratha, Gujarathi and Canarese, of treatises on algebra, geometry, trigonometry, grammar, history, natural philosophy, general knowledge and moral

admitted, the debate tended to centre on the difficulties of translation when preparing instructional material. The implicit tendencies towards a laicised vernacular literacy promised advantages to both government and the emerging intelligentsia. These interests were not identical, yet this minimal discursive space between state and society contained strong imaginative stimuli suggesting shifts in the distribution of cultural and political opportunities which would eventually pave the ground for new hegemonic possibilities. Despite constraints on the articulation of egalitarian principles within official discourse, and despite their self-interestedness, native elites showed their awareness of what liberal universalism promised. Consider the address by native princes and chiefs to the Education Society meeting called in November 1827 to hand over native subscriptions[40] for two English professorships in Bombay. It spoke admiringly of the government's intentions to extend learning among all classes of natives:

> But having beheld with admiration ... the encouraging manners, the freedom from prejudice, the consideration at all times evinced for the interests and welfare of the people of this country ... the constant endeavours to extend amongst them the inestimable advantages of intellectual and moral improvements, the commanding abilities applied to ensure permanent amelioration in conditions of all classes and to promote their prosperity *on the soundest principles*.[41] (emphasis added)

The new vernacular discourses would soon contain similar references to universal categories like *sarv lok*, though, for reasons outlined, it would be premature to read these as an enunciation of egalitarian principles.

In trying to extend the reach of new discourses through the vernacular press, especially newspapers and 'useful' journals, intellectuals began

---

instruction.', Col. Sykes, *Statistics of Educational Institutions of the East India Company in India*, 1844, p. 73. See also fn. 19 above.

[40]By the end of 1827, the subscription for the establishment of Elphinstone professorships had yielded Rs. 2,29,656 in Bombay currency. Some of these contributions came from outside Bombay, including places as far as Bengal. See *Fourth Report of Bombay Native Education Society for 1827*, Bombay, 1828, p. 35.

[41]Ibid., p. 33.

to show interest in spreading the new knowledges and enlarging the audience for new ideas. The impact of these new ideas and cultural practices was not confined to upper-caste intellectuals and elite circles. Rather, they were more likely to be avidly received by groups beyond the privileged circle that colonial educational discourse chose to address. In Western India, especially, it was not long before native groups not represented within the structure of the Native Education Society began to stake claims to the new opportunities, using the current communicative strategies and vocabularies. Some of these attempts by elite and non-elite groups to stake their claim to the new literacy and sites of vernacular production reveal the emerging modes and patterns of contestation within the public arenas of colonial politics.

Extending the Colonial Public Sphere: Laicisation and the Possibility of a Caste Alliance in pre-1857 Western India

By invoking norms that transcended particularistic boundaries and sectarian identities, the new proposals contained covert but potent possibilities to suggest social bonds outside localised, community-specific affiliation. Although pre-modern ways of mapping perceptions of selves and others remain under-analysed, it may be argued that such notions of universal and equal rights radically challenged the limited scope for the emergence of non-particularistic or secular tendencies within the pre-colonial social order. Official discourse did not foreground notions of universal literacy: nevertheless, the project of colonial education invoked egalitarian norms to the extent that it echoed ideas of a common, general system of knowledge.

Petitions and Regulating Access

Native attempts to negotiate educational policy took the form of petitions addressed at first to the Education Society and later to the Board of Education—the centralised authority that determined the admissibility of claims for the entire Presidency. Petitions fell into three main categories: claims by educated/literate persons seeking government patronage for their compositions, usually in the form of a request that their compositions be included on the official curriculum or purchased for government reading rooms; petitions from relatively homogeneous, politically-aware groups seeking sanction for a government-aided school for the community; and petitions from contending groups for a share in funds allocated for certain specified purposes. Standardised vernacular education through state initiative certainly represented a novel scenario. With the education bureaucracy being the main civil interface with colonial power outside the courts, it was not surprising that native groups showed alacrity in demanding access to new schools. Wherever persons with some English could be found, except perhaps among the recently displaced ruling classes, petitions for a government-patronised school in the area to teach the new 'useful' learning were common.[42] Having ostensibly acquired the 'consent' of native communities by successfully creating a demand for the new knowledges, colonial power proceeded to establish a centralised system to regulate native claims over education.

The Board's Regulations of 1845 specified the procedure for establishing new schools. Inhabitants of towns or school districts, whose estimated population was not less than 2000, could petition the colonial government provided they were prepared to meet the following conditions:

first: The petitioners must agree to provide and keep in repair a school house, and the building for which being neither a temple, *chowree* or any other place of public resort, must be sufficiently spacious ...
second: The petitioners must agree to furnish the schoolhouse with a small wooden table, two plain chairs, and a plain box with a padlock for the preservation of the schoolbooks.
third: The petitioners must also agree that each boy would pay one *anna* monthly.[43]

[42]Especially in the early decades, the nature of requests in such petitions could vary quite widely and the official response, too, was far from standardised. Sometimes the plea was to make available a schoolmaster who could teach in a language appropriate to the local community, which could range from Persian to Portuguese. At other times, the government was petitioned for the Collector's recommendation for a local school to be taken over by the Education Society.

[43]On the other hand, English schools could be established in *zillah* towns, provided Board funds allowed, and the local community showed sufficient zeal

Vernacular Literacy and Contestation over the Dakshina

As the preceding discussion has emphasised, early education policy in Western India could not avert its dependence on instruction through the vernacular. Intellectuals here were quick to detect the new orientation that educational policy gave to vernacular textuality, just as they realised that access to the new sites of vernacular production would determine status and privilege within the new political order. This accentuated the significance of the vernacular sphere, even as it focussed attention on its vulnerable destiny in the shadow of English. Either way, the vernacular sphere seemed in risk of political ignominy: the subordination of the vernacular under English seemed inevitable, while severance from English could now only lead to marginality and intellectual impoverishment. Yet the emerging vernacular sphere owed its very existence to the inherently elitist limits of the English sphere, and the vernacular even assumed critical importance. In fact vernacular education and textuality emerged as the locus of diverse, contesting, and often irreconcilable claims

A prolonged debate over the distribution of the *dakshina* represented one of the most significant attempts from the Marathi-speaking *moffussil* areas to negotiate the centralised cultural authority vested in the Education Department. With various groups in and around Pune staking their claims, the story of the *dakshina* fund is important. It reflects the trajectory of official designs almost formulaically, as well as shifts in structures of patronage and contestation produced through educational policy. The record of *dakshina* under British rule[44] also poignantly captures

---

to bear a portion of the expenses. The latter would have to 'subscribe a sum of not under Rs. 500 for the purchase or erection of a schoolhouse', upon which, subject to the report of its Superintendent, the Board would advance a similar sum and proceed to establish a school according to the set terms and conditions. See 'Rules and Regulations of the Educational Establishments under the Board of Education, 1845' in J.A. Richey, ed., *SER*, Part II, pp. 161–3.

[44]For details on the significance of the *dakshina* fund, see fn. 26 above. Elphinstone's 'Report on the Territories Conquered from the Peshwa' declared the British intention to continue supporting the annual *dakshina* awards, as a mark of their 'respect for traditional native learning'. However, the size of the fund was reduced from five lakh rupees in the Peshwa period to Rs 50,000 in the years after

the ironies of the simultaneous laicisation and subalternisation of the vernacular sphere. Quick to realise the significance of the *dakshina* in the cultural politics of the region, Elphinstone declared at assumption of power that the British intended to continue giving out alms to learned brahmins.[45] However, the fund was substantially reduced and was now to be used to promote proficiency in the more 'useful' branches of native learning, like law and mathematics, by appointing a small number of professors to teach these subjects at the new Poona Sanskrit College. Established in 1821, the Poona College, like its counterparts in the other Presidencies, became the site for engineering shifts in the definitions and modes of native knowledge, before eventually paving the way for the introduction of colonial education and modern discourses through English.[46]

When the Poona Sanskrit College was established, it was decided to divide the reduced *dakshina* monies amounting to Rs 50,000 into

---

the take-over, the administration of the fund was the responsibility of the Office of the Deccan Commission, a little later it was handed over to the Poona Collector, and in 1834 the college was entrusted to the Agent for the Sardars in the Deccan. See 'Minute on the Dukshina' by W.J. Hunter and Major Thomas Candy dated 30 April 1850, in J.A. Richey, ed., *SER*, Part II, pp. 166–9.

Finally when official policy towards vernacular production underwent a major shift with the establishment of the University of Bombay in the late 1850s, the *dakshina* was turned into monthly stipends for deserving students seeking a college education in English.

[45] Elphinstone, 'Report on the Territories Conquered from the Peshwa', in G.W. Forrest, ed., *Selections from the Official Writings of the Hon. Mountstuart Elphinstone*', p. 335.

[46] Mr. Chaplin, the Commissioner of the Deccan, who had a hand in the inception of the Poona College, stated its objectives as 'the encouragement and improvement of the useful parts of the Hindoo learning and also to introduce, as far as possible, the means of communicating to our new subjects such branches of European knowledge as they may be able and willing to receive ...' quoted in 'Extract from Major Candy's Report of the Poona Sanskrit College' in J.A. Richey, ed., *SER*, Part II, p. 155.

Students and professors at the Poona Sanskrit College were employees of the government on monthly stipends and salaries. Attempts were also made to standardise instruction through the adoption of bureaucratic procedures such as prescribed courses of study, regular timetables and examinations.

two parts, of which, Rs 20,000 was for the Sanskrit College and the rest was meant to be distributed in the customary fashion to traditional pandits and *shastris*. However, gradually, from the 1820s, citing various reasons, chief among them being the unacceptability of hereditary claims, the government attempted to curtail grants of the latter category.[47] To begin with, the Poona Sanskrit College had a total of 8 *vydicks* and *shastris* with 10 assistant teachers and 100 stipendary students.[48] Soon, moves were afoot to introduce changes. In 1824 an English class was attached to the college. More changes followed. Over 1834–36 Major Candy replaced the native head of the college as the college superintendent, besides passing orders to dismiss the *vydicks* from their positions as professors. Alongside, a native professor in Marathi was appointed, ostensibly so that students would not leave the college 'with a contempt for their mother tongue and without the ability to write even a common letter in it with propriety'.[49] Notwithstanding the facetiousness of such claims, this step to patronise a system of learning with tendencies towards laicisation marked a distinct shift in the prevailing literate practices.

The main controversy over the *dakshina* occurred in 1849 on the

[47]The committee of *shastris* which scrutinised applications was dissolved in 1836, when Major Candy took over as the College Superintendent. It was announced that no new candidates would be admitted into the list of *dakshina* awards; instead, Candy's pay would be defrayed out of the *dakshina* fund monies. These measures provoked a series of petitions from the brahmin community of Pune and the surrounding areas who protested that 'the non-admission of candidates utterly changed the whole face of the *dakshina* and the whole brahmin community was thrown into consternation as if deprived of a great and accustomed indulgence which continued to be shown to them from the beginning of Peshwa power and which was best calculated to benefit the Hindoos and bless the government', quoted from 'Petition from brahmin inhabitants of Poona and the adjacent towns', January 1849, No. 1687 in 'Proceedings of the General Department for 1849'.

[48]At first, the College was headed by Raghuacharya, who was also the Professor of Nyaya. The staff comprised of five professors of the *shastras* employed at Rs 60 each; three professors of the Vedas at a combined expense of Rs 125 per month; ten assistants, each employed at a salary of Rs 20 per month and 86 students, whose stipends amounted to a monthly sum of Rs 430.

[49]Captain Candy's 'Report on the Poona Sanskrit College', in J.A. Richey, ed., *SER*, Part II, p. 158.

issue of patronage, when the authorities tried to replace the study of traditional, brahmanical texts by the pursuit of modern 'useful' learning through the vernacular. Until then, policy had been determined by the fear that the total abolition of grants for *vydick* and *shastric* studies would provoke large-scale resentment in the brahmanical circles of Pune. But in 1849 word got around to the English-educated group,[50] who met regularly at the Native General Library, that deliberations were on regarding the use of a sum of Rs 3000 accumulated through some lapsed grants. The entry of the students of the Poona English School into the fray marked the real turning point in the contestation over access to the *dakshina*, indicated by the political vocabulary and tone of their petitions. Arguing that the situation had changed substantially since the British government first took over the disbursement of *dakshina*, the English students claimed that Sanskrit scholars could no longer claim a monopoly to official patronage:

> The *dakshina* is an educational fund and the rules on which the premiums were to be given were made some years ago when there were few or no English students to compete for the *dakshina* premiums. ... Hence the premiums were directed to be given to the students of Sangscrit [*sic*] alone; these circumstances have long been changed and there are many brahmins who will write vernacular books on the most useful subjects such as the natives most urgently want and who are acquainted

[50]Gopal Hari Deshmukh (1823–90), alias Lokhitawadi, was employed as the Second Clerk in Office of the Agent for the Sardars in the Deccan, through which the *dakshina* was administered. Apparently, he got wind of the government's plans on this sum of Rs. 3000. It was this information that provoked the petition from the 'reformed' Poona School students. See Bhavani Shankar Sridhar Pandit, ed., *Raosaheb Keshav Shivram Bhavalkaryanche Atmavritta*, Nagpur, 1961, p. 103.

Gopal Hari Deshmukh was born into a *deshasth* brahmin family. His father had served under Bajirao I. Deshmukh studied at the Poona English school. He became well known for his trenchant critique of brahmanical practices in his *Shatapatre*, published as a series of letters in the Bombay weekly, *Prabhakar* from 1848 onwards. He helped set up the Native General Library and a branch of the anti-caste Paramhansa Mandali—in Pune. He also edited the Pune *Dnyanprakash*. Later in his career, he held many important positions, including those of the Assistant Inam commissioner, Joint Judge of the Nasik High Court and Member of the Law Council. He grew increasingly sympathetic towards the Arya Samaj.

with European sciences although they do not know Sangscrit [*sic*]. Your petitioners are willing to offer their services as translators and authors and the least expensive way to encourage them will be to allot some of the present premiums to your petitioners which they do not doubt your Lordship-in-Council will prefer to these premiums being granted as sinecure.[51]

Despite their common brahmanical background, 'colonial' brahmins sought to distance themselves from the old system of learning. They argued that their lack of training in Şanskrit could no longer be held against them as a mark of intellectual disadvantage. The skills that they had to offer were far more pertinent to the needs of the times, as compared to the exclusive, esoteric Sanskrit learning of the *vydicks*. Showing a shrewd grasp over changed political idioms, these petitioners argued that it was indefensible for students of a 'dead' language to secure a life-long access to an educational fund meant for the public promotion of 'useful' and liberal learning. Rather than entertaining contradictory criteria in making the grants, they urged the government to adopt a single set of uniform conditions for all awardees of the *dakshina*.[52] Claiming that continued support to Sanskrit learning was antithetical to the government's claimed objectives of establishing a system of 'national' education through the English schools, they argued:

> If encouragement of learning be the object then your petitioners respectfully suggest that the condition of producing Marathee original works or translations into it should be *simultaneous* with the exclusion of the *vydicks*, who being mere reciters of the *Veds* shall immediately be silenced and shall have no ground to complain of the injustice of government. On the contrary, granting of the *dakshina* premiums as sinecure life grants to Sangscrit [*sic*] scholars alone on the present

[51]'Petition signed by Students of the Poonah English School', dated 8 November 1849, Bombay Government Files, 'Proceedings of the General Department for 1849'.

[52]See 'Petition of the English students of Poona', dated 22 October 1849, Bombay Government Files, No. 1412 in 'Proceedings of the General Department for 1849.'

occasion will not only give unnecessary offence to all brahmins, *vydicks* and others included, but shall also give a final blow to the cause of national improvement and the interests of the English schools.[53]

This petition set in motion a flurry of counter-claims from contending groups of *bhats, shastris* and *vydicks* from Pune and the outlying areas stretching as far as South Konkan, Nasik, Wai, Satara, Maholee, 'Telinga', the Carnatic,[54] each trying to voice their collective discontent at the imminent changes. There were also unsuccessful local attempts to pressurise the signatories to withdraw their names from the petition.[55] But this small group of colonial intellectuals already had a keen sense of their own significance in the new literate arrangements. And yet their evident political acumen is not sufficient reason to infer that this fledgling intelligentsia had also internalised and accepted the norms of a liberal rationality. This was clearly borne out when, in a subsequent

[53]Ibid.

[54]'Petition from the *vydick* brahmins and the surrounding areas from Poona' dated 23 February 1850, No. 145, received in the Persian Department; an English translation of this exists in the 'Proceedings for the General Department for 1850'. Once the new policies concerning the *dakshina* were announced, another petition of protest dated 25 June 1850 with 3000 *modi* signatures was submitted by another group of brahmins, describing themselves as *vydicks* of Poona, but signed by a Vishnubhatt on their behalf. The large number of signatories would suggest that they may not have been 'real' *vydick* scholars but 'ordinary' *bhats* (priests). Claiming that they had been paid till 1839, they protested that their patronage was being discontinued, although they had done nothing to meet with the disapproval of the government. They shrewdly based their demands on their claims to command 'more' popular respect, and their larger numbers.

[55]In his personal memoirs, apparently written sometime in the late nineteenth century, Keshav Bhavalkar (1831–1902) recounts his stay in Poona, where he taught in the Government English School during the years 1849–1860. During this time, he was an active witness to the controversies and several petitions for patronage from the *dakshina*.

Bhavalkar was born in a poor brahmin family from the town of Junnar. Having trained as a schoolmaster at the Normal School in Bombay, Bhavalkar claims, Dadoba Pandurang, the Superintendent of Native schools, had selected him for the important vacancy in preference to local candidates. Apparently, he was chosen because of his reformist inclinations and was entrusted with the responsibility of trying to form a branch of the organisation, Paramhansa Mandali in Poona.

petition, untroubled by the irony of projecting themselves as the agents of a 'general enlightenment', this minuscule group asserted: 'Should the distribution of the *dakshina* be made upon a proper system it is capable of being turned to the *greatest advantage of the public* at large and disseminate new knowledge and true science *among all classes of the Hindoo nation.*'[56] (emphasis added)

Evidence suggests that around this time Phule had personal ties with some upper-caste individuals with reformist inclinations. Despite his contact with English and modern ideas through his education at the missionary school in Pune, it is unlikely that he was a regular at the small 'public' meetings of high-caste men at the Native Library in mid-nineteenth-century Pune.[57] Yet it seems that the only immediate social support to the petition by the English school students came from Phule and his caste fellows.[58] This created a controversy within Pune society,

[56]'Petition from the English students of Poona', dated 8 November 1849, Bombay Government Files, No. 1418 in 'Proceedings of the General Department for 1849.'

[57]For details of Phule's life and political career, especially his early links with upper-caste, reformist intellectuals, see chapter one, fn. 112. Bhavalkar's account speaks of Phule's presence in the meeting on the day before the crucial *sabha* called at Vishrambaagwada, where eight of the English school petitioners were to appear before the traditional intellectual establishment of the city. However, apparently, Phule was not one of the signatories to the petition. He narrates how, on the day of the meeting the group was met with angry insults along the way, as they proceeded to the *Dnyanprakash* office, where they were met by Phule and his followers, who escorted them up till the library rooms in Budhawarwada. From here, an additional police escort was provided. The entire party continued on to the *sabha*, but Phule and his men waited outside while the eight upper-caste petitioners proceeded to defend themselves. See Bhavani Shankar Sridhar Pandit, ed., *Raosaheb Keshav Shivram Bhavalkar Yanche Atmavritta*, pp. 106–8.

[58]Bhavalkar claims to have been personally involved in drawing up the above petition. Unfortunately, this very moving account of the efforts to organise the petition and the subsequent furore it raised within Pune society survives only in an incomplete form. A few of the petitioners were willing to face the penalty of excommunication. But most felt that it would be unfair for only a few to be subject to such a harsh punishment. Apparently, to save the brahmin students the ignominy of being made out-castes, Phule offered to take the responsibility for having organised the petition upon himself. On being questioned in the

despite which these 'neo-brahmins' found it necessary to accept the proffered help. Their decision to overlook opposition was propelled by the realisation that their political position was no longer entirely contingent upon their local influence. Rather, it was backed by their ideological links with English-educated groups produced through the network of colonial schools throughout the Presidency. If forced to, and in circumstances where it was expedient to do so, such neo-brahmins could temporarily even ally with 'inferior' castes. The move paid off, for the decisive Minute on the *dakshina* showed that the government had been more than mindful of the compromise formula suggested by the English school students:

> Your Petitioners understand that three classes of Brahmins have come forward to claim shares in the *dakshina*, viz. students of English, students of the *Shastras* and Sanskrit, and students of the Veds, and they respectfully suggest that a distribution to all these three classes in equal portions of thousand rupees each under condition of translating and composing useful works in vernacular languages will be a good measure and justice to all classes in the event of the Government not being disposed to carry out the plan proposed in the first petition of the English students dated 22 September last.[59]

Thus, the vexed circumstances under which possibilities of laicisation unfolded in colonial Western India witnessed intense contestation over the meagre official patronage available for the preparation of vernacular texts. In keeping with the general thrust of policy initiatives to control the vernacular sphere, albeit through rapidly diminishing investments, this round of re-structuring again saw a further reduction in the total allocations of the *dakshina*. The total disbursements aimed at 'cultivating' the vernacular now amounted to less than a paltry Rs 6000 per year. The government retained the division of the *dakshina*

---

sabha, we barely read that Bhavalkar named Phule as the person responsible for the radical petition, at which point the narrative is cut off, literally in mid sentence! See also fns. 55 and 57 above.

[59]See 'Petition of the students of the Poona English School', dated 11 November 1849, Bombay Government Files, No. 1418 in the 'Proceedings of the General Department for 1849'.

into two parts of Rs 1500 each, but all these grants were now earmarked for the printing of texts in the vernacular. Another Rs 1500, divided into eleven separate shares of different denominations,[60] were to be given away as prizes to Marathi writers and translators. It is at this point that we find an uncharacteristically explicit mention of the principle of universal access within the official discourse: 'These shares or prizes are to be open for competition to all classes and castes of Natives of India, and shall be given as rewards for the composition of original useful works in Marathee, or for translation into it of useful works from other languages.'[61] Despite assurances that the grants to traditional native learning would be continued, the last part of this Rs 1500 was now to be used to 'most widely benefit the country' through plans for the 'improvement and extension of native education and literature'.[62] The Poona Sanskrit College and the present Government English School were to be amalgamated and a sum of Rs 1200 per annum from the previous year's balance was to be spent on creating a professorship of the Vernacular Language for the 'cultivation' of the Marathi language. A native scholar with a competent knowledge of English, Sanskrit and Marathi would hold this chair. Any remaining money would be divided between various measures[63] aimed at 'producing great benefits

[60]Two prizes of Rs 200 each were announced for a work of 'not less than 150 octavo pages in some useful subject of Science or general literature of correct style and composition.' Four shares of Rs 150 each could go to a similarly 'appropriate' work of 100 octavo pages. Five awards for a third class prize of Rs 100 each would be given a similar works of 75 octavo pages. See 'Minute on the Dukshina' by W.J. Hunter and Major T. Candy dated 30 April 1850, in J.A. Richey, ed., *SER*, Part II, p. 166. See also fn. 63 below.

[61]Ibid. A similar phrase suggesting the tendency towards laicisation is repeated again towards the end of the Minute. We are told that the translation exhibitions to be held in Poona College were also to 'be opened to all natives of India'.

[62]Ibid., p. 168.

[63]The measures included endowments for four translation exhibitions, each of 40 rupees a month, to be held by 'young men possessing a competent knowledge of English and Marathi and rudimental [*sic*] knowledge of Sanskrit' who would teach part-time at the College and use the rest of their time in doing translations under the supervision of the Head of the College, Major Candy. These provisions would cost an estimated Rs 1920 per annum. The remainder Rs 774 was to be constituted in to a General Fund for the Encouragement of Native Literature

to the general body of the Marathi people'.[64] Once approved, these new rules were to be publicised in the Government Gazette and in the native and other local papers.[65]

As the preceding discussion shows, the contestation over the *dakshina* fund dramatically reflects the appropriation and displacement of old systems of learning through the introduction of the new cultural and cognitive norms and their institutional elaboration under colonial rule. Colonial policy initiatives to redefine prevailing forms and content created gaps for the articulation of contesting claims from sections of the old intelligentsia and the newly-schooled elite. Importantly, this scenario shows the implications of the extension of colonial literacy which, in principle, represented an unprecedented opportunity for a less hierarchical distribution of knowledge. However, conceived as a pedagogic project and administered monologically through a centralised apparatus that responded with profound bureaucratic indifference, the extension of modernity into the hinterland had deeply undemocratic implications. Unlike their counterparts in Bombay, with few external avenues like trade and finance to establish their influence with the colonial government, the emerging intelligentsia in Poona depended almost directly on the British government for their position within local society. Such direct links between modern intellectuals and state power were not surprising in the colonial situation, where the displacement of political modernity meant that norms of mediation and representative government informed political practice merely in principle.

These events highlighted the tussle between traditional learning, based on the hierarchies of *jati*, and the emerging community of colonial-educated intellectuals. They also showed that for reasons linked to but discontinuous with the earlier cultural order, the new intelligentsia too was an elitist minority. Numerical marginality placed the new elite at a disadvantage that the older intelligentsia did not have to confront. The new elite had to base their legitimacy upon bourgeois

and Education, which was to be used to encourage the composition and printing of vernacular texts and to reward meritorious vernacular school masters. See ibid., pp. 168–9.

[64]Ibid., p. 169.

[65]Ibid., p. 167.

principles of being bearers of 'useful' skills to promote 'general enlightenment'. Evidently, there were constraints upon this bunch of officially selected 'trainees' at the Poona English School when projecting themselves as agents of a laicised order. Consequently, their advocacy of an egalitarian vernacular culture represented more a programmatic imaginary than a concrete ideal. The articulation of the hegemonic function within colonial society was thus beset by profound contradictory tensions. Intellectuals had to claim a mediating function between the colonial government and their 'unreformed' compatriots from a position that was politically privileged but numerically insignificant. Consequently, in asserting their leadership within a political order based on principles of representative legitimacy, this minuscule group had to rely upon the support of 'lesser' groups outside their limited circle. Curiously, as the 'neo-brahmins' of Pune quickly found out, their minority status apparently also held definite advantages. Their position as political intermediaries made them aware of the uniqueness of their cultural capital and its potential to establish a monopolistic ideological affinity with state power. Consequently, their discourse acquired an aggressive tone not quite commensurate with their numerical strength or actual influence over state policy.

The dispute between the 'traditional' and new 'colonial' brahmin groups created a marginal space for the emergence of a lower-caste voice in the colonial public arena. The juncture at which the exclusive provision of official patronage for vernacular production was announced also saw a short-lived opportunity for a caste alliance between the English-school elite and the lower-caste constituency, comprising mainly of the *mahar* and *mang* communities under Phule's leadership in Pune. But the possibility of this critical alliance was limited: though the new brahmins could advance their claims only with the help of the lower-caste constituency under Phule's leadership, the tragic irony of these processes were soon evident. For, a few years later, the same *dakshina* prize committee which had been set up through 'outside' support from the lower-caste constituency[66] refused to admit Phule's manuscripts, citing aesthetic and literary grounds.

[66]See fns. 57 and 58 above.

Despite the shift in legitimating values and their dependence on non-elite groups, the new upper-caste intelligentsia retained almost exclusive control over cultural production. With the exclusion of the lower-caste voice from the primary arenas, the possibility that the dissemination of the new literate order might lead to a socially inclusive discourse reflecting heterogeneous interests also receded, and the emerging arena of public discourse and contestation was less than likely to allow for the accommodation of lower-caste interests. Phule's next step suggested that he had read these signs in the *dakshina* episode of 1849–50 quite clearly. Hence, it is appropriate to look at Phule's efforts to provide literate skills to students from lower-caste communities by invoking the principles of voluntary association. Close on the heels of the *dakshina* dispute, in 1852, the Society for the Promotion for the Education of the Mahars and the Mangs was established in Pune. With great difficulty, the Society secured some support from the *dakshina* fund for its schools for a few years.[67] The Society's efforts attracted both publicity[68] and local opposition,[69] and although the government feted Phule for his contribution,[70] in the end there was little help forthcoming either from official policy or from the upper-caste intelligentsia.

The position of modern intellectuals and their role as mediators between the government and the lay public is crucial to the communicative structure of modern societies. The normative emphasis on networks of consensual rationality within the political discourses of modernity[71] is premised on such relations between power and knowl-

[67]See fn. 83 below.

[68]See fns. 70 and 78 below.

[69]See fn. 80 below.

[70]The colonial government presented Phule with a set expensive shawls, the traditional symbol of intellectual honour, in a public ceremony in Pune on 20 November 1852. This ceremony was widely reported by the Marathi missionary papers.

[71]In a sub-section entitled the 'The Basic Blueprint', Habermas notes how, by virtue of being tied to the critical-public exercise of reason, modern power undercuts the very principles by which pre-modern regimes rule. He elaborates: 'The principle of control that the bourgeois public opposed to the concentration of powers of command, namely, publicity—was intended to change domination

edge. Arguably, the modern university represented the institutionalisation of bourgeois ideals of communicative rationality and general enlightenment. Equally, it may be seen as the crystallised image of pedagogic assumptions intrinsic to political modernity, especially the exercise of representative government. Such ideologies of individual improvement and general enlightenment were built into the project of colonial education in even more complex ways, for Indian modernity afforded only minimal possibilities for the development of large-scale, inclusive and consensual social bonds. The rise of colonial higher education, in this respect, echoed the emergence of modern educational systems in the West. Pierre Bourdieu's work on education and linguistic standardisation has shown how these processes assisted the reproduction of social hierarchy in modern Western societies.[72] Such insights into the conservative biases of modern education supplement studies that documented how modern education systems were put in place by bourgeois governments as a response to lower-class demands for political rights.[73] Colonial policy sought to delegitimise norms based on a pre-print cultural order in favour of standards that purportedly aspired to the general enlightenment of the colonised population. Nevertheless, as events in mid-nineteenth century Pune showed only too well, the new arrangements contained few provisions to support claims to

---

as such. The claim to power represented in rational-critical public debate, which ... renounced the form of a claim to rule, would entail, if it were to prevail, more than just an exchange of the basis of legitimation while domination was maintained in principle.' Habermas, *The Structural Transformation of the Public Sphere*, 1989, p. 28. See also chapter five, fn. 45, of the present book.

[72]Pierre Bourdieu, *Language and Symbolic Power*, Cambridge, 1991.

[73]See Pierre Bourdieu and Jean-Claude Passeron, trans. Richard Nice, *Reproduction in Education, Society, Culture*, English edn., London, 1990; Andy Green, *Education and State Formation in England, France and the United States of America*, London, 1990; Brian Simon, *Studies in the History of Education 1780–1870*, London 1960; Fritz Ringer, Detlef Muller, Brian Simon, eds, *The Rise of the Modern Education System: Structural Change and Social Reproduction, 1870–1920*, Cambridge, 1987. For an account of the role of the discipline of English Literature in university education in nineteenth-century England, see Terry Eagleton, *Literary Theory: An Introduction*, Minneapolis, 1983 and Chris Baldick, *The Social Mission of English Criticism: 1848–1932*, Oxford, 1983.

literacy from sections that had been excluded from pre-colonial literate communities.

The Society for the Promotion of Education of the Mahars and the Mangs, Established Pune, 1852

Even if the emerging public discourses showed few signs of accommodating lower-caste interests, they were restructuring collective identities and modes of negotiating marginality. In a bold move, soon after the *dakshina* episode, Phule decided to organise lower-caste interests through the formation of an association that would take up the cause of education for boys and girls in the *mahar* and *mang* communities. Voluntary associations had been a critical element in the creation of large-scale networks within Western modernity. In the colonial context, associational principles were invoked with respect to access to colonial education. Whereas in the West these ideas had signified the creation of communicative, social and economic ties extending beyond narrow bounds, an important aspect of voluntary associations in Western India was their use to safeguard community interests and foreground the claims of particular identities.

Phule's initiatives, well-known in the writings on the political history of nineteenth-century Maharashtra,[74] highlight his astute understanding of the new literate regime and power structure. Phule's first step was to start schools for girls in 1851,[75] the first such native initiative in Pune. By 1852 he had also been able to organise three schools for lower-caste boys, which was probably unprecedented at the time anywhere on the subcontinent. Apparently there were 237 pupils on the rolls in the three girls' schools, out of which the average attendance was just a little less

[74]For a detailed account of Phule's career and writings in the context of nineteenth-century colonial politics in Western India, see Rosalind O'Hanlon, *Caste, Conflict and Ideology*.

[75]Girls were first admitted into the missionary-run schools. The first native schools for girls in Bombay had been organised through the vernacular *sabhas*, the *Marathi* and the *Gujarati Dnyanprasarak Mandalis*. The Marathi girls' schools were supported by Jagannath Shankarseth, the well-known trader and banker. As a lower-caste initiative, the girls' schools started by Phule had greater political significance.

than 200,[76] as against 270 boys on the rolls in the three lower-caste schools in 1857, out of which 213 presented themselves for the annual examination.[77] These figures are not the best index of the impact these schools would have had on the public imagination. In thinking of the repercussions of these moves, it is important to remember the enhanced visibility these schools enjoyed through the ceremonial staging of their annual examinations as public occasions that demonstrated the government's 'benevolence'.[78] Phule's own association with both these projects lasted for about ten years,[79] and these initiatives were remarkable for the emergence of non-brahmin agency in the sphere of public action. They also represented an uneasy but unprecedented alliance between brahmin and non-brahmin agents. These efforts faced serious difficulties and opposition.[80] Nevertheless, it was significant that the schools were

[76]'Report of the Second Annual Examination of the Native Female Schools in Poona', held on 12 February 1853, reprinted in Phadke *et al*, eds, *MPSV*, p. 619.

[77]Appendix No. 1 and Memoranda to the 'Report of the Public Examination of the Poona Mahar and Mang Schools held on 2 February 1858' in Bombay Presidency General Department Files, Vol. No. 38 of 1858, reprinted in ibid., pp. 639–40 and pp. 647–51.

[78]It seems that the government was more favourably disposed towards Phule's contribution to the education of girls than his efforts to start schools for lower-caste boys. The public honour extended to Phule was for his work in setting up girls' schools. Moreover, the examinations and ceremonies for the girls' schools took place amidst much fanfare in the quadrangle of Pune College, a hallowed site for the staging of colonial politics in the city. On the other hand, the public examination of the lower-caste students seems to have been a far less spectacular affair, being held at a peripheral location at Babajee Munajee's Coach Factory near the Civil Hospital. See ibid., pp. 617–18 and 635.

[79]In his testimony to the Hunter Commission, Phule wrote of having worked in the school for *mahar* and *mang* boys for about ten years after it was established. He is less specific about his association with the girls' school; we only learn that he and his wife worked there for 'many years'. Apparently, these schools still existed at the time when Phule was recording his testimony, but had been taken over by the Educational Department. See 'Memorial addressed to the Education Commission' recorded by Jyotirao Phule in Poona on 19th October 1882 in *Report of the Education Commission, Bombay*, Vol. II, Calcutta, 1884, reprinted in ibid., p. 233.

[80]The missionary paper, *Dnyanodaya* of 15 September 1853 carried an extensive report on the public examinations at the lower-caste schools. In his

run through joint efforts from disparate sections of colonial society.[81] The managing bodies of both these schools had a few common patrons, including some prominent brahmin intellectuals and colonial officials. The adoption of Western principles of voluntary association facilitated dealings with the colonial government, but equally, the organisational form allowed individuals from different backgrounds to come together on the basis of shared concerns. Going by the relative size of official grants to girls' and boys' schools, it seemed that the colonial state was far keener to exhibit itself as the champion of female education rather than risk supporting the general lower-caste cause. Whereas the Managing Committee of the Female Schools at Pune was granted Rs 75 per month from the *dakshina* fund,[82] the lower-caste boys' schools run by the society received a much smaller grant,[83] despite clear signs that donations and

---

speech, Phule referred to the difficulties he had faced: both he and his wife had to leave home because of his father's disapproval. There was criticism from within the *mali* caste as well. People were unwilling to lend them the space needed to run the school, and the money for a new building was even more difficult to find. Moreover, it was not easy to persuade *mahar* and *mang* families to send their boys to the school. At that point, apparently, Sadashiv Govande helped with funds and Ranba Mahar and Lahuji bin Ragh Raut Mang explained the benefits of education to their respective communities. See report in *Dnyanodaya* of 15 September 1853 quoted in ibid., p. 611.

[81]Describing the reasons for forming the society, the above letter by Moro Vitthal Walwekar, the secretary of the society, observed: 'Ignorance is the great affliction of this nation [*desh*]. Any one hoping to find a remedy is confronted by the obstacles of caste [*jatibhed*] and language [*bhashabhed*], differences that no one dares remove.' The letter explained: 'Having realised that to educate the *mahar* and *mang* communities constituted the foremost benefit to the nation/region [*desh*], it had been Jyotirao's endeavour for some time now to work towards this end. But it is by far preferable that such work be carried out as joint effort between more dedicated persons rather than by just one conscientious person.' Translated from the original Marathi quotation, excerpted in ibid., p. 612.

[82]The account for receipts and disbursements for the Poona Native Female School Fund from 1 March 1852 to 28 February 1853 shows that Rs 900 of the expenses for this period came from grants from the *dakshina* Prize Committee and Rs 1072 from private subscriptions. The audited statement of accounts was signed by Krishnashastri Chiplunkar and Kero Laxman Chattre. See ibid., p. 632.

[83] We learn from the above-mentioned *Dnyanodaya* report of 1853 that the lower-caste boys' schools drew a monthly grant of Rs 25 from the *dakshina* Prize

subscriptions from native quarters would be far more difficult to secure in the latter case. The issue of the ways in which the caste divide figured in the arenas of colonial cultural politics is important, for it is a preliminary to discussing the hegemonic aspirations of this colonial intelligentsia who, by the 1880s, eventually emerged as the prime authors of nationalist discourse.

Marginality, Translation and Subaltern Literacy

It would be interesting to look more closely at the implications of Phule's attempt to organise lower-caste claims to education, especially by tracing what became of these low-caste students after they left school. Data on this front is not easy to come by, and when looking for divergent views on the politics of colonial literacy we have to rely on Phule's own writings. As an intellectual from a non-elite caste background, Phule's perceptions were different from those of upper-caste vernacular discourse. His writings constantly reiterate the importance of education to any lower-caste self-assertion. Another related theme in it is the role of colonial education in determining the structure of domination emerging in native society. Education as a whole forms the main theme of several of his important texts: his earliest available composition, a play entitled *Tritiya Ratna*, written in 1855 but which remained unpublished; the *povada* entitled *Vidyakhaatatil Brahman Pantoji*, published originally in the *Satyadeepika* of June 1869; and *Gulamgiri* (Slavery) published in 1873. The last-named contains an English preface and a whole chapter in the main Marathi text that dwell on education. Phule's remarkable

Committee. Soon after the public examination in February, 1858, the Society petitioned for an increase in the grant as private support had been diminishing. The society's letter dated 23 February 1858 asked for the entire monthly cost of Rs 109–3–1/4 for running these schools. However, the Department of Public Instruction replied that the grant would be increased only to Rs 50 per month and any further increase would be subject to a personal visit made by the President, Mr Howard. See letter dated 3 June 1858, No. 1265 in Bombay Presidency General Department Files, Vol. 24 of 1858. The 'Report of Poona Mahar and Mang Schools', cited above, mentions that, besides the monthly grant of Rs 25, the government had also sanctioned Rs 5000 for a new school building. See report reprinted in ibid., p. 637.

deposition in an English statement to the Education Commission in 1882 again shows his intense preoccupation with the significance of education to modern politics.

On first impression, the major difference between Phule's writings and upper-caste discourse may appear to be the fact that, unlike the latter, they do not really discuss the benefits of the dissemination of the new knowledge. Nor do the divisive effects of bilingual literacy figure as an explicit theme in Phule's writings, as they do in the vernacular writings of many upper-caste early intellectuals.[84] Yet it would be naive to see this simply as a lacuna in Phule's grasp of the nature of colonial politics. This apparent 'lack' needs to be related to Phule's strong sense of his political position and purpose.

At one level Phule's work is acutely informed by an awareness of the way the politics of language worked in the colonial world, although it could be said that his later work shows an even greater acknowledgement of this reality. Clearly realising the significance of publicity within colonial politics, Phule made it a point to attach English translations of his title pages and dedications, whereas the main text, except for these first few pages, was only in Marathi. This became his regular practice, especially after he published his *Chatrapati Shivaji Raje Bhosle yanche Povada* in 1869 from Bombay. Phule's major text, *Gulamgiri*, best brings out his strategy to straddle the linguistic divide that characterised colonial politics. Its title page was boldly translated into English as 'Slavery—In this civilised British Government under the cloak of Brahmanism exposed by Jotirao Govindrao Fule'. In order to emphasise his political intentions, he attached an English preface to elaborate his main theme, namely the suppression of lower castes at the hands of the brahmanical order from 'ancient times' to 'the present'.[85] This

[84]For an analysis of the representations of the bilingual divide in vernacular discourse, see chapter three, pp. 127–38.

[85]As O'Hanlon's study has shown, through a skilful appropriation of orientalist historiography Phule's efforts aimed to consolidate a lower-caste public identity within the arena of nineteenth-century colonial politics. O'Hanlon's work emphasises Phule's great rhetorical dexterity as a writer and political leader. See Rosalind O'Hanlon, *Caste, Conflict and Ideology*; for an argument about Phule's strategic engagement with philological and orientalist discourse, see chapter one, pp. 52–4.

English preface intended to bring the book directly to the notice of government, especially as by this time the administrative machinery and apparatus of publicity were already dominated by upper castes.[86] This showed Phule's shrewd grasp of the dynamics of representation in the colonial public sphere, his keen awareness of the linguistic divide that characterised colonial politics. Phule's primary concern was with representing the everyday circumstances and the marginalisation of illiterate, lower-caste, labouring and rural communities to the colonial government. Thus, in apparently reducing the bilingual hierarchy within the colonial power structure to something like a cryptic formula, Phule's work is profoundly suggestive of the emerging linguistic and political divisions within native society. This puts in perspective the apparent lack of discussion on the importance of translation and the accumulation of knowledge for the enrichment of the vernacular in his writings. Moreover, despite his emphasis on universal primary education, Phule's writings do not disparage the upper-caste led translation project[87] or the pursuit of higher learning. The schools he helped start had to rely on vernacular texts[88] prepared by brahmins affiliated to the Bombay

[86]Phule's testimony to the Hunter Commission, which was entirely in English included excerpts from this Preface. The following statement shows Phule's deliberate use of English: 'I wrote some years ago a Marathi pamphlet exposing the religious practices of the brahmins and incidentally among other matters, adverted therein to the present system of education, which by providing ampler funds for higher classes only, aims to leave the masses wallowing in ignorance and poverty. I summarised the views expressed in the book in an English preface attached thereto, portions of which I reproduce here so far as they relate to the present inquiry.' 'Memorial Addressed to the Education Commission, a statement for the information of the Education Commission dated 19 October 1882, by Joteerao Govindrao Phooley, Merchant, Cultivator and Municipal Commissioner, Peth Joona Ganj, Poona', reprinted in Phadke, *et al.*, eds, *MPSV*, pp. 233–4.

[87]By the time Phule recorded his testimony to the Hunter Commission in 1882, he was greatly disillusioned with the upper-caste reformist project and bitterly resented brahmanical dominance in the colonial bureaucracy. Yet he remained firmly convinced that the extension of colonial education would be central to redressing the marginality of lower-caste groups.

[88]However, some of the brighter students at the girls' school were taught basic reading and counting skills in English. See 'Report of the Second Annual Examination of the Native Female Schools in Poona', reprinted in ibid., p. 625.

Education Society. In developing his critique of brahmanical dominance through the monopolisation of intellectual, ritual and political power, Phule was not underestimating the necessity of learning but was attacking the elitist orientation of colonial education. Speaking on behalf of the large numbers who remained unprovided for in allocations for literacy, Phule's concerns were bound to differ from the responses of upper-caste intellectuals who possessed the advantage of belonging to communities with literate backgrounds. Given these historical and political constraints, Phule's discourse had to remain aloof from the translation project and the production of modern discourses in the vernacular.

However, as the shaping of a bilingual literacy was primary to the making of the colonial public sphere, it is crucial to note that Phule's initiatives to provide education to lower-caste children nevertheless left these communities excluded from the sites of translation and the making of vernacular discourse. Despite their blend of incisive analysis, rhetorical vigour and proximity with the everyday lives of ordinary people, Phule's writings were bound to remain something of a marginal feat within the structural limits of the colonial-liberal public sphere. The whole poignancy of the situation was quite apparent when, in 1855, the very *dakshina* Prize Committee that had been set up through support from Phule and his associates refused to admit his play *Tritiya Ratna*[89] into the 'open' competition which was meant to encourage the composition of modern vernacular texts. There is tragic irony in the fact that it is neither within policy documents, nor in the upper-caste discourse, but rather in Phule's writings that we have one of the most unequivocal and clear-sighted enunciations of the idea of universal access. Testifying before the Hunter Commission in 1882, and opposing the government move to cut down spending on primary education—ostensibly as a way of curbing the overcrowding of bureaucratic professions—Phule's response struck a forthright and balanced note:

> Although the number of students presenting for the Entrance Examination is not at all large when the diffusion of knowledge in the country

[89]See *Gulamgiri*, Pune, 1873, reprinted in ibid., p. 182. Much of Phule's important work, including his ballad on Shivaji, was first published in the missionary paper *Satyadeepika*, or privately through the help of friends.

is taken into consideration, it looks large when the requirements of Government are concerned. *Were the education universal and within easy reach of all*, the number would have been larger still, and it should be so, and I hope it shall be so hereafter.[90]

In the light of this analysis, we shall look more closely at asymmetries underlying the bilingual relation between English and Marathi and the political implications of these divisions within colonial society.

[90]'Memorial addressed to the Education Commission', reprinted in ibid., p. 243.

3

Colonial Education and the Cultivation of English and Marathi

Hierarchies of Language and the Emerging Political Structure

Introduction

Having argued that the transfer of liberal discourses as colonial ideology was connected to asymmetries in colonial bilingual relations, I will now argue some of the important ways in which colonial bilingualism shaped the emerging political hierarchy. Post-colonial theory has much to offer here, but an understanding of alternative modernities will have to go beyond general insights on the connections between colonial power and the appropriation and 'othering' of native textual traditions within the self-narratives of post-enlightenment Europe.[1] Homi Bhabha's writings[2] have invoked post-structuralist perspectives, especially the notions of difference, discontinuity and displacement in conceptualising the links between modern modes of inscription, colonial power and the production of colonial-modern subjectivities. Similarly, Cohn's essay on the Orientalist study of Indian languages[3] drew on ethno-historical perspectives and methodologies to provide insights into the role of linguistic objectification in undoing the internal

[1]Edward Said, *Orientalism*, New York, 1978.
[2]Homi Bhabha, *The Location of Culture*, London, 1994.
[3]See Bernard Cohn's essay cited in chapter one, fn. 97.

coherence of 'primitive' ways of life and cultural practice. Given the complex intersections between the colonial project and the politics of language, scholarship on the impact of colonial rule in India has been understandably concerned with the consequences of the entry of English. Bhabha's writings[4] were among the earliest to suggest that to think of colonial power is to map the meanings that the English book and the printed word acquired for those who did not possess the requisite linguistic skills. The circulation of the white man's books, the subalternising influence of colonial literacy and the apprehension of colonial power were linked in complex ways, affecting those who were 'schooled' as well as those who suffered the ignominy of being neglected by the education project.[5] Tejaswini Niranjana has shown how the project of translation became one of the main sites through which colonialism acquired its discursive power by enabling the insertion and subordination of native texts into Eurocentric cultural narratives.

Yet in trying to understand the cultural and intellectual transactions underlying colonial power, the fact that colonialism worked by altering discursive and linguistic norms and practices seems to have prevented scholars from attending to the *institutional* dimensions of these discursive interventions. Indigenous cultural norms were reshaped through radical and *irrevocable* shifts in existing linguistic practices. Colonial cultural policy altered institutional structures, which meant that these changes endured.

Said's work showed the manoeuvres within Western post-enlightenment thought to harness difference via the logic of 'othering', while Bhabha's oeuvre has emphasised the *mutability* of liberal structures and their potential to produce difference through colonial displacement and translation. These perspectives open ways of investigating the institutional dimensions of the colonial impact through its moves to telescope and reproduce Western modernity as colonial-liberal discourse.[6] The

[4]Homi Bhabha, 'Signs Taken for Wonders: Questions of Ambivalence and Authority under a Tree outside Delhi, May 1817', *The Location of Culture*, pp. 102–22.

[5]Tejaswini Niranjana, *Siting Translation: History, Post-structuralism and the Colonial Context*, Berkeley, 1992.

[6]As mentioned in chapter two, fn. 1, some work by the Subaltern Studies

previous chapter has sketched how the construction of colonial ideology involved processes of translation across cultural and linguistic divides.[7] This suggests that the idea of translation did not just account for the means by which the West appropriated the authority to generate a judgmental discourse on native cultural traditions, but that it was intrinsic to the colonial encounter in more fundamental ways. The ability of colonial power to reproduce and disseminate the authority of Western norms and notions of culture, communicative exchange, and cognition impels us to think of translation as absolutely *endemic* to the construction of colonial discourse, and by implication to the very processes that underlie the creation of a colonial intelligentsia. The construction of colonial power was founded on the ability of the bourgeois imagination to posit a direct relation between the Western enlightenment and non-Western ways of life. This relation was conceived as a brusquely established intercourse between the respective languages. They were ostensibly 'in dialogue', despite their significant conceptual and cultural dissimilarities. Coded into these processes of translation and redefinition was the central tension underlying the journey of liberal ideas to non-Western societies, namely their *simultaneous* presence as signifiers of Western cultural imperialism and the spread of modern discourses outside their context of origin.

On the one hand, native languages were placed in a relation of direct subordination *vis-à-vis* English and, on the other, colonial translation made it appear as though, in principle, English and vernacular publics

---

collective has addressed questions of displacement of liberal discourse as colonial ideology. In addition to the works cited there, see also Dipesh Chakrabarty, 'The Difference/Deferral of (a) Colonial Modernity—Public Debate on Domesticity in British Bengal', *History Workshop Journal*, No. 36, September 1993, pp. 1–34; Gyan Prakash 'Writing Post-Orientalist Histories of the Third World: Perspectives from Indian Historiography', *Comparative Studies in Society and History*, No. 32, 1990, pp. 383–408; Partha Chatterjee, *The Nation and its Fragments.* For a more general sampling of issues that have gained prominence in the study of nineteenth-century South Asia since Said's *Orientalism*, see Carol Breckenridge and Peter van der Veer, eds, *Orientalism and the Post-Colonial Predicament: Perspectives on a South Asian World*, Philadelphia, 1993.

[7]See especially sub-section 'Colonial policy, bilingualism and general access' in chapter two, pp. 71–9.

could be endowed with symmetrical expressive and cognitive repertoires. This was far from true. The disproportionate sizes of these reading audiences and the authority they enjoyed compounded the asymmetry between English and the vernacular spheres. Thus, despite the apparent homology that official policy sought to establish between English and the vernacular, there remained an inherent contradiction between the modern, universalist norms upon which English sought to base its claims as a language of superior rationality and the circumscribed English-knowing audience. Knowledge of English introduced native intellectuals to a hoirzon of new intellectual, cultural and political choices, but it also placed them severely at odds with their own social world.

A small class of intellectuals, exclusively endowed with the skills of translation and mediation, came into being. The paradox between the *illegitimacy* of privilege and the *elitist* concentration of the intellectual means to generate normative discourses constitutes a crucial tension within the political discourses of modernity. This tension appeared in the colonial context in the form of the limits of translation between English and the vernaculars. The position of modern intelligentsias has been determined in part by their potential to negotiate the possibilities of dissemination and representation within the world of literate politics. With language as a site in the construction of state–society relations, the relation between the English sphere and the vernacular publics was vital to the hegemonic efforts of the intelligentsia.[8]

English represented both a language and a system of knowledge against which native cultural and social practices were to be measured and then reformed.[9] Arguably, the fact that the political repercussions of colonial bilingualism have not been sufficient thematised in South Asian history is itself a sign of its enduring legacies. Sudipta Kaviraj[10]

[8]For a discussion of how the significance of linguistic divide entered the political calculations of the emerging colonial intelligentsia in nineteenth-century Western India as they sought to further their hegemonic aspirations, see chapter five.

[9]Gauri Vishwanathan, *Masks of Conquest* and Tejaswini Niranjana, *Siting Translation*.

[10]Sudipta Kaviraj, 'The Imaginary Institution of India' in P. Chatterjee and G. Pandey, eds, *Subaltern Studies VII*, Delhi, 1992.

points out the connection between India's political modernity and the linguistic reinscription of the native world under colonialism. He shows that Indians derived ideas as modern political beings from the experience of colonialism, and that contemporary linguistic-regional identities were also fashioned during the colonial period. The initial years of colonial rule in Western India saw a stress within official policy on instruction through the vernacular to an extent not seen in other parts of the subcontinent, especially Bengal. Consequently, quite uniquely perhaps, the first few decades of colonial rule had seen the emergence of a native discourse reflecting critically the cultural and political possibilities of the colonial world. Differences were beginning to emerge on the location and political position of the sites of production for vernacular and English discourse, with critical implications for the capacity of a colonial intelligentsia endowed with a two-tiered, bilingual capacity.

This linguistic hierarchy was internalised most actively through the pedagogic experience of the colonial classroom, but also through the asymmetry in financial outlays for English and vernacular instruction. Shifts in official patronage of translation exemplify the importance of vernacular literacy within colonial policy. The metaphor of the European Renaissance figured prominently within official and native discourse to describe shifts in linguistic hierarchy emanating from English. Native discourse too displayed a preoccupation with the importance of translation and the 'accumulation' of knowledge through the vernacular; the efforts of native intellectuals to come to terms with the bilingual divide will be discussed at some length. From the mid 1850s, as the education project developed into a system of higher education, the policy towards the vernaculars showed shifts as plans for the establishment of Bombay University emerged and as budgetary allocations were divided between vernacular (Marathi) schools and schools where the medium of instruction was English. When the already parsimonious scale of allocations to vernacular education further reduced, it was clear that changes in education policy were a sign of the tightening control upon avenues for social mobility. The subordination of the vernaculars to English had never been in doubt, but now the emergence of higher education in English was further expression of the elitism of the education project, which fixed the vernacular into a secondary position despite its 'popular' significance. By the latter half of the nineteenth century, the vernaculars had been subalternised within the education system, as had the status of the Marathi school-educated intelligentsia *vis-à-vis* the university/English-educated elite. These divisions affected not only composition in Marathi but also the possibilities of forging a popular anti-colonial alliance. By the first phase of overt nationalism in the 1880s, the structural contours of the arrangements of privilege and marginality were institutionalised. The intelligentsia had indeed learnt its 'lessons' and relinquished whatever radical aspirations they may have harboured for a less hierarchical society.[11]

Bilingualism, Translation and Colonial Literacy

From 1822, education policy in Western India had to work with the assumption that, at least initially, only the vernaculars could sustain a modern literate culture necessary for the dissemination of colonial ideology.[12] This would be a more efficient way of introducing Western learning, besides providing preliminary training in the cognitive skills that the study of English would require. Official initiatives thus had to maintain an uneasy stance between its espousal of modern, Western learning and the compulsion towards dissemination through the

[11]The Hunter Commission was appointed to review the state of education throughout the subcontinent. It submitted its *Report on Education in India* in 1882. The purpose of this exercise was to explore the possibility of encouraging private investment in the field of higher education, which, until then, had been under strict government monopoly. Further, by 1882, there was ample evidence that the colonial intelligentsia had reached the historical limits of its 'progressive' phase. For instance, in 1885, the Sarvajanik Sabha, the most influential 'liberal' political association of the time in Western India, vehemently opposed the government's announcement to allot a small number of scholarships annually to deserving students from the lower castes. For an argument about the increasing orthodoxy of the intelligentsia as they 'progressed' towards articulating an explicit nationalist position, see chapter five. For the testimony of upper-caste intellectuals on the distribution of government funds for native education, see *Report of the Bombay Provincial Committee of the Education Commission*, Calcutta, 1884.

[12]For a discussion of the early emphasis on vernacular education in the Bombay Presidency, see chapter two, especially fns. 19 and 39.

vernacular. Society schools were 'primarily for the conveyance of knowledge in the languages of the country' and for 'providing suitable books of instruction' for use in the native schools' in the several languages.[13] Unlike pre-colonial relations between Sanskrit, Persian and Arabic, and the vernacular traditions, the new high language was now invested with normative functions in order to actively mould vernacular textuality in its own image. This was a difficult balance to maintain and already by 1824 the move to introduce English in a *separate* school had been made, where English would be 'taught classically' and 'here instruction might also be given in that language on History, Geography and the popular branches of science'.[14] This made it clear that the cultivation of the vernaculars entered the purview of education policy basically as a *prelude* to English education. Shifts in policy in the 1850s formalised the dominance of English in the education system, but the ground was already being paved: 'a Mahratta, a Guzerattee and an English School should be established at the Presidency but scholars not be admitted into the latter till after they have received instruction in one of the others.'[15] A large part of the Education Society's work would be to provide reading materials in the vernacular schools through translation. Given the urgency, pedagogic efforts could not await the preparation of texts; these processes would have to take place simultaneously. Consequently the ambitious colonial pedagogical mission could not proceed from prepared texts, and, even when these were available, translation formed the core of the circular teaching method as students were drilled to acquire new skills simultaneously both in English and the vernacular: 'The first class of the Mahrattas consisted of 12 boys. ... They read short polysyllable lessons in English from Murray's Spelling and Reading Exercises, and translated them into

[13]Resolutions passed at a general meeting of the subscribers of the Education Society on Thursday 10 August 1820, 'Sixth Annual Report of the Bombay Education Society, 1821', pp. 33–5, in R.V. Parulekar, ed., *SERB*, Part II, p. 30.

[14]Letter No. 362 dated 10 March 1824 from the Secretary to the Government to the Committee of the Bombay Native School Book And School Society, 'Extract from the Bombay Secretariat Records, General Department Files, Vol. 8 (63) of 1824', in ibid., p. 61.

[15]Ibid., p. 59.

their own tongue. They also translated short pieces of Mahratta into English, and had gone through an abbreviated course in English grammar.'[16] Instruction would have to proceed through what Jervis went on to describe as 'tuition by double translation'. Significant amounts of time in the classroom were spent on teaching the two languages.

These attempts to yoke English and the vernaculars also sought to erase continuities between the emerging standardised forms and their pre-colonial pasts. Habits of reading required by colonial curricula had not been part of the modes of instruction within pre-colonial literate traditions. Imperial imperatives to minimise echoes of the pre-colonial cultural past would have rendered the experience of simultaneously learning the new 'high' language and the emerging standard vernacular forms even more alienating. Print and standardised literate practices altered prevailing conceptions of learning, language and literacy, while the selective nature of the bilingual relation meant that long after students were familiarised with the elements of the two languages, much of the further instruction had to proceed through constant translation between English and the vernacular. This reinforcement was most necessary as the entire exercise was intended to advance the notion that a sufficient degree of transferability existed between English and the vernaculars. Despite philological scholarship, these laborious endeavours in the colonial classroom showed that there was little evidence on the ground to back up claims that South Asian vernaculars and modern European languages were linked by underlying bonds of primeval affinity.

Imperial reasoning on education led to an apparently firm belief in the efficacy of successive rounds of translation and retranslation. Such attempts to link English and the vernacular were expected to produce the means to rapidly and comprehensively reconstitute native commonsense. Its logic ran thus: if an English education was meant to advance skills that students had acquired through reading vernacular—material prepared mainly through translations from English 'originals'—

[16]Report dated 6 July 1826 from George Jervis, Secretary of the Bombay Native School Book and School Society to James Farish, Secretary to Government, 'Extracts from the Bombay Secretariat Records, Educational Department Files, Vol. 2 of 1826' in ibid., p. 90.

then the only proof of English learning could be their ability to successfully translate their lessons into the vernacular! Such oral and, where possible, written translation exercises formed the core of class tests and public examinations. The disingenuousness of such prescriptions seemed to be directly proportional to the huge ambitions of the project. It was not surprising that students who made it to the English schools were frequently under-prepared to adapt to instruction in English. Complex contradictions marked the transition from a knowledge circumscribed within particularistic religious traditions to a system of education premised on general principles of laicised learning, especially when it was couched in an unfathomable language. Balshastri Jambhekar's Report as Assistant Professor at the Elphinstone Institute in 1838 was one of many instances that bear this out. His remarks on the teaching methods reveal a lamentable shortage of vernacular books, and cruel constraints under which master and pupils struggled to internalise lessons doled out in unfamiliar languages through the process of translation:

> To show the difficulty that is now experienced by the different classes, for want of books with translations, I beg leave to state ... that most of my time, and the time of my assistants is employed in explaining to boys of different sects, and in each class, the meaning of what they read, in their own languages. A passage is first read by one of the Hindoos and explained to them in Mahratha; then it is similarly explained to the Parsis in Goozeratee, and lastly to the Mohammeddans in Hindoostanee, till everyone in the class has understood it. This is found necessary not only in the lower class, but even in the highest class. ...[17]

We learn from Bhavalkar's autobiographical account of his experience in the early 1840s that similar processes of translation formed a crucial part of the pedagogic method adopted in the Normal School where native teachers were trained. With the teacher–student ratio such that, usually, a single teacher was responsible for *all* students in the school, students could not even hope to learn from producing

[17]Report by Balshastri Jambhekar on the Junior School, Elphinstone College dated 21 August 1838 in 'Extract from the Bombay Secretariat Records', General Department Files, Vol. 444 of 1838, in R.V. Parulekar, ed., *SERB* (1826–40), Pt. III, Bombay, 1957, p. 236.

their own translations. Class lessons simply comprised copying out translations prepared by the teacher or from a shared rare printed specimen of an abridged translation. His memoirs recount that part of their lessons each Wednesday was an assignment to copy out a translated account of Hume's *History of England* in the Marathi *modi* script, and on Saturdays the same exercise had to be copied out in the Marathi *balbodh* script. But as there were only abridged accounts of the history of Hindustan and of England available in Marathi, students were forced to transcribe a detailed oral account given by Balshastri in class, with the only help available from a few English books that formed the school library. Translation was not just confined to the learning of languages; it formed the very basis of the instructional method adopted for other subjects as well.

Given the discrepancy between the radical expectations that the colonial class-room was invested with and the shabby means it was allotted, there was constant slippage between what was sought to be taught, the language through which that learning was to be transmitted, and the type of learning skills to be inculcated. At best, colonial pedagogy could vaguely clarify whether the texts used for study were meant to train the student towards a better grasp of the language or advance his skills of reading and composition or aid his comprehension of the subject. Translation was thus burdened with multiple cognitive functions: it was meant as a somewhat hapless substitute for a substantive elucidation of ideas and concepts, even as it was meant to drill students in habits of writing and reading. Translation was used pretty much like a hold-all pedagogic tool to reduce the learning of several unfamiliar skills and competencies to a circular pattern of activity that would eventually deliver results through mechanical repetition.

However, despite all these attempts to link English and the vernaculars through schools, the competencies acquired by the new intelligentsia were in no way symmetrically distributed between the two languages. If anything, the deficiencies in the training of the average student of these colonial schools were commensurate with the enormous ambitions of the education project. Mr Green, a much-respected headmaster of the English School at Surat and Educational Inspector of the sub-division, had some telling observations[18] to make on the education that a student ended up with after an average of four to six years spent at school. Such a student could be expected to possess a good general knowledge of geography, a considerable amount of history, and he would have gone through a course of popular physics and mathematics that included study of quadratic equations and six books of Euclid. It was likely that he would understand an easy English book and he would have been taught the 'best' books in his vernacular language. If he were a Hindu, he would have acquired the rudiments of Sanskrit. Green went on to observe that although this might seem like a lot, despite—or perhaps, *on account* of—his training, the student remained lacking in the basic linguistic means through which to pursue his education, nor could he hope to attempt any level of self-expression:

> We are compelled, however, to remember that after all these years of study, the pupil for any purposes of future self-education, *is really without a language*. His vernacular tongue with which he is tolerably well-acquainted, contains almost nothing worth his reading, and English is so difficult, to an Asiatic mind that he is still unable to study in it without resistance and unlikely to acquire the habit of reading for general information.

If this debilitating scenario was indeed the case, students are not likely to have had any illusions that their training endowed them with symmetrical capacities to carry out the range of cognitive functions through either or both languages. Impelled by the mismatch between normative liberal precepts invoked by the colonial order and their own place within its hierarchy, vernacular intellectuals were actually quick to become alert to the possibilities of a vernacular discourse within the public domain. Signs of an emerging social self-reflexivity testified to the existence of communicative channels between the colonial administration and native intellectuals. The self-representations of colonial power as well as native discourse showed that the imagined

[18]Mr Green's remarks were offered during his stint as Acting Principal at the Elphinstone Institute Bombay in 1849 and are found in the *Report of the Board of Education* (henceforth, *RBE*) *of 1849*, Bombay, 1849, pp. 4–5.

links beween eighteenth-century Europe and the indigenous social order played an important part in creating these discursive channels. These imagined links were partially able to disguise the political and economic intentions of colonial rule and allow it to create a countervailing colonial-modern culture.

English and Laicisation in the Vernaculars: A Colonial 'Renaissance'

Despite its avowals to preserve native beliefs and practice, colonial authority was aware of the radical nature of its intervention. It needed a framework through which to harness indigenous cultures to the narratives of European history in ways that would legitimise Western intervention, at least to itself. Colonial ideology worked through casting the native as the primitive Other of the white man, in whose image the former would have to be recreated through being administered extracts from Western history and doses of a curtailed variant of liberalism. Non-Western cultures were represented within colonial discourse through a powerful dynamic that fixed their position *and* difference within normative structures derived from a Eurocentric modernity. In doing this a discursive trope was required to articulate the desirability of reforming the native to measure up to the norms of the modern West. The Renaissance and Reformation provided the trope for these ideological ambitions. This is not to suggest that the analogy entered colonial discourse simply as a motif to foreground Western superiority. It figured as a strong motif within the self-narratives and official stances of colonial power because it resonated with its objectives to secure political ends through altering the distribution of learning and language on the subcontinent. In fact the Renaissance trope served at least two functions within the imperial imagination. First, it allowed the 'benevolent' conferment of modern knowledges on non-Western peoples to be presented as a counterweight to the radical disruptions of metropolitan capitalist interests. Second it was a crucial element in the construction of a continuous narrative from the 'origin' of Western civilisation to its present world-historical phase, suggesting thereby that interventions by the Western bourgeoisie to remake other societies in its own self-image were for the purposes of an evolutionary improvement. Far from suggesting that the Renaissance was 'chosen' for its analogic appropriateness, I suggest that the memory of the rise of modern vernacular literatures in Europe provided vital imaginative stimuli in conceiving of possible 'solutions' to the ideological problems created through yoking dissimilar cultural worlds. Crucial to the making of the self-image of modern Europe, reminiscences of the Renaissance and its discursive legacy now helped reduce the profound discontinuities between eighteenth-century Europe and South Asia by relocating them as a 'mere' linguistic problem. Print was also crucial to possibilities that the colonial ruling class could imagine. It allowed them to alter and regulate cultural production within the native world, even as it enabled them to represent the colonial enterprise as an opportunity to universally extend developments like the laicisation of culture produced by the European Renaissance into the rest of the world.

Such ambitions put English in a somewhat paradoxical position. It was expected to establish itself by delegitimising existing classical literary traditions but also simultaneously demonstrate its power to stimulate general enlightenment by engendering a body of modern, 'useful' texts in the South Asian vernaculars. English was the arch-signifier of a Western modernity and imperial consciousness, but it was also to be the inspiration for a laicised knowledge within native society. As the vehicle of a secularised worldview, it had to measure up to the task of challenging the esoteric traditions of Sanskrit, Persian and Arabic on their own ground, although it was always clear that it could never hope to replace these as the high languages of worship in South Asia. If the vernaculars were to develop enlarged lexical and syntactic capabilities to compare with the achievements of English, part of the inspiration had to come from the indigenous classical languages. Their value could not be easily dismissed; the possibilities opened by English and the entry of print meant they were likely to emerge with altered but renewed significance. Ostensibly, English was the elevated symbol of a vastly superior culture, but it was also expected to actively transform the cognitive and affective habits of large numbers. The ultimate irony was that this combination of roles that English had to play out was subject to the allocations of a parsimonious colonial state. Even so, these cultural shifts were profoundly transformative because, for the first time, the vernaculars were elevated to a position where, in principle, they were thought capable of being the carriers of socially significant, learned discourses.

On both sides of the colonial divide, within official and native discourse, the expectations from English were not without internal contradictions. These tensions are evident in the multivalent emphases through which the European Renaissance and Reformation were evoked. In the whole range of ideological positions, from Anglicism to the 'vernacular lobbies' within official and native circles, the use of the Renaissance metaphor became subject to regional variations. In Bengal, the Orientalists were the strongest advocates of the argument that colonial discourse should project itself through the vernaculars. The dissemination of colonial ideology would not be half as efficacious if transmitted directly through English; instead, it ought to overwrite vernacular textuality so that native speech would truly reflect Western rationality. Therefore the Orientalists advocated following 'the forms of speech which they [natives] already understand and use. These must be applied to the purpose, either by direct translations, or which is preferable [*sic*], by the representation of European facts, opinions and sentiments in an original native garb.'[19]

If Western learning was to appeal to the native mind as a practical necessity, the study of English would need to be introduced alongside the study of Sanskrit and Arabic. However, in trying to abruptly supplant the pre-colonial high languages in a social context that had not seen the emergence of a secularised world-view, English could only partially foreground its position as an instrument for creating a laicised cognitive structure. It hoped to begin this task by insinuating itself into the world-view of traditional native intellectuals:

> In the history of all philosophical and religious reformation, it will be found that the most effective agents have been those who had been

[19]Letter from Horace Wilson from Fort William, quoted in Willoughby's letter dated 27 May 1850 to Secretary to the Bombay Government, Appendix XI, *Report of Department of Public Instruction* (henceforth, *RDPI*) *for 1848–50*, Bombay, 1850, p. 183.

educated in the errors they reformed. ... Bacon was deep in the fallacies of the Schools. Luther had preached the doctrines of the church of Rome and an able *Pundit* or *Maulvi* who should add English to Sanskrit and Arabic, who should be led to expose the absurdities and errors of his own systems and advocate the adoption of European knowledge and principles, would work a greater revolution in the minds of his unlettered countrymen. ...[20]

Such plans to accommodate English alongside patronage to classical Sanskrit and Persian studies in colonial colleges met with native resistance. Interestingly, it was not the move to introduce English that was opposed; rather what was questioned was the rationale of the government's attempts to divide its allocations between traditional learning and education through English. For instance, there is Rammohan Roy's well-known letter of 1823,[21] where he strongly denounced the government's plans to patronise Sanskrit learning on account of its elitist bias, and because of what he considered its moribund and speculative character. By comparing traditional native scholarship to the theology of the European schoolmen, his response showed how allusions to the European Renaissance within official policy were simultaneously internalised and deflected by native discourse. Making an implicit connection that English was the language of modern rationality and science, Roy urged the government to promote liberal scientific education through English.

In Bombay native patrons of the Education Society made a similar plea to make available 'the European Arts and Sciences to the Natives'. Their expectations from English varied somewhat from those in Roy's letter. They did not emphasise English as the language of scientific rationality but their hope was that English would invigorate native education by a general diffusion of the new learning through the vernaculars:

by the study of the English language ... [the natives] do not contemplate the supercession of the vernacular dialects of the country in the

[20]Horace Wilson quoted in 'Minute by Willoughby dated 12 January 1850' in ibid., pp. 183–4.

[21]Rammohan Roy's 'Letter to Lord Amherst, dated 11 December 1823', quoted in J.A. Richey, *SER*, Part II, pp. 98–101.

> promotion of native education; but they regard it merely as a help to the diffusion of the European Arts and Sciences among them, by means of translations by those who have acquired a thorough acquaintance with it; and as a branch of classical education to be esteemed and cultivated in this country as the classical languages of Greece and Rome are in the Universities of Europe.[22]

The emerging native discourse seemed to concede the status of English as the new high language of learning. The comparison between the position of English in the colonial situation and that of the classical languages of Greek and Latin suggested that native elites did not see English as displacing the vernaculars; rather, they hoped that the diffusion of Western knowledge through translation would eventually urge English into a position of elevated marginality, making it resemble European prestige languages as showpieces within the university system in the West.

Tendencies towards laicisation were more emphatically played out via the vernacular in Western India than in other parts of the subcontinent. As the late 1840s saw shifts away from vernacular instruction, the debate on the future course of policy again cohered around references to the European Renaissance. The new president of the Board of Education, Sir Erskine Perry, held strong Anglicist views and his aim was to discourage emphasis on the vernaculars. Differences over policy shifts resulted in acrimonious exchanges between Erskine Perry and George Jervis who, as translator of numerous schoolbooks on mathematics, and as the initiator of the Vernacular Engineering Class in Bombay, nurtured a strong belief in the greater efficacy of instruction through the vernaculars. The argument for a greater Anglicist accent within policy was as much a result of the underlying paradoxes in projecting colonial education as a re-enactment of issues in the European Renaissance. This led to acute practical difficulties in the preparation and publication of vernacular schoolbooks. Little could

[22]Letter from the Committee representing the Native Community to the Secretary, Bombay Native Education Society, dated 1 December 1827, 'Extract from the Fourth Report of the Bombay Native Education Society for 1827', pp. 39–47 in R.V. Parulekar, ed., *SERB*, Part II, p. 109.

be done to dispose off these immediate obstacles, and the debate came to rest upon general considerations of the place of English and the importance of cultivating the vernaculars. Jervis' position was similar to that of the Orientalist lobby in Bengal. He argued that English could only remain an elite language and the Anglicist view that it would soon become generally familiar was no more than a fond hope. Ironically, the most enthusiastic support for colonial rule as a re-enactment of the European Renaissance came from fervent advocates of instruction through the vernacular. To Jervis it seemed clear that to proceed with English as the medium of colonial ideology, the government would be neglecting—

> the benefit of three hundred years' experience in Europe and we are retrograded to the days, in which the Latin was the sole language of literature; and when in consequence, knowledge both temporal and spiritual, was confined to a few Monks, a few Divines, a few Men of Letters. Until such an exclusive agency was put an end to—until the modern tongues of Europe were emancipated—the PEOPLE could never learn, or know for themselves. On the abrogation of the exclusive use of the Latin language, on the inauguration of the language of the People, the acquirement of knowledge was made accessible to all ... *all* men could be taught, *all* men could be teachers, and how wonderful has been the advancement, in morality and literature, by such a change in Europe.[23]

We have here a most lucid exposition of connections between the laicisation of learning witnessed in early modern Europe and the extension of bourgeois rationality as colonial ideology. Jervis believed that the alienness of English need not impede the expansionist ambitions of colonial rule. Colonial authority could hope to transcend the limits of its influence via Western knowledge in the vernacular. This 'liberal' argument to promote the vernaculars through state-backed initiatives was part of the design to maximise the assimilation of colonial ideology by the largest possible numbers. To this Perry responded with arguments reminiscent of Francis Warden's position,[24] namely that the supervision

[23]George Jervis, 'Minute of 24 February 1847' in *RDPI for 1848–50*, p. 48.
[24]See chapter two.

of general education in the colony was not part of administrative obligations. The administration could secure its ideological interests through measures that used English to stimulate a 'thirst of knowledge' among the native population, apparently much as Latin had done for Europe. To promote the 'demand for enlightenment', Perry suggested making a knowledge of English obligatory for employment in colonial offices. Within this view, progress was a function of the laissez-faire principles of gradualism and private initiative. The teaching of English through print would, in course of time, lead to an adequately large reading public and it ought to be left to native 'men of genius' to come forward to 'address their fellow-men through their mother tongues'.[25] On the other hand, Jervis felt that it was precisely because conditions were not suitable for the emergence of such native private initiative that it was imperative for the state to take the responsibility of producing appropriate reading material through an officially-funded translation project.

The prospects for modernity within the colonial context thus came to depend largely upon translation. As native discourse realised, the pedagogic transfer of Western knowledge needed to be backed by an officially sponsored translation project—on this depended a laicised cognitive order. Discussion on shifts in the distribution of *dakshina*[26] has shown the trend in official initiatives and the extent of patronage to encourage vernacular production. However, as the following argument will elaborate, the establishment of the University of Bombay in 1857 saw important changes in the position of the vernacular sphere and the official support now available to it. An analysis of the official patronage for translation into Marathi shows that, by the 1860s, the state had already relinquished its interests in the vernacular sphere, ostensibly because its interventions had secured the required structural shifts. From then on, vernacular production was the responsibility of native private initiative, though the government continued to exercise its authority to determine the size and the quality of the vernacular public by regulating the content and allocations to vernacular education.

[25]Minute by the President of the Board of Education, Sir Erskine Perry, dated 14 April 1847 in *RDPI for 1848–50*, pp. 59–61.

[26]See chapter two.

Shifts in Official Patronage to the Translation Project

From 1821, the preparation of reading material and printed books in Marathi had begun through the efforts of the *shastri mandali* of the Bombay Education Society. These efforts were aimed at rectifying the 'total' absence of 'appropriate' reading material in the vernacular. The initial publications covered a range of subjects but were all meant for the use of students in the engineering and medical class in Bombay, or in the vernacular schools in the capital and the outlying areas of the Presidency. The depository list of books stocked by the Bombay Native Education Society in 1839 had 86 titles in Marathi and Gujarati.[27] It included works on practical geometry, algebra, logarithms, trigonometry, primers, a treatise on the management of schools, geography, astronomy, the history of England, natural philosophy and chemistry. Among the titles were an atlas containing nine maps, Marathi–English dictionaries and anthologies of stories, and tracts considered exemplary reading material for beginners and young readers. Alongside, the Poona Sanskrit College, after acquiring its lithographic press in 1829, began contributing to the effort of preparing 'useful' Marathi texts and even became the major official venue for producing these for the next few years. The college was reorganised in the 1840s to demote the importance of traditional Sanskrit texts, and Major Candy was appointed as college superintendent, signalling the government's intentions to assume direct charge of supervisory arrangements to regulate vernacular forms and determine appropriate usage for the new 'reformed', standardised Marathi. Ironically, Candy's main task was to correct and revise vernacular readers prepared by native staff at Bombay and Pune.

Part of the reorganisation of Poona College was the creation of a Vernacular Department consisting of exhibition translators, appointed exclusively to expedite the task of making 'useful' printed texts in Marathi. Despite the biased power structure of these institutional arrangements, within a few years after efforts to produce a standardised Marathi script, by the late 1840s and the early 1850s, vernacular intellectuals were engaged in rendering important texts and ideas of political economy

[27]For the prices of some of these titles, see chapter four, fn. 52.

into Marathi.[28] These translations showed sophisticated awareness of the conceptual and linguistic complexities involved in transplanting the discourses of modernity. Consider the following remarks by Krishnashastri Chiplunkar[29] in the preface to his translation of Mill's work, entitled *Arthshastraparibhasha*, published in 1855 from Pune:

> The following text has been formulated on the basis of work of the renowned English writer, Mill. There are numerous thoughts in the original work that the present author has decided to leave out of the present work as they apply only to Europe and would not be easily comprehensible here, neither would they be very useful. Similarly,

[28]These treatises on political economy in Marathi were not 'strict' translations in the modern sense of the term; rather, I prefer to see them as attempts to vernacularise the discourse of political economy. At least four Marathi intellectuals attempted such essays on political economy in the vernacular. They were Krishnashastri Chiplunkar, Gopal Hari Deshmukh, Hari Keshavji and Vishwanath Narayan Mandlik. These treatises are republished in D.K. Bedekar, ed., *Char Marathi Bhashetele Arthashastragnya*, Pune, 1969.

[29]Krishnashastri Chiplunkar (1824–1876) was born in Nasik in a *chitpavan* brahmin family. Apparently his father, Haripant was a *karkun* in Pune. Krishnashastri began studying the *vedas* from a very young age. He joined the Poona Sanskrit College, where he studied under the well-known Moreshastri. When the Poona College was re-organised in the 1840s, Krishnashastri was appointed Professor of Marathi. While at the Poona College, he composed many Marathi prose texts, including a version of Mill's work on political economy, the *Arabian Nights* and a biography of Socrates. He contributed to the first Marathi weekly from Pune, *Dnyanprakash*, besides editing the anti-missionary paper, *Vicharlehari* started in 1852 and the *Shalapatrak* published by the Education Department. Krishnashastri was a reputed scholar of English and Sanskrit. He was probably associated with the Dakshina Prize Committee when Phule's manuscript was rejected in 1855, but he supported Phule's initiatives in starting schools for lower-caste communities. Krishnashastri was also involved in the activities of the Sarvajanik Sabha. Once the Translation Department was moved out of Poona College, Krishnashastri became the Reporter on the Vernacular Press. His son, Vishnushastri, edited the well-known literary periodical, *Nibandhmala*, but the latter's ideological vision was, in many respects, much narrower than his father's. For a biographical account on Krishnashastri Chiplunkar, see Appendix Two, '*Krishnashastri Chiplunkaryanche Charitra*' in Bhavani Shankar Sridhar Pandit, ed., *Raosaheb Keshav Shivram Bhavalkaryanche Atmavritta*, pp. 118–27.

the original text draws examples pertaining to England to illustrate some of its principles; they have been changed to refer to situations here so as to be easily accessible to Marathi readers and other alterations of the same order have been made.[30]

Krishnashastri's preface is remarkable for its underlying tone of assurance, and its awareness that use of the vernacular implied a critical mediation between two historical contexts yoked by colonialism. At the same time, the new supervisory arrangements at Poona College were meant to establish norms for what constituted acceptable and 'cultivated' usage for Marathi on matters of grammar, syntax, idiom and style. Major Candy's rulings over what constituted 'correct' linguistic practice in Marathi often aimed to cast vernacular idiomatic usage and syntax in the mould of English patterns. This would only reinforce the argument that the modern form of the native vernaculars were determined by multiple levels of translation from English, a point most well brought out by the title of Potdar's study on the making of modern Marathi style, *Marathi Gadyacha Ingreji Avataar*,[31] or 'The English reincarnation of Marathi prose'. The translation section of the Poona College vernacular department sought to consolidate the work done until then by the *shastri mandali* in Bombay by enlarging and 'correcting' those early books to form a graded, 'complete' series for each subject prescribed on the vernacular school curriculum. Vernacular materials were to be prepared also in geography, morals, mathematics, natural philosophy, political economy and history.[32] Similar materials

---

For other examples of attempts to engender a modern vernacular rationalistic discourse, see discussion on the native press in chapter four.

[30]Translated from Marathi, Krishnashastri Chiplunkar, *Prastavana* to '*Arthshastraparibhasha*' in D.K. Bedekar, ed., *Char Marathi Bhashetele Arthashastragnya*, p. 265. This text on political economy prepared by Krishnashastri was used in the higher vernacular classes both in Poona and Bombay, until the establishment of the university brought such attempts to teach 'advanced' subjects in the vernacular to an abrupt end.

[31]D.V. Potdar, *Marathi Gadyacha Ingrezi Avataar*, Poona, 1922.

[32]For details on the revision procedures adopted by Candy, see the 'Annual Report of the Poona College for the year 1854' in the *RDPI for 1854–55*, Bombay, 1855, pp. 12–15. Apparently, the method followed was for Candy to 'correct'

for Gujarati schools and a further set, if possible, for Canarese schools were to be produced in the vernacular department of the Pune College.

Given the general rationale underlying the patronage towards vernacular production, it was not surprising that Poona College, especially the vernacular department and translation section, underwent further restructuring with the establishment of the University of Bombay in 1857. The establishment of a university led to a reassessment of the official goals of the education project. With the emergence of a centre of higher learning in the Presidency capital, internal arrangements at Pune College had now to be modelled more closely along the lines of Elphinstone College in Bombay. Higher education meant that the position of the vernaculars would need to be renegotiated, especially as official circles were unlikely to be enthusiastic about native languages developing as the medium of higher instruction. Soon after the emergence of Bombay University, the Office of the Marathi Translator was detached from Poona College and, in 1862–3, it was moved out of Pune to Sion Fort in Bombay as an autonomous unit.[33] This showed that during the space of a few years, the official expectations from the translator's office had changed rapidly. Its primary objective was no longer to produce educational material. It was now meant to serve more bureaucratic functions consistent with its authoritative supervisory purposes: the translator's office was no longer entrusted with the 'liberal' task of augmenting vernacular textual repertoires, its work now lay in the translation of samples extracted from vernacular publications for purposes of official surveillance.[34]

---

the earlier translations produced by the Education Society's *shastri mandali* in Bombay or those by the translation exhibitioners employed in the Poona College.

Candy's appointment to supervise the production of Marathi texts at the Poona College was severely criticised in the vernacular press, especially by Bhau Mahajan's *Prabhakar*. Candy responded to these attacks through the missionary paper, *Dnyanodaya*. Bhau Mahajan challenged Candy to a public contest over his Marathi and translation skills, but it seems the latter declined the challenge. See 'The Late Govind Kunte alias Bhau Mahajan, a Sketch by Keshav Bhavalkar' in G.G. Jambhekar, *Memoirs and Writings of Balshastri Jambhekar* (henceforth, *MWBJ*), Appendix 3, Vol. 3, Pune, 1950, pp. 45–52.

[33] *RDPI for 1862–63*, Bombay, 1863, pp. 175–7.

[34] Such weekly summaries of the contents of native vernacular newspapers

Some translation activity continued within the routine functioning of the Board of Education. Alongside these shifts in the structure of translation office and the extent of patronage to the production of Marathi books, there were signs of changes in the type of subjects and titles now to be chosen for translation and considered fit for dissemination among a colonial vernacular audience. Maya Paṇdit's study[35] on translations in nineteenth-century Maharashtra points out that financial assistance in the form of modest prizes from the *dakshina* fund for worthy translations of educational materials into Marathi was withdrawn during the 1850s. These prizes were now offered for original, 'literary' compositions—novels, lyric poetry, dramas and translations and adaptations of such works in Marathi. This was meant to 'create a taste for reading among the masses' that would hopefully supplant the great delight they took in 'mere myths'.[36] The composition of imaginative vernacular literature was beyond the purview, and surely the capabilities, of a bureaucratically managed government department. Quite aptly within this logic, the translation exhibitioners were rendered redundant when the translation department was moved out of Poona College and absorbed elsewhere in the colonial bureaucracy!

At one level, these moves seemed to indicate the government's intention to divert its patronage for a wider purpose than just the preparation of schoolbooks used by only a small section of the population. However, this withdrawal of official assistance for the translation of vernacular educational materials was backed by policy moves aimed at conclusively fixing the place of the vernaculars as fit only for an elementary, and basically inferior, preparatory training to 'higher' education in English. These shifts signalled that the limits for the development of a modern critical vernacular discourse through official support had already been reached. From now on, education policy

---

and periodicals were eventually forwarded to the offices of the colonial establishment in London.

[35]Maya Pandit, 'Translation Culture and the Colonial Discourse in Nineteenth Century Maharashtra', in Milind Malshe, Madhav Apte, P.N. Paranjape, eds, *Explorations in Applied Linguistics*, Pune, 1995, pp. 169–81.

[36]Department of Public Instruction Files, Vol. 6 for 1856 and Department of Public Instruction Files, Vol. 15 for 1862–3, quoted in ibid., p. 174.

measures showed little substantial commitment or interest in patronising the extension of modern knowledge through the vernaculars. Evidently the ideological objectives of the official patronage to the vernaculars had been realised. From then on, although vernacular production was still strictly controlled through the Office of the Marathi Translator, once the task of establishing standardised linguistic practice had been accomplished under close colonial supervision, policy apparently lost interest in supporting the composition of vernacular texts. These moves to gradually relinquish direct involvement in vernacular production in favour of private initiatives, once the initial tasks of forging a monopolistic normative structure had been put in place, were indeed part of a larger pattern exhibited by educational policy. A similar logic impelled policy after 1880 to hand over the responsibility of starting more schools to native private operators. The administration's lack of interest in the vernacular sphere was borne out by its decision effectively to exclude the study of vernacular languages from the colonial university within a few years of its being established in the 1860s. Its predominant interest in the vernacular sphere now was to keep as strict a vigil upon it as resources permitted, and after 1864, one of the chief functions of the vernacular translators'office was the compilation of weekly summaries of the contents of all the vernacular newspapers and periodicals published in different parts of the Presidency.

From this point on the vernacular sphere was left to develop outside of official patronage. But with the overall spread of literate skills being insufficient to make vernacular publishing a commercially viable proposition, the vernacular sphere was left with no option but to allow itself to be shaped by the minimal official patronage still available. This was almost entirely directed towards the creation of modern imaginative writing in Marathi loosely modelled on a select range of Western texts.

The laicisation and general diffusion of learning in the West had resulted in the increasing specialisation of modern knowledges and a growing differentiation between rational and imaginative discourses. This disjunction between the analytic and the aesthetic aspects of modern thought takes on a very different form in the trajectory of a laicised colonial culture, where it is primarily determined by shifts in official patronage. As a result, the discourse of the post-1857 generation of vernacular intellectuals reveals a different set of emphases from those in the writing of early colonial vernacular intellectuals like Balshastri Jambhekar, Bhau Mahajan, Krishnashastri Chiplunkar, and the young Lokahitawadi. From the 1860s, vernacular discourse was increasingly concerned with determining appropriate aesthetic and literary norms for modern Marathi, but these processes of aestheticisation coincided with an increasing tendency towards political intolerance within the vernacular sphere. To briefly anticipate the argument of the last chapter, one of the important reasons for this was the fact that, compared to the vernacular discourse of the pre-university generation, from the early 1860s the vernacular Marathi intelligentsia showed a significantly weaker interest in appropriating the discourses of modern scientific rationality and liberal political ideology. So much so that, by the period of the 'vernacular Renaissance', Marathi writing did not even seem to remember the work of early intellectuals. This later body of vernacular writing, aimed at defining the criteria of modern literary taste with respect to Marathi, was marked by two important features: firstly, it was mainly the work of men whose formal training did not extend to a college education; and secondly, its self-consciously 'literary' style owed much to Sanskrit, with few signs of having been equally influenced by the discourses of modern scientific or political rationality. As it was at this point that vernacular discourse was wakening to its potential to contest the legitimacy of the colonial state, these temporal, linguistic and ideological divisions in colonial consciousness had political implications, especially for the possibilities of constructing an anti-colonial hegemonic alliance. This required intellectuals to assess the possibilities to be negotiated through optimal choices made at key points that would represent their own group interests as coinciding with those of anti-colonial nationalist ideology. To discover this we need to see how early vernacular native discourse perceived the colonial bilingual divide.

Translation and the 'Diffusion of Knowledge': The Emergence of a Native Vernacular Discourse

The argument until now has delineated how a specifically asymmetrical bilingualism formed a constitutive feature of the colonial public sphere and was crucial to the distribution of power within colonial society.

Many of the early comments on the relation of English to the vernaculars were about disparities in the levels of intellectual and cultural 'wealth' accumulated respectively by English and the vernaculars. Early vernacular discourse was preoccupied with the need to 'improve' native society by developing the vernaculars. It would be hasty to dismiss such concerns as an artless internalisation of colonial ideology, for even early native writings showed that intellectuals had glimpsed the political possibilities inherent in the use of standardised linguistic forms. Given the general argument here about the colonial public sphere and the vernacularisation of liberal discourses, an analysis of some key concerns of native vernacular discourse would help ground the cultural imperialism argument and allow us to theorise the possibilities of agency, mediation and hegemonic influence within colonial modernity. The intelligentsia's representations of the emerging social structure is important to an understanding of their efforts to articulate a counter-hegemonic discourse to the state.

The first native intellectuals associated with the Native Education Society in Bombay were particularly impelled by the need to appropriate the discourses of secular, 'useful' learning into the vernacular. For example, there are the introductory remarks to *Bal Mitra* by Kashinath Chatre—considered among the ablest Marathi translators to have worked with the Native Education Society in Bombay in its early years. One of the first 'readers' for students in the new Marathi schools, *Bal Mitra* was published in 1828. It was a translation of a work titled *Children's Friend*. Chatre's preface articulated his perceptions of the differences between the modern European vernaculars and Marathi:

> The *Bal Mitra* was originally a composition in French, and from which it came into English and now the Marathi is based upon that. If one thinks of the French and the English languages, one realises that they have been undergoing improvement for centuries. There exist books in them on every topic, and in them there are words to express almost every thought occurring to the mind; they are known to all the great intellectuals and therefore Marathi can hardly have the same lucidity that is possible in these languages. A language in which no one has composed grammars or dictionaries until now, in which no great

scholars have taken interest, whose vocabulary is limited and its spoken style is not matured either.[37]

The great learning of the new rulers, the wealth and variety of books available in their language, and the facility of print apparently made a deep impression on the imagination of native intellectuals. It is principally on these counts that claims towards the legitimacy of colonial rule and its radical difference with previous regimes are acknowledged. To view these impressions as merely naive or obsequious would echo stereotypical colonial representations of the native character. It would also be a reductive misreading of the impact of the new discourses, for often these laudatory comments about the cognitive sophistication of the new regime were accompanied by carefully articulated arguments for the need to use the colonial encounter as an opportunity to derive benefit from these ideas for native society.[38] Notice for example the views expressed in the *Bombay Durpan*, the first native Marathi newspaper to be established in 1832, published from Bombay. The efforts of the government's Education Society were praised, but the editorial comments drew attention to the openings for intellectual enrichment and opportunities for the negotiation of political power under the new regime:

> Under a government which patronises literary improvements and encourages the diffusion of useful learning among its subjects, the cultivation of the mind is prosecuted with more ardour and with greater success than under a ruling power that is despotic. The result of such

[37]Translated from Marathi, Sadashiv Kashinath Chatre, *'Prastavana'*, *Bal Mitra*, Pt. 1, Bombay, 1828, n.p.

[38]The terms used to identify its community of readers by the first Marathi newspaper, the bilingual paper, *Bombay Durpan* (1832–40) vary between *'lok'*, '*hya deshatele lok*' (people of this *desh*), *ettedeshiya lok, etheel lok* (people living here). The paper followed a deliberate policy of religious neutrality. Although the *Bombay Durpan* probably did not remain bilingual beyond the first two years of its life-span, the vernacular parts of the *Durpan* adopted a determinedly neutral tone even while reporting on the missionary campaign against native religious practices. For a further discussion of the impartial editorial policy of the *Bombay Durpan*, see chapter four.

pursuits is to improve the literature of the country and to add to the stock of knowledge possessed by the people. The discoveries of one generation lead to others by the succeeding one, thus the arts and sciences flourish, and civilisation then advances with rapid strides. But it does not so much depend upon the ruling power as with the people themselves to improve their intellectual condition.[39]

The *Durpan* was critically aware of the importance of the vernaculars for its vision of maximising benefits from the education project. The value of extending the circulation of the new knowledge by augmenting the range of reading material available in Marathi formed a crucial part of its agenda,[40] besides also informing much of the other work undertaken by its editor, Balshastri Jambhekar.[41] The significance of Balshastri's initiative as editor of the *Durpan* extends far beyond the fact that it was the first native newspaper in Marathi. The *Bombay Durpan* represents a unique, historic moment in the story of the cultural impact of colonial intervention. By publishing the paper as a bilingual venture that used both Marathi and English, Balshastri was signalling his awareness of the importance and centrality of the bilingual relation to the colonial world.

Although the first, the *Durpan* was not the only newspaper of the

[39]*Bombay Durpan*, 2 March 1832 in G.G. Jambhekar, ed., *MWBJ*, Vol. 2, p. 30.

[40]See, for example, the Prospectus/*Prastavana* and the opening article explaining the value and purposes of the periodical press in the first issue of 6 January 1832, reprinted in G.G. Jambhekar, ed., *MWBJ*, Vol. 3, pp. 1–5.

[41]In his short life-span of thirty-six years, Balshastri (1810–46) contributed immensely to modern education in Western India and to the making of modern Marathi. Upon the establishment of the College Division of the Elphinstone Institution in 1834, he was appointed Assistant Professor of Mathematics. Jambhekar was made the Educational Inspector of the Southern Division when the Board of Education was created in 1840. As Educational Inspector, he had to tour the province to establish a regional network of schools. He also taught at the Normal School attached to Elphinstone College, besides being responsible for the preparation of vernacular teaching materials in a wide range of subjects, including astronomy, geography, history, grammar and mathematics. For a chronology of Balshastri's life and important correspondence, see G.G. Jambhekar, ed., *MWBJ*, Vol. 1. For a discussion of his position as an early, 'progressive' vernacular intellectual, as well as his role in the controversy over Shripat Sheshadri's conversion to Christianity, see chapter four.

colonial period to be published from Western India using both English and Marathi. However, it also differed from all the subsequent bilingual English–Marathi papers, in the unique structure of the bilingual relation it proposed.[42] It chose a format where each page was divided into two vertical halves, seeking to reproduce the exact equivalent of every reported item in both English and Marathi. In choosing a format with symmetrical columns in English and Marathi, the *Durpan* was virtually fearlessly trying to posit equality between the status of English and the vernacular. Of course, in stating its aim to encourage a pursuit of *vilayati vidya* (Western knowledge) among natives, the paper did implicitly acknowledge the superiority of Western knowledge. And yet in introducing itself to its untested audience, the tone of the Prospectus displayed no sign of nervousness or awe; instead it was amazingly brisk and business-like in outlining the goals set by its editors:

> Though the publication is undertaken, chiefly, with the object of promoting amongst the Natives the study of European literature, and the diffusion of European knowledge, and consequently with the intention of being conducted in the English language; the sphere of its usefulness will not be limited to such only as are conversant with that language, but will be extended to all who are acquainted with Murattee, as it is proposed to have two columns in each page, one English and the other Murattee. Communications received in the former will be accurately translated into the latter and vice-versa; and the originals and translations published in opposite columns.[43]

Further, in declaring, on more than one occasion, that it would not allow itself to be disfigured either by personal, petty differences or by servility towards the new rulers,[44] the *Durpan* gave ample evidence

[42]For an argument on the changing structure of the bilingual relation as seen in the native press initiatives after 1860s, see chapter five.

[43]*Prastavana, Bombay Durpan*, quoted in G.G. Jambhekar, ed., *MWBJ*, Vol. 2, p. 2.

[44]In its opening issue of 6 January 1832, the *Bombay Durpan* declared, 'Personality shall not disfigure, nor servility stain the pages of the *Durpan*, which the conductors actuated by honest intentions, will steadily, temperately and firmly endeavour to render, deserving of the good will and support of every lover of truth and virtue.' See ibid., p. 4.

that the new political principles had been internalised in ways that allowed the fledgling intelligentsia to take up critical positions[45] *vis-à-vis* both native society and the colonial government. The *Durpan* did not hesitate to either censure the government about the arrogance of colonial officials[46] or to take issue with an Anglo-Indian paper, the *Bombay Gazette*, when it criticised the Society's schools for allowing the study of 'absurd [native] fables' through the class books instead of religious instruction.[47] Similarly, in 1832 the *Durpan* castigated the

---

Similarly, commenting on the influence of a free and impartial public press, the *Durpan* observed: 'Of the various workings and effects of a public press, there is none perhaps more valuable, or more extensively beneficial, than the check which an independent and impartial publication never fails to exercise on the abuse of power, or the misconduct of persons vested with authority. This salutary effect however, can be only produced by scanning the measures of public men, condemning what is improper in their conduct and making known such of their acts as are of a beneficial character. And the conductor of a public journal must not shrink from this important part of his duty, either from dread of the anger of any party, or tenderness for the feelings of the individual of whom it may be necessary to speak.': see *Bombay Durpan*, 26 October 1832, in ibid., p. 64.

[45]Among the important instances of the early critique of colonial rule in Western India was the series of eight long letters by Bhaskar Pandurang Tarkhadkar, written under the pen name of 'A Hindoo' in the *Bombay Gazette* between 30 July 1841 and 27 November 1841. Evaluating the injustice and inequities that marked British rule, the letters included a criticism of the work of British historians like James Mill, and themes such as the highly discriminatory attitude of the British administration, the cunning the British had displayed in depriving the native princes of their kingdoms, the absolutist nature of Company rule, the ruinous economic drain effected through colonial policy and the great miserliness of education policy. For a detailed account of these letters, see J.V. Naik, 'An Early Appraisal of the British Colonial Policy', *Journal of the University of Bombay*, Vols. XLIV & XLV, Nos. 81–2, 1975–6, pp. 243–70.

[46]See a reader's letter protesting against the rude behaviour of the Government Secretary, and proposing to petition the English Parliament. *Bombay Durpan*, 15 June 1832, files held at the Bombay Archives, Vol. 1, p. 150; see also report, 'Misbehaviour of the Police Establishment of the Central Division' in *Bombay Durpan*, 10 May 1833; Report on 'Native Gentlemen Equally Entitled to the Same Civility as Europeans' in *Bombay Durpan*, 25 April 1834 in G.G. Jambhekar, ed., *MWBJ*, Vol. 2, pp. 104–6.

[47]Reply to a letter in the *Bombay Gazette* by a 'Friend' of the Native Education

Bombay Government over its decision to limit the expenditure on native education to a fixed annual sum instead of the practice followed until then of simply paying for the total annual costs of the Society's work.[48]

The cogency, coherence and consistency of Marathi columns in the *Durpan* attest to the determination and capabilities of its editorial team,[49] with Balshastri being its most important member. What is impressive about its achievement is the total absence of all complaints on the underdeveloped state of the vernacular. This contrasts with the work of Vishnushastri Chiplunkar as editor of the *Nibandhmala*. Despite differences between the materials published in the *Durpan* and the *Nibandhmala*,[50] it is interesting that the latter contained repeated expostulations describing the difficulties of sustaining a vernacular journal and the difficulties faced by native editors and publishers. It seemed to be part of Balshastri's heroic project not to admit differences

Society, *Bombay Durpan*, 4 September 1835 in G.G. Jambhekar, ed., *MWBJ*, Vol. 2, p. 120–1.

[48]*Bombay Durpan*, 9 November 1832 in ibid., p. 38. An article on the proposed measures to economise on native education ends on this sharp note: 'We cannot conclude these observations without expressing our surprise and regret that this society which represents so imposing an appearance and partakes of a national character [*svadeshiya hithartha guna dakhavite*, which translates literally as 'displaying qualities contributing to the welfare of our region], should, as it has done since its institution, not depended upon its own resources, but upon persons of Education whom misfortune or indiscretion might have induced to enlist in the army, and come out to this Country. Such a system is surely unworthy of an Institution supported by public liberality ... this system ought to be abandoned, and an able Master engaged at once, on a salary which will be an adequate remuneration for the services of a properly trained person. ... Such a change, we are persuaded, would conduce greatly to the respectability of the Society and the efficiency of the Institution.'

[49]The other two editors of the *Bombay Durpan*, Janardhan Vasudev and Raghunath Harischandrajee, were both *prabhus*. For information about Raghunath Harischandrajee see G.G. Jambhekar, ed., *MWBJ*, Appendix 2, Vol. 3, p. 385. As a sub-brahmin caste with a history of literate skills, the *prabhu* community was quick to respond to the new professional and public-political opportunities under colonial rule: see chapter four.

[50]See chapter five.

between the status of English and the vernacular,[51] between the alien government and native society. Given that his entire professional life was devoted to the work of cultivating the vernacular to create a modern, 'useful' discourse in Marathi, it seems improbable that Balshastri actually believed in an audience with symmetrical literate capacities in English and Marathi. Besides his pioneering work in setting up the bilingual *Durpan* and sustaining it over eight years, he started the first periodical monthly in Marathi, *Digdarshan*.[52] The Prastavana to the first issue of the *Digdarshan*[53] stated its belief that knowledge was power, and that learning (*vidya*) was essential for all. It professed not to address scholars alone, but to introduce the subjects of useful learning (*vyvaharopyogi shastre va vidya*) like geography, history, physics, chemistry, with relevant maps and illustrations as well as literary subjects, to a more general audience. Balshastri's next venture after the closure of the *Durpan* shows his commitment to enlarging the repertoire and market for the vernacular, and his awareness of the social implications of the changing linguistic economy as well as the dangers of Marathi being subordinated by the English sphere. On more than one occasion, the *Durpan* reiterated the need for native intellectuals to be well versed in both English and the vernacular, especially on account of the increasing tendency to regard knowledge

[51]Records suggest that the *Bombay Durpan* could not sustain itself as a bilingual publication beyond 1834. The later issues seem to have been entirely in English. However, it would unfair to construe this, or its ultimate closure in 1840, as evidence of the editors' incompetence; the colonial native press had to contend with structural constraints of an ideological and financial nature.

[52]Plans to start a 'useful' periodical had been announced in January 1839. The *Digdarshan* saw itself as a journal devoted to detailed articles, either in the form of translations or original compositions for a general audience on various subjects such as geography, history, chemistry and general knowledge. The first issue came out in May 1840 and the periodical probably survived until March 1845, with a long gap between October 1842 and January 1844. Priced at Rs 6 per year or Rs 5 if paid for in advance, it included lithographed maps and illustrations. Apparently, the journal had a circulation of 300 copies, out of which, probably, a third were government and missionaries subscriptions. See G.G. Jambhekar, ed., *MWBJ*, Appendix 3, Vol. 3, pp. 85–6.

[53]See G.G. Jambhekar, ed., *MWBJ*, Vol. 2, p. 191.

of English as sufficient qualification for higher bureaucratic positions.[54] Opposing moves to romanize the Indian alphabets, the *Durpan* was forthright in outlining the disastrous social and political implications this would have:

> If translations are to be written in the Roman character, we see very little good from their being used as a medium of imparting knowledge to the natives of India. In the event, therefore, of the new plan being adopted, the principal object of the School-Book societies here and elsewhere which is to educate the mass of the population by means of easy translations, must be entirely abandoned. ... That is every hope of spreading useful information by means of translations, must be given up. And all this for what? For the convenience of a handful of Europeans, who find it troublesome to get into their heads, the fifty simple characters of the *Devnagiri*, but who nevertheless are supposed to have enough patience to go through the conjugations of two thousand and two hundred verbs of theSanskrit language.[55]

Realising the need to create a sufficiently large literate audience in Marathi, he had hoped to sustain the *Durpan* by conflating his two audiences—derived from official circles and the small segment of colonial-modern native intellectuals—into an ideal, imaginary, colonial public characterised by its apparently homogeneous, bilingual capacities.

[54]The following comment occurs in a piece entitled 'Qualifications necessary for superior offices' in the *Bombay Durpan* of 17 March 1838: 'For let us candidly examine what advantage a person possessing no other qualifications than an acquaintance with English can have over a European properly educated at Aylesbury [Haileybury?]. The latter is decidedly more competent to do all in which the knowledge of the English language is requisite; whereas the former having but imperfect acquaintance with the languages of the country cannot prove more efficient than he in the examination of records, documents or witnesses that he may have occasion to institute, in the course of his duty. Such a native is inferior to a European in general information and intelligence, while at same time he is deficient in the qualifications of local knowledge, and proficiency in the native language, which alone can make him more useful than a foreigner.' See ibid., p. 136.

[55]*Bombay Durpan*, 5 February 1836, quoted in *The Oriental Christian*, March 1836 in G.G. Jambhekar, ed., *MWBJ*, Appendix 2, Vol. 3, p. 616.

The *Durpan* has been discussed at length for it helps us appreciate the social self-reflexivity shown by the emerging native discourse. Such early initiatives also help mark shifts in the structure of bilingualism, resulting from changes in official policy to formalise hierarchical distinctions between English and the vernacular within the education system after the 1850s.

Balshastri Jambhekar was not exceptional in his concern with disseminating a vernacular critical discourse. Similar considerations underlay the formation of the vernacular wing of the Students Literary and Scientific Society, the *Upyukt Marathi Dnyanprasarak Mandali*. In an address to its inaugural meeting on 1 September 1848—later published in the Sabha's Marathi journal for a larger audience—the President, Dadoba Pandurang described their aims: 'The Sabha's main intentions are to undertake and enable through this body of compositions in the mother-tongue [*svabhasha*] on subjects of a classical and useful nature, and thus enable the spread of useful knowledge within our land [*svadesh*].'[56]

To draw on a final instance, a remarkable article appeared in the same journal, *Marathi Dnyanaprasarak*, in 1852, less than three years after it began publication. Translated, its title meant, 'Reflections on educating natives through the local languages alone and the benefits of giving them the same education [*vidya*] through both English and the local language'.[57] The main arguments underlined the centrality of the language question within the debate on colonial education. The article also indicated the extent to which a centralised education policy had altered the linguistic field even since the time of the *Durpan* in the early 1830s. It pointed out that the greatest merit of Western useful (*upyogi*) learning was its divergence from the particularistic traditions of Hindu and Muslim learning. Specifically, British rule was commended for replacing a taste for ancient tales from the puranas (*prachin puranik katha*) with knowledge about the efforts of men (*purush*) who worked

[56]Translated from Marathi, Dadoba Pandurang, *'Prastavana'* in *Marathi Dnyanaprasarak* (henceforth, *MD*), Vol. 1, No. 1, 1850.

[57]*'Ettedeshiya lokans keval svabhashechachdvara vidya shikavili asta labh konkonte, va teech jar English va svabhasa ya dohanchyadware shikavila tar konkonche yacha vichar'*, *MD*, Vol. 3, No. 9, December 1852.

for the general (*sarv lok*) welfare.[58] Evidently, dissemination was already, at least partially, a social practice and value. For, despite claiming that the diversity of opinions in the medium-of-instruction debate detracted from the efforts to spread education, the article went on to elaborate an argument about the advantages of vernacular education. The vernaculars would cover a larger demographic compass, which would enhance the interest people would take in issues of local administration. Showing a close familiarity with official correspondence and details of the divergent educational policies pursued in the Bengal and Bombay Presidencies, the article even remonstrated against the unfavourably small allocations for education in Bombay.[59] Knowledge of English was essential if the essence (*rasa*) and significance (*mahatva*) of complex texts were to be fully appreciated in that language.[60] English was indispensable for the spread of education in Hindustan and there was little wrong in acknowledging this. History showed several examples of people learning a language that they were convinced would bring benefits.[61] English was also important because it was the channel for communicating with the highest levels of judiciary and bureaucracy, and in business.[62]

Having established the significance of English, the article went on to highlight the poor condition of Marathi schools. Already, it would seem, the vernaculars were regarded as inadequate for the dissemination of useful knowledge and vernacular education was strategically being underdeveloped, through official measures, to make it the cheap, low-quality option for instruction on a 'popular' scale.[63] The article lamented government measures to reduce expenditure on the training of teachers and the preparation of vernacular texts. It noted the disparity and

[58]Interestingly, the collective subject of the above *Dnyanaprasarak* article is alternately represented as *'hindulok'* and the more neutral, inclusive, *ettedeshiya lok*. The accent on the aspect of religious community in the former term suggests a shift from the non-particularistic policy followed by the *Bombay Durpan*, see fn. 38 above.

[59]See table on p. 138 below.

[60]*MD*, Vol. 3, No. 9, December 1852, p. 269.

[61]Ibid., p. 267.

[62]Ibid., p. 274.

[63]Ibid., pp. 274–9.

disjunctions between the English and Marathi spheres. On the one hand, the *pantojis* in the Marathi primary schools had no standard books to teach from, nor did their heavy burden of duties leave them with time to read in English. On the other, those who studied English hardly had the time or the financial means to attempt translations into the vernacular.[64] The dismal rewards available to native translators could only jeopardise the translation project, especially as the translations done by colonial officials were neither popular nor effective.[65]

Making a strong connection between translation and the spread of modern discourses, the article argued that reform was *necessarily* a bilingual project. Students who learnt only English were likely to become shallow braggarts. A chauvinistic fear that English would destroy the local languages and pride in native culture (*svadeshabhiman*) was most inappropriate.[66] Nevertheless, the article revealed that prevailing common sense accepted hierarchical discontinuities between the cognitive and political status of English and Marathi, and the resulting dependence of the vernacular sphere. Admitting that both English and the vernaculars were vital as means of communication between the rulers (*rajyakarte*) and the ruled (*praja*),[67] it likened English and the vernacular to the brick and mortar needed to build a 'reformed house'.[68] A higher English education was most necessary for the elite and influential middle classes (*madhyam pratiche va varishta lok*). Given the very real constraints, however, it might be an inescapable decision to invest limited funds available in instructing influential groups within native society.[69]

[64]Ibid., p. 279.

[65]Ibid., p. 287. Commenting that Europeans failed to understand the character of native languages and often wrote and spoke them much like English, the article was especially critical of Major Candy's work. It observed that his translations were appreciated neither by popular nor scholarly audiences.

[66]Ibid., p. 289.

[67]Ibid., p. 305.

[68]Ibid., p. 306.

[69]Revealing the alertness of colonial intellectuals to emerging shifts in social hierarchy, the article remarked that, in the present context, *madhyam* and *varishta lok* referred mostly to brahmins, whose traditional importance had, however, been diminished. Instead, the term referred to those who had gained social prominence,

By the mid-1850s, colonial intellectuals were beginning to sense that their position in the emerging hierarchy depended on the small size of the reading public and its internal divisions. This implied that they had also admitted an inability to change the directions of official policy or substantially enlarge the literate community. Upper-caste intellectuals had begun to realise the political advantages of a two-tiered education system where the vernaculars would be reserved for a basic general instruction and only the higher classes would have access to a 'full' English education. Having thus shown a willingness to accept the status quo and the subordination of the vernaculars within education and the public domain, vernacular discourse from now on showed only a diminishing interest in egalitarian ideals and the general spread of education. Consequently, by the time of the 'vernacular renaissance' of the 1870s, the dominant agenda in the vernacular sphere was a conservative defence of the hierarchical structure of native society. The establishment of a university and the emergence of English as the sole language of higher education embedded the bilingual divide within the social hierarchy.

The Emergence of Bombay University: Instituting Colonial Bilingualism as Social Hierarchy

The bilingual divide, gradually but irrevocably, acquired the dimensions of a concrete social reality. A preliminary glance at the relevant statistics shows that there were significant differences between allocations for English and Marathi, even in the early decades of the education project when, ostensibly, official policy was more inclined towards encouraging instruction through the vernacular. Claims that the colonial bilingual relation was founded on egalitarian premises were belied by the inequality in allotments. These differences show that the number of students in English schools was less than ten per cent of the total enrolment in Presidency schools. Between 1826 and 1842, four government English schools had been established in the Bombay Presidency as against 201 vernacular schools with 761 and 9702 students

either through their affluence, government support or intelligence. Ibid., pp. 314–19.

	Bengal Presidency	Bombay Presidency
Population *	37 millions	10 1/2 millions
Total Receiving Govt. Ed.	5,570	10,616
Receiving English Ed.	3,953	761
Funds applicable to Ed.	Rs. 4,77,593	Rs. 1,68,226

* We are told that these figures were taken from a table in the last edition of the *Encyclopaedia Britannica's* article on Hindustan.

respectively.[70] By 1848 the number of English schools had gone up to 7. At this point the number of vernacular schools had come down to 166, but the number of vernacular students had remained almost unchanged, with 9708 students on the rolls,[71] indicating that the government was attempting to reduce the already paltry sum being spent per student in the vernacular sector. A comparison with developments in Bengal[72] for the corresponding period appears below.

These figures suggest that the early emphasis on vernacular education had allowed policy in Bombay to be more broad-based than in Bengal. They also show a marked imbalance between the numbers in English and vernacular schools in Bombay, raising serious questions about the elitist position that English education was assuming in Western India. Such huge discrepancies in the capacity of the English and vernacular schools in Bombay meant that, for a large percentage of these students, colonial education offered only the prospect of an elementary vernacular training, which included perhaps only a bare sprinkling of English reading skills. Left with virtually no chance of making it to a liberal, higher education in English, this significant number represented what may be termed the colonial literate under-class.

As President of the Board of Education, Erskine Perry mooted these changes ostensibly to tackle this internal asymmetry between vernacular and English education. However, the changes suggested actually aimed to make education policy in Bombay even more elitist by increasing the scope for instruction through English. Perry believed that the

[70] *RBE for 1845*, Bombay, 1845, p. 11.
[71] *RBE for 1857–58*, Bombay, 1850, p. 35.
[72] *RBE for 1845*, p. 146.

'information of the modern times could only be conveyed to the natives, at the present, through the medium of English'. For him, the task of improving the vernaculars was best left to the upper classes of natives.[73] Arguing against his proposals, the staunch ideologue for vernacular education, George Jervis, pointed out how the existing situation was already heavily balanced in favour of instruction through English. Even before Perry's proposals, official figures for the year 1846–7 showed that whereas a sum of Rs 45,419-5-4 was spent on 8225 students in the vernacular schools, the sum expended on teaching English to a much smaller number of 1395 was Rs 1,02,769-0-8.[74] Almost a decade later, despite much talk of starting more English schools, the proportion between students studying English and those studying through the vernaculars had, in fact, grown more skewed. The following table summarises the comparison between these two sectors of the colonial education system in the Bombay Presidency in 1855–6:

	Total no. of English Schools			Total no. of Vernacular Schools		
No. of schools	17			322		
No. of pupils	2,851			22, 950		
	Rs.	a.	p.	Rs.	a.	p.
Amount of fees paid	21,487	4	0	10,822	3	10
total cost of education	1,14,320	6	4	75,990	13	5
Average cost per pupil per annum	40	1	7	3	4	11

Thus, while a 'full' training in English emerged as the acme of the progression of rewards, the divide between the high language and the vernacular assumed serious social dimensions. This meant several things. With a college or university education in English established as the most conspicuous realisation of intellectual aspiration and opportunity possible within colonial society, the intellectual hierarchy between

[73]Minute by the President of the Board, Erskine Perry dated 14 April 1847, *RBE for 1848–50*, p. 59.

[74]Minute by Colonel G. Jervis dated 9 May 1848, *RBE for 1848–50*, p. 81.

English and the vernaculars was acquiring a substantial institutional basis.

Although education policy in the 1850s showed signs of redefining the emphases of its early statements, in real terms these changes hardly represented a radical deviation from the basic assumptions of the project of colonial literacy. The hierarchical bias in favour of English had been clear from the start, colonial policy having consistently demonstrated its capacity for a calculated ambivalence intended to give room for manoeuvre at all points. The changes of the 1850s only accentuated the assumptions always implicit in earlier policy documents. For example, the list of rules for educational establishments under the Board of Education formulated in 1845, even before the Perry–Jervis controversy of 1848, had put the matter quite bluntly:

> ...5. The educational establishments under the control of the Board are divided into mainly two classes, somewhat but not wholly, corresponding to the primary and superior schools of Europe.
>
> 6. The first class is intended to meet the wants of the great bulk of the population, who have but little time to devote to school instruction, and the information there conveyed is consequently of an elementary character, and is conveyed in the vernacular tongues.
>
> 7. In the second class the English language (except at Sanskrit College) and the superior branches of education are taught.[75]

The very structure of the education system symbolised the internal asymmetry in the relation between English and the vernaculars. By 1858 the basic structure of the education system was visible in its 'mature' form. At the very bottom of the scale were village vernacular schools. From here the student would proceed to second-grade anglo-vernacular schools, of which there would be one for every *taluka*. The superior anglo-vernacular school at the *zillah* place came next in the hierarchy. The handful of English 'high' schools were to be located in the bigger towns, where it was proposed to supply at least one European master for each school. These were to form the top layer in the pyramid of the school structure. As against this, it was decided to keep the number

[75]'Rules and Regulations of the Educational Establishments under the Board of Education, 1845', J.A. Richey, ed., *SER*, Part II, p. 159.

of colleges at two in 1858; these colleges represented the very top rung of colonial education and taught entirely through English.

The emergence of English as the sole language of higher learning meant the relegation of the vernacular as fit only for primary education. Thus, part of the colonial student's training taught him to understand that, in his situation, aspiration to intellectual merit involved something of a summary transcendence, if not outright disavowal, of vernacular literacy. This fixing of vernaculars within the intellectual hierarchy was bound to have a major impact on social structure: It meant the funnelling of a select few for a 'full' liberal training in English. It also meant an effective subalternisation of the vernacular intelligentsia within the colonial hierarchy.

Study of the vernacular was no longer to be given even a secondary emphasis in the way that it had hitherto, and was now all but excluded within higher education.[76] This met with opposition from many among the English-educated elite but failed to affect official rulings on the matter. The hierarchisation of the education system also affected the level to which a vernacular school training equipped students for a college education. More importantly, it influenced the intelligentsia's efforts to imagine and articulate the nature and limits of the new communities emerging through the impact of colonial policy. Now, only the best graduates could be expected to possess sufficient English to attempt translations into the vernaculars; their command and fluency within the vernacular was not such that they would choose the latter as their primary medium of expression. Consequently, it is not surprising to find official reports on vernacular literature from the late 1860s noting regretfully that graduates hardly figured in lists of vernacular authors; such lists almost entirely comprised pre-university or even barely-schooled men.[77]

These changes to upgrade colonial education into a 'full' system of higher education were accompanied by two other tendencies that

[76]For a good account of the changes in educational policy in Bombay from 1850 onwards, see R.V. Parulekar's essay, 'Medium of Instruction' in J.V. Naik, ed., *The Educational Writings of Shri R.V. Parulekar*, pp. 1–40.

[77]M.G. Ranade, 'A Note on the Growth of Marathi Literature', 1898, rpt. in *The Miscellaneous Writings of the Late Hon. Mr. Justice Ranade*, New Delhi, 1992, pp. 1–55, especially pp. 42–52.

increasingly characterised education policy from then on. After 1858, policy was not interested in allowing unhindered expansion in the numbers enrolled in schools. Until now, petitions for a vernacular school had been heard, provided they came from a locality with a population of at least 2000 inhabitants willing to provide and maintain appropriate premises[78] and who undertook the payment of the fee of one anna per month by each student. But now, under pressure from the Government of India at Calcutta, official policy was that, in principle, it wished to distribute its grants mostly to support *existing* schools that satisfactorily imparted a non-religious education. This step was mainly to check the expense to the administration on account of its earlier 'liberal' policy which, it was feared, would have 'witnessed the foundation of new schools, probably in increasing numbers, until every village, had been supplied with its own vernacular public school'.[79] Of course, policy could not reject all applications for the opening of more schools, and funds were subsequently released for elementary vernacular schools. But the more general point being made here is that, from the mid-1850s, and especially after 1857, coinciding with the establishment of universities, educational policy had effectively turned the corner from its earlier 'radical' phase. Funds purportedly claiming to support the general dissemination of modern, useful and scientific knowledge were now taken up to make graduate courses taught by European professors available at the university. As policy shifted its attention to consolidating what had already been achieved, it developed a clearly elitist and conservative bias. Arguing that a widespread modern education among the colonial population could be politically dangerous, Lord Ellenborough, President of the Board of Control, advised that education policy needed to be more carefully elitist:

> Education and civilisation may descend from the higher to the inferior classes, and so communicated may import new vigour to the commu-

[78]For details of conditions under which permission was given for a vernacular school, see chapter two.

[79]See 'Annual Report by Director of Public Instruction, E.I. Howard' in *RDPI for 1856–57*, Bombay, 1857, pp. 9–11. Howard's Report notes that this check on the expansion of the school system was part of the directive received from the Government of India.

nity, but they will never ascend from the lower classes to those above them; they can only if imparted solely to the lower classes lead to the general convulsion, of which foreigners would be the first victims. If we desire to diffuse education, let us endeavour to give it to the highest first ... by founding colleges to which the higher classes alone shall be admitted.[80]

The increasing attention to higher education did not mean that deficiencies within the programme of colonial literacy, some of which have been alluded to, had been addressed or removed. Instead, they were now regarded as being too large and fundamental to be remedied within the considerations and paradigms underlying policy. Official statements either tried to gloss over these difficulties or took them as inevitable to the colonial situation; or, at worst, represented them as arising from the recalcitrance of native students. Alongside these shifts, the college curriculum developed a marked literary orientation that included the re-introduction of Sanskrit as a 'classical' literature in place of the earlier emphasis upon cultivating learning through the vernacular. The most significant difference in the content of the Sanskrit courses prescribed now—from those prescribed previously as part of the Sanskrit studies in Poona College—was that the later syllabi largely ignored the systems of philosophical and ethical thought available through Sanskrit. Students' knowledge of Sanskrit now was to be predominantly built around a 'literary' curriculum. However, prominence in the liberal arts college curriculum was to be given to the English literary component and the study of European history. As against this, prior to the changes of the mid-1850s, students at the Elphinstone Institute and Poona College had had the opportunity to balance their readings on English literature and European history with a study of texts on science and mathematics in the vernacular. It must be remembered that these changes, which weakened even the limited emphasis within colonial education on the cultivation of a rational, critical temper, occurred alongside increasing discontinuities between the 'high' and the 'low' linguistic

[80]Letter from Lord Ellenborough, President of the Board of Control to the Chairman of Court of Directions dated 28 April 1858, in *RDPI for 1857–58*, Bombay, 1858, p. 12.

spheres created by colonial bilingualism. All this made for the shift towards conservatism evident in the ideological stances taken by the intelligentsia in the post-1857 period, as well as a growing gap between the orientation of the English-educated and the vernacular sections of this intelligentsia. Despite their differences, they shared certain elements, for example a growing mutual distrust of each other, as also a prominent tendency in both to articulate the pre-colonial past through Sanskritic ideology.

Western India's educational policy and history thus offer an interesting contrast to the historical development of the *mentalité* of the Bengali *bhadralok*. Educational policy in Bengal worked almost exclusively through an emphasis on English, and therefore the development of university education in English did not require a shift from earlier policy. In the Bombay Presidency, on the other hand, the more broad-based thrust of initial policy was one of the reasons that made for a discursive space allowing the emergence of a figure like Phule as a champion of lower-caste interests. But the inevitable betrayal of even this shallow stress on general literacy through the vernacular had two important consequences for the making of the modern political temper in Western India. Firstly, it meant that the structural limits of subaltern assertion within the colonial public arena were quickly reached. With the switch to English, upper castes could consolidate their hold over scarce educational opportunities at a much faster pace than was possible for those communities who barely had previous access to formal education. In the long run, the uneasy balance between vernacular and English education in Western India also severely affected the levels of preparation and intellectual training among the upper-caste intelligentsia.

4

Colonial Power, Print and the Re-making of the Literate Sphere

Colonial Power, Print and Publicity

Print was obviously indispensable to the making of colonial ideology and governance. Quite early on, post-colonial literary theory drew attention to the significance of the English book in enhancing the operations of colonial power and the ambivalent meanings it acquired for those who could not comprehend its contents.[1] In the colonial imagination[2] education presupposed a system of learning centred on print and individuated reading practices. Education policy was in that

[1]See Homi Bhabha's essay, cited in chapter three, fn. 4.

[2]The discovery of unique strategies of social and cognitive control coincided with the emergence of modernity in the West. Processes of 'Othering', objectification and enumeration formed some of the essential elements of the epistemological and ideological apparatus through which the West asserted its ascendancy over non-Western societies. The term 'colonial imagination' is used here as shorthand to refer to this discursive configuration.

Foucault's impressive analysis of modern power does not take into account the colonial context. Nevertheless, his emphasis on the role of intellectuals and the human sciences in the dissemination of modern power holds important insights for an understanding of the displacement of liberalism as colonial pedagogy. For an analysis of the relations between modern knowledge and power see Z. Bauman, *Legislators and Interpreters: Modernity, Post-modernity and Intellectuals,* Cambridge, 1989; Michel Foucault, *Language, Counter-Memory and Practice: Selected Essays and Interviews*, New York, 1977; Michel Foucault, *The Order of Things: An Archaeology of the Human Sciences,* London, 1970.

sense a rubric for a whole set of inter-related assumptions and practices about knowledge, cultivation, textuality and identity inherent within Western modernity and necessary to the elaboration and maintenance of colonial power. To what extent would the processes of objectification and discursive control have been possible without print? This is not to suggest technological determinism; rather, it is to suggest that the introduction of print as part of the colonial encounter led to complex shifts in existing ideological norms and structures. At the cultural level, it introduced radical shifts in assumptions about language, literacy and the 'literary'. But print also altered the structure of the political world, for the principle of publicity led to shifts in the universe of ideas, the structure of social communication, and the norms and distribution of political power. A rich and detailed literature on the new knowledges, mentalities, cultural and political identities associated with rise of print in the West[3] highlights the great promise of power contained in the encyclopaedic accumulation of knowledge since the Renaissance and its organisation into internally coherent but discrete segments. In our own colonial context, what were some of the ways in which intellectual norms and possibilities, represented by print, design colonial power?

Despite work on the political significance of early colonial efforts to codify native knowledges and languages (this presumes a print-based literacy), the connections between the implicit rationale of print and its effects within colonial modernity remain untheorised. It would be appropriate to begin by discussing some of the paradoxes and shifts underlying the introduction of print in Western India. One of the earliest instances of a literary society along Western lines was established in Bombay. Intended as a discursive space for learned conversation, the Bombay Literary Society was set up in 1804, more than a decade before the British formally assumed control over the region. It was meant for the benefit of 'cultivated' gentlemen among colonial officials in Bombay who were, in the words of James Mackintosh, the society's first president, 'detachments from the main body of civilised men sent out to levy contributions of knowledge, as well as to gain victories over barbarism'.

[3]See chapter one, fn. 3.

He told his audience, in his inaugural address, that the idea of establishing such a society had occurred to him even before he left England. He saw himself as 'a representative of Europe's curiosity' in India and assured the gathering that similar sentiments would inform all plans for the society's activities and inquiries. The society was structured according to principles of voluntary non-personal association and followed modes of learned conversation premised on the advantages of circulation and reading habits through print. Such ideas about an abstract, non-particularised public realm had already been implicit in attempts by orientalist scholars to produce a body of authoritative texts that recorded norms pertaining to various native cultural and social practices.[4] And yet, ironically, the 'public' for these early printed texts denoted a limited and exclusive circle of officials and personnel in the colonial establishment, with perhaps a somewhat larger, curious audience back home. The introduction of print on the subcontinent thus created its own cognitive domains, roughly definable by the intellectual appetites of metropolitan audiences and the interest of colonial authorities. Mackintosh's inaugural address exemplifies quite perfectly the tensions underlying the creation of a colonial public realm. It was no mean task to reconcile the ideas of publicity and the notion of a modern republic of letters with the size and nature of the audience for texts produced through the colonial establishment: 'the smallest society brought together by the love of knowledge is respectable in the eye of the reason; and the feeble efforts of infant literature in barren and inhospitable regions are in some respects more interesting than the most elaborate works and the most successful exertions of the human mind'.[5]

In principle, of course, anyone who could read could have access to this commonwealth of printed texts. In practice, admission was contingent upon certain qualifications, of which the possession of

[4]See Bernard Cohn's essay cited in chapter one, fn. 97 and also his 'The Census, Social Structure, and Objectification in South Asia, in *An Anthropologist Among the Historians and Other Essays*, New Delhi, 1987.

[5]James Mackintosh, 'Inaugural Address delivered to the Literary Society of Bombay', in 1804 in *Transactions of the Literary Society of Bombay*, London, 1817, pp. xi–xxvi.

'good sense' was one of the most important requirements.[6] In this way print was instrumental in creating a literate sphere quite distinct from that presupposed by the pre-colonial world of cultivated and learned exchange, although this new sphere was too small and exclusive to supplant the existing structure of native literate and learned practices. Nevertheless, the coming of print and colonial discourse resulted in definitive shifts in the structure of native literate/learned norms and practices, especially in what constituted the cognitive domain and in the ways of being an intellectual.

Advocating the pursuit of subjects that had hitherto been the domain of government, Mackintosh urged the society to undertake the collection and classification of information on all aspects of native life. In making such a plea he was drawing upon knowledge of the enhanced possibilities of accumulation, dissemination and control enabled by print. These had led to the celebration of abstract reasoning and the rise of expert knowledge in the West. Mackintosh acknowledged that in this part of the world the society's project represented a new experiment. But he anticipated the possible benefits of the publication of statistical information thus compiled with enthusiasm:

> tables of political arithmetic have not yet been made public in any tropical country ... I shall mention only an example of their value that they must lead to a decisive solution of the problems with respect to the influence of polygamy on population, and the supposed origin of that practice in the disproportional number of the sexes. But in a country where every part of the system of the manners and institutions differs from Europe, *it is impossible to foresee the extent and variety of the new results, which an accurate survey might present to us.*[7] (emphasis added)

He felt such knowledge ought not to be the exclusive preserve of government. This was not out of any desire for intellectual freedom but because he was confident of a 'reasonable' agreement between the ends of government and science. Information confined to government was lost forever; whereas the existence of a public domain helped maintain the best interests of government by making important and

[6]Ibid.
[7]Ibid.

valuable information available to it. He was evidently untroubled that such direct complicity between the society's intellectual efforts and governmental ends would undermine the principle of publicity:

> this knowledge is a control on subordinate agents for government as well as a control on government for their subjects. And it is one of those which have not the slightest tendency to produce tumult or convulsion. On the contrary, nothing more clearly evinces the necessity of that firm protecting power by which alone can order be secured. The security of the governed cannot exist without the security of the governors.[8]

This early discourse on the founding of a modern literate sphere in Western India elucidates the usefulness of print for the ideological relations that colonial power intended to establish. Upon assuming political control in 1818 the British were quick to draw up comprehensive proposals to selectively extend the colonial literate sphere to carefully chosen social groups as the first step in cultivating a new intelligentsia. By introducing similar steps throughout the subcontinent, they aimed to produce a standardised moral code suited to a secular colonial civil order. A single organisation, the Native School and School Book Society, was responsible for various aspects of the new literate order. Gauri Vishwanathan has shown that the project of native education[9] did not proceed from a ready, 'home-made' model which could be replicated in the colony with modifications. She points out that the British Parliament committed state funds for the education of its colonial Indian subjects even before formalising similar steps for its home population. While this establishes the impossibility of treating the histories of modernity in metropole and colony as discrete narratives, chronological priority by itself is not ultimately significant. For the question really is: What enabled the colonial state to arrive at the radical idea of an education project as ideological strategy, despite their lack of previous experience? According to the argument here, the answer lies in new assumptions about language,

[8]Ibid.
[9]Gauri Vishwanathan, *Masks of Conquest.*

reading and learned practices that were introduced through print, which helped colonial power define links with a new intelligentsia and, through them, with the rest of native society.

Reading as Reform

As Foucault's work has taught us, the management of power through an internalised regime of control had become an important part of the repertoire of the Western state with the early modern period. The colonial imagination inherited these ideological strategies and saw their potential in establishing control over other, dissimilar social worlds. Control was to be exerted not through force but primarily through authority over the norms of discursive production, reception and dissemination. This would clear the space for altering forms of language and redefining notions of collective and self-identity. Scholars working on the rise of print culture in the West have pointed to the important part played by the shift in reading practices and the ensuing laicisation of culture in the formation of modern subjectivity and collective identities. Among the most important concerns in the earliest administrative plans was the great emphasis on *reading* as a measure to neutralise native resistance and cultivate compliance. Initially, colonial policy was somewhat wary of introducing English and Western literature, but the overall ideological advantage that it stood to derive from the regulation of literate practices through the introduction of print is evident from the following extract of Elphinstone's Report of 1818:

> I do not perceive anything that we can do to improve the morals of the people except by improving their education. There are already schools in small towns, and in many villages; but reading is confined to *brahmins, banyans,* and such of the agricultural classes that have to do accounts. I am not sure that our establishing free schools would alter this state of things, and it might create a suspicion of some concealed design on our part. It would be more practicable and *more useful to give a direction to the reading of those who do learn, of which the press so easily affords the means.* ... Books are scarce, and the common ones probably ill-chosen; but there exist in the Hindu languages many tales and fables that would be generally read, and that would circulate sound

morals. There must be religious books tending more directly to the same end. If many of these are *printed and distributed gratuitously, the effect would without doubt, be great and beneficial.* It would however be indispensable that they should be purely Hindu. We might silently omit all precepts of questionable morality, but the slightest infusion of religious controversy would secure the failure of the design.[10] (emphasis added)

Similarly, reading had an important place in the pedagogic practice of missionary schools. Learning to read was seen as much more than simply acquiring a cognitive or linguistic skill; it was as much a process through which people could be *improved* and made 'better' human beings. Even more than in early modern Europe, standardised reading practices within the colonial curriculum were an ideological instrument, advocated for their potential to reform native self-perceptions, especially with respect to the political and moral authority of the colonial state. These objectives are also apparent in early records for the first English schools established in Bombay to provide Christian instruction to natives. Getting 'young tender minds' to read parables containing 'simple, moral truths' of Christian belief was deemed the most suitable method of instruction, far more efficacious than direct preaching. The acquisition of information was not the only object of these reading lessons. Reading was as an act of moral self-discipline, requiring students to carry out the activity in an upright posture of attention. They were sufficiently significant to classroom activity to be described at some length in the Second Annual Report of the Education Society in 1817:

the benefits to be expected from these [reading lessons] ... are many and important. Regarded merely as reading lessons, their recommendations are not inconsiderable, since from the diversified nature of their subjects, they add greatly to the learner's stock of words, and introduce a pleasing variety into his lessons ... The chief excellence however of these tracts is that they inculcate the purest principles of

[10]Mounstuart Elphinstone, 'Report on the Territories Conquered from the Peshwas' in G.W. Forrest, ed., *Selections from the Official Writings of the Hon. Mountstuart Elphinstone*, p. 334.

morality in the way of example, which is precisely the way that is most likely to engage and influence the minds of children. These affecting narratives propose examples of the use of and application of right principles and situations similar to those in which the greater part of the children may themselves be hereafter placed. They have the advantage moreover of being written with great feeling; and moral instruction never makes so lasting an impression nor is ever so cordially received, as when laying aside the formal didactic method, it condescends to address itself to the heart and affections.[11]

Reading extended beyond a standardised classroom: 'appropriate' materials circulated through print opened out political possibilities. As a highly visible site of ideological manoeuvring, the classroom could arouse resentment and resistance whereas print allowed a more general circulation for colonial discourse even as it promised a convenient degree of impersonality. The impersonal but extensive reach of the printed word was not only efficacious as communication but had the hardly inestimable advantage of being relatively cheap. As plans on the future use of the *dakshina* funds noted: 'the circulation of a few well-chosen books, such as ... are already being printed at Calcutta, would have a better and more extensive effect than a regular college, and would cost much less to the government.'[12]

Print Capitalism in a Colonial Society

The new print slowly supplanted literate traditions and 'remedied' the lack of 'appropriate' books and reading material in the school system. The introduction of English and the opening of schools evoked interest in some sections because of employment opportunities. If that interest was to be taken advantage of, the new schools had to be provided reading material: 'A few tracts should be framed in a popular way on general history, natural history, geography and astronomy and considering the great commercial pursuits of many native inhabitants

[11]'Extract from the Second Annual Report of the Bombay Education Society for 1817', pp. 17–24, quoted in R.V. Parulekar, ed., *SERB*, Part II, p. 5.

[12]Mounstuart Elphinstone, 'Report on the Territories Conquered from the Peshwas' in G.W. Forrest, ed., *Selections from the Official Writings of the Hon. Mountstuart Elphinstone*, p. 335.

of this Presidency, an elementary treatise on navigation and a description of the countries connected with this port would be highly useful and could not fail to interest them'.[13]

The report of the Native Education Society for 1821 complained that there was little interest in English outside the island of Bombay. In order to bring the provincial population within the ambit of the new literate and discursive practices, education would need to be systematically extended into mofussil areas. This brought up the further question of the use of native languages. The education project could not achieve its ambitions by confining itself to English. What would be needed were 'plain and useful school tracts in the languages of the country ... one of the first objects towards improving the education of the natives, must be the preparing and publishing some *unexceptionable school tracts in the native languages.* These languages will for the most part be the Mahratta and Guzeratee ... '

The extension of colonial ideology thus entailed the selection of certain languages as most suited to performing the new functions. A 'direct' discursive connection between the new 'high' domain of '*Ingrezi vidya*' (English knowledge) and the 'low' realm of the native vernaculars began to take shape. However, in trying to sustain itself by cultivating small sections within native elites, colonialism introduced fundamental discursive and institutional ruptures within indigenous structures. These discontinuities were also underwritten by a series of starkly asymmetrical demographic relations, firstly between the new rulers and the size of the subject population, but even more crucially between the new indigenous elites and their 'unreformed' compatriots. To maintain itself, colonial power needed the means to outwardly bridge these divides so that the new government could, however imperfectly, suture itself to several layers of the indigenous social fabric. Thanks to the relatively easy reproduction and dissemination of ideas with print, the project of transmission of colonial discourses into the vernaculars appeared distinctly feasible. It seemed to colonial administrators that printing and circulating simplified books containing the 'vast riches'

[13]'Extract from the Fifth Annual Report', 1820, pp. 10–12 in R.V. Parulekar, ed., *SERB*, Part II, p. 22.

of European literature and science might be an effective strategy to span cultural and ideological differences between the two sides of the colonial encounter. The Report of the Native School Book and School Society for 1824–5 points to this logic:

> The extreme dissimilarity of ideas prevalent in Asia and Europe, or rather the greater abundance of ideas which European civilisation has created, renders conveying a knowledge of European literature, science and morality, in the native languages, a task of the utmost difficulty. At the same time, the various meanings which belong to many English words, incapacitate a native though it [*sic*] possesses a very considerable acquaintance with the language, from translating any English work written in a style in the least elevated above the familiar style of conversation. ... If however, any Gentlemen conversant with the manners and modes of thinking of the natives should take the trouble of composing original treatises on European literature, science and morality in a style suited to their comprehension, which requisite alone would render them easy to be translated, such works should be of the greatest value. ... But the obstacle (the slowness of printing) to the speedy and extensive circulation of books, which is indispensable for promoting the objects of this institution, has also been obviated by Government having with its wonted liberality presented to the Society four Lithographic presses and by two fonts of types ... besides ordering Printing Presses and types (English and *balbodh*) from England for its use ... the natives evince an admirable capacity for acquiring the requisite knowledge and for applying it with all the exactness that can be wished.[14]

Cultural and political differences *vis-à-vis* the South Asian social world were to be managed by establishing discursive correspondences—by the strategic use of translation and the remaking of native linguistic forms.[15]

[14]'Extract from the Second Report (1824–25) of the Bombay Native School and School Society', pp. 11–15 in R.V. Parulekar, ed., *SERB*, Part II, pp. 73–4.

[15]Bernard Cohn makes a similar argument in his essay 'The Command of Language and the Language of Command', though not specifically about the importance of print to the making of colonial ideology. For the full reference, see chapter one, fn. 97.

The magnitude of change signified by the project of colonial literacy through the introduction of print was also apparent to native intellectuals who came in contact with the new literate forms. The unexpected inclusion of a discussion on the origins of printing at the end of an early lithographed textbook on the wonders of geography and astronomy illustrates the deep impression made by the circulation of printed texts. Using the *devnagari* script for both Marathi and Gujarati versions,[16] the Marathi version came out in 1832 from Poona, while R. Prera lithographed the Gujarati translation for the Bombay Native Education Society in 1833.[17] The final chapter in this takes the form of a dialogue between a teacher and pupil to tell the story of the invention of printing. The unprecedented simultaneity and speed of communication enabled by printing evokes the following question:

> I have another question about the printed books that I have seen in so many of the schools of this city and which are also being simultaneously printed in many other languages. This age is unrivalled [*uttam*] in its ability to enable the spread of knowledge through these means, and this [*desh*] certainly did not have anything of the kind before. Therefore, I shall be much obliged if you could tell me more about the invention [*yukti*] of printing.[18]

The student was rewarded with an account of the invention of printing in Holland before the lesson ended, with a somewhat sly reference to the 'era of darkness' until the invention of the press enabled European books to spread everywhere.

[16]The four sections are devoted to the fundamentals of geography, an account of Hindustan's past, a brief description of the parts of the various continents and a concluding descriptive section on astronomy. The last section starts with a series of chapters describing the solar system (*surya mala*). However, the sequence of themes in the concluding chapters is interesting: chapter 13 discusses the qualities of the Divine Creator; followed by an account of magnets, with the last chapter devoted to an account of the emergence of printing: evidently, printing was seen as an important aspect of the accumulation of modern 'useful' knowledge. See *Dialogues on Geography and Astronomy*, Poona, 1832.

[17]*Dialogues on Geography and Astronomy*, Bombay, 1833.

[18]Translated from Marathi, '*Chaapnyache Yuktichi Utpatti*' in *Dialogues on Geography and Astronomy*, Poona, 1832.

Obliquely, such texts sought to pare down the cultural and metaphysical disparities underlying the colonial divide into questions that could be simply posed as a hierarchical relation between the 'achievements' of English and the vernaculars. Represented in this way, it became conceivable to rectify the 'deficiencies' of the latter via extensive translations from English. Early native intellectuals became aware of the political possibilities under colonial rule in terms of the hegemonic potential of the standardised forms of the vernaculars and the project of translation. But equally, in cultivating small groups of native intellectuals to serve as its ideological representatives, colonial power was creating an arena of interests and influence quite distinct from its ties with native trade networks. The hiatus between the emerging intelligentsia and native bourgeois interests created by colonial influence had, as we shall see, important consequences for the story of vernacular publishing, especially in its early phases.

Except for the Parsis in Western India, the emerging colonial bourgeoisie, in marked contrast to the modern West, was indifferent to the new literate order. With native bourgeois groups disinclined to invest in publishing ventures or in developing the commercial potential of an enlarged audience for printed materials, both the size of the new literate native audiences and the output of vernacular books remained tied to the directives of colonial policy for a long time. In principle, the entry of print, especially native initiatives to establish a newspaper and periodical press, were intended to extend the size of the audience for the new discourses beyond the small 'schooled public' of colonial classrooms. In actual fact, with few possibilities for acquiring the new linguistic and cognitive skills outside government or missionary schools, the audience for the new textual forms remained largely confined to those attending such schools. Benedict Anderson's thesis about print capitalism and the growth of modern vernacular cultures needs modification with respect to the colonial situation, where print entered as part of a modern capitalistic order but grew under circumstances inimical to the development of an indigenous market. If the extension of native literate communities were subject to such structural constraints, it followed that limits were put upon the meanings that the principle of publicity could assume within colonial society. All these factors created a situation biased in favour of groups that had prior access to literate skills. And given the circumstances of vernacular standardisation, groups that had first access to the new arenas were likely to have an abiding influence upon the forms and ideological orientation of the new public vernacular discourses.

If the native languages were now to be primarily oriented for use through print, then the forms that could become current as 'commonly' intelligible—as standardised written practice—were nowhere available: they had to be devised. In the West, print had precipitated the standardisation of scripts and helped fix linguistic norms like spelling and grammatical usage through dictionaries and grammars in the second half of the eighteenth century. Attempts to create a standardised mass-education system had followed half a century or more later. In contrast, the entry of print into the colonial context saw the inauguration of urgent official efforts to standardise codes and fix scripts for the native languages so as to rapidly transform indigenous textual traditions, which were hitherto current mainly through oral transmission. One of the arguments made about the shift in literate practices through print in the West is that the new mode of textual transmission created its own audiences, it did not simply address pre-existing ones. This was even truer in the colonial context, for the introduction of print occurred through bureaucratic efforts to develop generally understood codes for the vernaculars. Ironically, such efforts preceded the dissemination and acceptance of these forms among reading communities.

Missionary Agents and the Early Public Sphere

Efforts to print vernacular texts had to begin with the cutting of printing type, which pre-supposed the fixing and standardisation of scripts. Not surprisingly, Christian missionaries were among the first to show the zeal needed for these arduous endeavours. Theirs was a many-sided involvement in the making of new discursive forms. Missionaries contributed not just as pioneers of vernacular print culture; their presence as primary agents in shaping the new public discourses also influenced the concerns and trajectory of subsequent discussion. Moreover, non-brahmin printer-publishers, who first acquired their skills in the missionary presses, were responsible for many of the important technical innovations in Marathi print.[19] Although official initiatives at printing and translating vernacular texts quickly subsumed and overtook early missionary efforts, and notwithstanding some common assumptions between the missionary and official schemes, the former acted as a distinct catalyst upon the reception of modern ideas by native intellectuals. The internal differences between missionary and official efforts often led them to target different sections of native society as potential constituencies for their respective propagandist and educational schemes. With the new literate skills being critical for negotiating the world of colonial politics, missionary initiatives brought long-standing social tensions to the fore and intensified the emerging patterns of contestation within native society. An outstanding example of this was Phule, who first encountered ideas of human equality and rights through the Scottish missionaries active in and around Pune, and emerged as an important subaltern leader and political figure in nineteenth-century Western India.

Missionary influence was thus important in the formation of the colonial public sphere. As agents with access to non-state funds, several missionary groups, including the Danish missionaries of the Tanjore area, the American Mission with establishments in Bombay and in the Ahmadnagar area,[20] the Scottish Mission in Bombay and Pune (best known through the figure of John Wilson[21]) and the Jesuits in Bombay contributed to the making of the new public domain and the creation of public opinion in Marathi. Missionary discourse tended to grossly exaggerate its own impact, especially in the early years, and similarly the figure of the ardent missionary given over to his propagandist cause must surely have been the object of some mirth. Yet the actual effect of missionary activity cannot be underestimated. The impact of

[19]See, fns. 95 & 96, and preceding text, below.

[20]For a history of the American Mission in Western India, see William Hazen, *A Century in India: The American Marathi Mission 1813–1913*, Ahmadnagar, 1913.

[21]For an autobiographical account of one of the prominent Scottish missionaries active in Western India, see J.M. Mitchell, *In Western India: Recollections of My Early Missionary Life*, Edinburgh, 1899.

missionary preaching, carried out in their own compounds or through street-corner meetings, or in the form of the larger public theological debates where Parsi or Hindu 'leaders' were challenged to defend their respective faiths,[22] cannot be judged simply by the number of converts. The effects ran much deeper. Missionaries showed untiring patience in engaging receptive minds in the hope of gaining converts. They had funds to establish educational institutions and engage in independent initiatives towards dissemination through English and the vernaculars. As such, they were important agents in the emerging intermediate sphere between state and society. They served as the initial grooming influence on many progressive upper-caste and non-brahmin students,[23] and their propagandist activities and criticism of native practices often set the agenda for discussion in the formative stages of the colonial public sphere.

A host of defensive responses in the form of *sabhas*, and published writings and organisations—which ranged from rationalist-progressive attempts to reform native practices in conformity with the missionary critique to others that were unabashedly revivalist—bear this out. A prominent instance was the controversy over the Shripat Sheshadri re-conversion case, discussed at length later.[24] Besides, the Christian influence was evident in the collective singing of prayer-songs at reformed Hindu organisations like the Prarthana Samaj. Similarly, in its breaking and sharing of bread, the initiation ceremonies of the

[22]Morobhat Dandekar, *The Verification of the Hindoo Religion,* Bombay, 1832; John Wilson, *An Exposure of Hindu Religion, in Reply to Morobhat Dandekar*, Bombay, 1832; *A Second Exposure of Hindu Religion,* Bombay, 1834, were the outcome of a series of public debates held in the Girgaum area, a predominantly Hindu locality of Bombay. Another series of publications from the pen of John Wilson, attacking the Parsi religion, included *a Lecture on the Vendidad Sade of the Parsis, Delivered at Bombay on the 19th and 26th of June 1833*, Bombay, 1833; *The Parsi Religion, as contained in the Zand Avasta, and Propagated and Defined by the Zorosastrians of India and Persia, UInfolded, Refuted and Contrasted with Christianity*, Bombay, 1843.

[23]For an account of the close links between the young Phule and his group of friends with the Scottish Mission in Poona, see Rosalind O'Hanlon, *Caste, Conflict and Ideology,* pp. 108–13.

[24]See below pp. 186–90.

anti-caste Paramhansa Sabha that met clandestinely in Bombay in the 1840s[25] resembled Christian baptism rituals. The missionary press actively helped publicise the few dissenting lower-caste voices that had access to the new means of public expression.[26] The extent of missionary influence can be gauged from the range of secular texts that were produced with some form of support from missionary quarters. These included Ganpat Lakshmanji's prize-winning essay, produced at the Bombay Scottish Mission school, on the superiority of bourgeois family norms;[27] the first Marathi novel, *Yamunaparyatan* by Baba Padmanji who formally converted to Christianity later; the detailed ethno-historical account of Bombay by Govind Narayan, *Mumbaiche Varnan*;[28] and of course the philological pieces on native vernacular linguistic structures by Reverend Stevenson.[29] Missionary impact thus went beyond the discussion of religious themes and left a lasting influence on reform initiatives and the emerging political domain.

The Beginnings of Print and the Making of New Languages

Print first came to the west coast, especially to the areas around Goa and Salsette, through Portuguese missionaries around the mid-sixteenth century. There are surviving specimens of their attempts to compose

[25]For a detailed summary of the Paramhansa Sabha, see. J.V. Naik, 'Early Anti-caste Movement in Western India: The Paramhansa Sabha', *Journal of the Asiatic Society of Bombay*, Vols. 49, 50 and 51, 1974–76, New Series, pp. 136–61.

[26]Phule's writings often appeared in the missionary periodical, *Satyadeepika* from Pune; similarly, the missionary paper *Dnyanodaya* was one of the few Marathi papers to report the activities at the lower-caste schools started by Phule, see chapter two, fns. 80 & 81. The *Satyadeepika* also published Phule's account of the two of the '*satyashodak*' weddings conducted without the aid of brahmin priests in Pune: see O'Hanlon, *Caste, Conflict and Ideology*, p. 241.

[27]Ganpat Lakshmanji, *Essay on the Promotion of Domestic Reform among the Natives of India*, Bombay, 1843.

[28]Govind Narayan Madgaonkar was a student at the Scottish Mission school in Bombay for many years, where he also studied theology along with Baba Padmanji. However, unlike the latter, Govind Narayan did not convert to Christianity. His *Mumbaiche Varnan* was first published in 1863.

[29]Rev. Stevenson, 'Observations on the Grammatical Structure of Vernacular Languages of India', *JBRAS*, Vol. III, 1849–51. See also chapter one, pp. 45–7.

and publish vernacular works as part of their proselytising mission.[30] Among these was the *Puranna da vinda e vida do christo* (*purana* of the advent and life of Christ), which became popularly known as the *Christapurana*. These texts uniformly used the Roman type, although some attempts had been made to print books in the 'language and the alphabet of the land.'[31] Around 1806 there were attempts to produce Marathi books like the *Balbodh Muktavali* with the help of Danish missionaries at the initiative of the Maratha king Sarfoji in Tanjore.[32]

English printing in Western India under British influence started in the last decades of the eighteenth century, with the earliest known specimen being an English calendar printed in 1780 'by Rustom Cursetjee in the Buzzer'.[33] The Bombay Courier press was, in all probability, the first important press in Bombay. Apparently it used English types brought from England and enjoyed a monopoly over printing jobs and advertisements for the Bombay government until the early years of the nineteenth century. Both the earliest English newspapers from Bombay, the *Bombay Courier* and the *Bombay Gazette*, that began to appear around 1790–1, were apparently published from the Bombay Courier press.[34]

[30]S.G. Tulpule, 'Christian Marathi Literature' in *Classical Marathi Literature from the Beginning to AD 1818*.

[31]Ibid., p. 380.

[32]Separate attempts at printing Marathi were made in Thanjavur. In 1806 Sarfoji Raje, the crown prince, who grew up under the influence of the Danish missionary Reverend Schwartz, had Aesop's fables translated into Marathi by Sakkhan Pandit. Apparently, Sarfoji was a great scholar, a patron of learning and an avid collector of palm–leaf manuscripts and inscriptions on copper. He established a printing press from where this translation was issued as *Balbodh Muktavali* in 1806. See G.B. Sardar, *Aravachin Marathi Gadyache Purvapeethika 1800–1874*, Pune, 1938, p. 7.

[33]This calendar had thirty-four pages and cost two rupees. See George Buist, *The Bombay Times and Journal of Commerce,* Vol. VI, No. 1172, 4 December 1855, quoted in A.P. Priyolkar, *The Printing Press in India*, Bombay, 1958, pp. 70–1.

[34]According to the *Bombay City Gazetteer*, Vol. III, Bombay, 1909, the *Bombay Courier* was started in 1790 and the *Bombay Gazette* in 1791; but it is Priyolkar's contention that, in fact, it was the other way round. See A.P. Priyolkar, *The Printing Press in India*, p. 72.

Gujarati was the first of the native languages spoken on the island to appear in print. This occurred in an advertisement in Gujarati characters in the *Bombay Courier* of 29 January 1797.[35] The credit for cutting these types went to Jeejeebhai Chapghar, who had worked at the Courier Press.[36] Soon after, Jeejeebhai also apparently cast the types for Malayalam characters for the printing of Robert Drummond's *Grammar of the Malabar Language*, published from Bombay in 1799. The first instance of Marathi print from Bombay appeared in an advertisement in the *Bombay Courier* of 17 July 1802. It used *modi*, the oldest of the Marathi scripts,[37] whose use dated back to the beginnings of Marathi textualisation in the late thirteenth century.

Simultaneously, attempts were made to print Marathi at Serampore. With the conquest of Vasai in 1803, the compilation of a grammar and the translation of the Christian scripture into Marathi were included on the agenda of Fort William College.[38] William Carey was in charge of teaching Marathi at Fort William. His first class was set up in 1804 in collaboration with Vaijnath Sharma, a Sanskrit scholar and Marathi pandit who had been under the patronage of Venirampant, a *vakil* at Calcutta for one of the Maratha *sardars*, Nagpurkar Bhosle.[39] With Vaijnath Sharma's help, a *Marathi-Ingrezi Kosh* (1810), apparently

[35]This advertisement apparently appeared in the *Bombay Courier* of 22 June 1797 in the *mahajana* script that was used for ordinary purposes and business communication. With an unbroken line joining the letters at the top, this script resembled the *modi* script, which had come to be used for non-classical Marathi texts. However, the *mahajana* script did not survive for long as the standard one for Gujarati, though it continued to be used in lithographed writings. See A.P. Priyolkar, *The Printing Press in India*, p. 74.

[36]B.B. Patel, *Parsi Prakash*, Vol. 1, Bombay, 1888, quoted in ibid., p. 73.

[37]The *balbodh* script, closer to the *devnagari*, had been used for classical Marathi texts. However, this pattern of usage was far from standardised, for classical Marathi manuscripts produced in the Tanjore region used the *modi* script. See ibid., p. 74.

[38]Letter by William Carey dated 7 September 1803, quoted in E. Carey, *Memoirs of William Carey*, London, 1837, p. 564.

[39]Vaijnath Sharma worked at Fort William College for many years and apparently taught several Europeans. See G.B. Sardar, *Aravachin Marathi Gadyache Purvapeethika*, pp. 4–5.

containing about 10,000 entries, was issued from Serampore, as was Carey's Marathi translation of *Panchtantra* and the *Hitopadesh*.[40] These were soon followed by the *Gospel of St. Matthew* and a grammar of Marathi that included 'dialogues on familiar subjects' which, though, were mainly in English. Unlike the earlier printed specimens from Bombay, the Serampore Marathi books tended to use the *devnagari* script. Evidence suggests that these efforts from the Serampore missionaries did not fare very well in Bombay[41] because, as can be imagined, there were significant variations between Vaijnath Sharma's Marathi and the variety prevailing in Bombay. *Simhasanbattisi* (1814) and *Raghuji Bhoslyanchi Vaunshavali* (1816) followed from the Serampore press, but using the *modi* script.[42]

Impelled by the poor reception of Serampore's edition of the Marathi scriptures and spurred by inter-missionary rivalry, the American Mission Press in Bombay launched plans to publish the Bible in the vernacular. By 1817 they had managed to issue a scripture tract of sixteen octavo pages and the Gospel of St. Matthew in Marathi.[43] By 1819 they had begun to print Marathi books for use in their schools in Bombay.[44] These developments sent out signals to the Bombay Government that they could not postpone plans for an official initiative towards the preparation of books and, in 1821, the Native School and

[40]The title-page of the 1810 Marathi-English *kosh* mentions Carey as Professor of Marathi and Bengali, and Vaijnath Sharma as the 'Chief Maratha Pundit' in the college of Fort William. The English introduction discusses the derivation of the regional vernaculars from Sanskrit and their importance to European scholars. See D.V. Potdar, *Marathi Gadyacha Ingrezi Avataar*, p. 12. The title-page of *Simhasanbattisi* published from Serampore in 1814 bears the remark, *'Vaijnathsharmanekriyate'* (composed by Vaijnathsharma), see ibid., pp. 12–13.

[41]'The Mahratta grammar by the Rev. Carey is in very few hands here, and in fact only a small proportion of that nation can read the *balbodh* or *nagree* character in which its parts are illustrated': Robert Drummond, *Illustrations of the Grammatical parts of the Guzerathee, Mahratta and English Languages* (printed at the Courier Press), Bombay, 1808.

[42]See G.B. Sardar, *Aravachin Marathi Gadyache Purvapeethika*, p. 6.

[43]William Hazen, *A Century in India: The American Marathi Mission 1813–1913*, pp. 8–10.

[44]Ibid., p. 8.

School Book Committee was formed as a branch of the Bombay Education Society.[45] Plans were made to print elementary grammars, common arithmetical tables and a selection of passages from 'native books suitable for general acceptance', besides a translation of Aesop's fables in 'Guzerathee and Maratha'.[46] A set of large wooden *devnagari* types was produced and initial publication efforts sought to pair 'Guzerattee' and 'Mahratta' through the use of the *devnagari* script for both languages, no doubt with a view to economise on labour and costs.[47] The first official publications in the two languages came out in 1822 and included a set of large letters to be displayed in the classroom; a collection of some short sentences, and a selection of fables in Gujarati and Marathi, all prepared by the School and School Book Society.[48] The *Panchopakhyan* followed later in 1822 and, in effect, was the first entirely Marathi book printed in Bombay.[49] *Vidurniti* was published

[45]In 1827, the name of this body was changed to the Bombay Native Education Society. See R.V. Parulekar, *SERB*, Part II, pp. 45–102. For a summary of early education policy in the Bombay Presidency, see chapters two and three, especially pp. 65–8 and pp. 117–19.

[46]'Seventh Annual Report of Bombay Education Society pp. 24–7' in R.V. Parulekar, *SERB*, Part II, p. 34.

[47]In a letter to James Henderson, Secretary of the Government, George Jervis declared' 'I am directed also to advert respectfully to the impossibility of making at this early period, any calculation of the expense for translating or composing original works for the Society ... The Society deem it a greater object to obtain a larger supply of Mahratta types and a new font of Guzerathee; the latter to be executed, like the new *balbodh (devnagari*); drawings of the letters might be sent home. They might afterwards be disposed to native presses, as there the works could be commercially printed'. The report of the Special Committee went on to add: '... the works that have already been issued ... [are] attended with exorbitant expense, and with many imperfections difficult to be removed in attempts to form printing types for characters that belong particularly to a free, open, writing hand'. See letter from Jervis, Secretary of the Society, to James Henderson, Secretary to the Bombay Government, dated 4 October 1823, Bombay Secretariat Records, General Department Files, Vol. 8 (63), pp. 91–6, in ibid., pp. 48–51.

[48]Seventh Annual Report of the Bombay Education Society for 1822; pp. 24–7 in ibid., p. 34.

[49]Apparently, Elphinstone distributed copies to various *sardars*, with a request

in 1823. The Society brought out its third book, *Simhasanbattisi*, in 1824. Lacking its own press, the Society issued these books from the Courier Press in a *balbodh* font imported from England. Interestingly, evidence shows these books from the Education Society were sold at different prices for English and native buyers.[50] The facility for rapidly producing translations had lent a deceptive appearance of equivalence between English and the native languages. Nevertheless, the fact that the books were sold at different prices to native and white customers showed that the colonial audiences for the two languages, as seems obvious, were neither homogeneous nor possessed similar material or cultural means.

Differential pricing showed it was not easy to attract buyers or find readers for the Society's books. Neither were the prices of these early publications particularly conducive to promoting the reading habit and the circulation of new vernacular forms. For example, in 1829 a *Maratha Grammar and Dictionary for the use of natives* cost Rs 40; the more extensive and prestigious *Maratha-English Grammar and Dictionary* compiled by Captain Molesworth was priced at Rs 90; a copy of the *Idiomatical Exercises in Maratha and English* cost Rs 12; a Marathi translation of Morrison's *Book-keeping*, Marcet's *Conversations on Natural Philosophy* translated by Hari Keshavji[51] and Berquin's

---

that it be perused with care. See G.S. Sardesai, *SPD*, Vol. 42, Bombay, 1934, p. 52, quoted in Priyolkar, *The Printing Press in India*, p. 89.

[50]An advertisement in the *Bombay Courier* dated 4 October 1823 stated: 'we have for sale a number of copies of Marathi books, *Panchopakhyan* and *Vidurniti*. The price of the former is Rs 8 for Europeans and Rs 3 for natives and that of the *Vidurniti* Rs 6 for Europeans and Rs 2 for natives', quoted in Priyolkar, *The Printing Press in India*, p. 90.

[51]Hari Keshavji (1804–58) was from the *pathare* community. Keshavji completed his primary education in the Robert Money missionary school. He worked as a clerk at the Engineering School established by Jervis in Bombay, followed by a stint as Head Clerk in the Thana Adaalat Court between 1829 and 1834. He had also apparently studied Sanskrit. Between 1831 and 1851, he translated and wrote textbooks for the Bombay Education Society. Among his translations were *Vidyeche Uddesh, Laabh ani Santosh* (in Gujarati from Lord Brougham's *Treatise on the Object, Advantages and Pleasures of Knowledge*), *Siddhpadaarthvigyan Vishayak Samvaad* (from Marcet's *Conversations on Natural*

Children's Friend were priced at Rs 12 each.[52] There were other problems too. From the beginning, one of the main problems was what official reports routinely described—as late as at the end of the nineteenth century—as 'the lack of original compositions'. Instructions to prospective authors circulated as part of an advertisement for generous rewards[53] offered to native writers hinted at the complex problems faced by official efforts to engender a vernacular print culture. In theory, print aimed at creating a community of readers and writers through promoting the circulation of a 'generally accessible' language. Yet, as the above-mentioned circular had to admit, the task of creating such a modern readership in the vernacular was ridden with difficulties:

Philosophy), *Rasayansamvaad* (from *Conversations on Chemistry*), *Yatrik Kraman* (from *Pilgrim's Progress*), *Deshvyavaharvyavastha* (from Mrs. Marcet's *Conversations on Mill*). His talents as a prose-writer and translator did not get the recognition they merited, probably because of his caste status. He was a member of the Student's Literary and Scientific Society, but later became intensely preoccupied with *Vedanta*. For a biographical account about Hari Keshavji, see D.V. Potdar, *Marathi Gadyacha Ingrezi Avataar*, Pune, 1957, pp. 42–6.

[52]See 'Appendix 3: Depository List of the Bombay Native Education Society's Works', *Fourth Report of the Bombay Native Education Society for 1827*, Bombay, 1828. However, the prices for these books in the Depository List for 1839 are much lower. The Marathi dictionary 'for the use of natives' was priced at Rs 18, the translation of *Conversations on Chemistry* at Rs 16, the Atlas cost Rs 1–8 annas. A copy of the *Murathee Bukhur*, a translation of Duff's *History of the Marathas* cost Rs. 6. A Marathi reader in geography was available for Rs 4, whereas a history of the Athenians or the Assyrians and the Babylonians could be bought for Rs 0–4 annas each. *Bal Mitra* cost Rs 3–8 annas, *Padaarth Vigyan* or *Conversations on Natural Philosophy* was priced at Rs 6, *Idiomatical Exercises in Murathee and English* and Morrsion's *Book-Keeping* cost Rs 2–12 annas and Rs 3–8 annas respectively. See 'Twelfth Report of the Elphinstone College and the School of the Native Education Society', pp. 76–81 in R.V. Parulekar, ed., *SERB*, Part II, pp. 193–9.

[53]The announcement appeared in a trilingual circular dated 8 April 1825, issued by George Jervis in Gujarati, Marathi and English. The prize money offered for composition of school books or translation using *balbodh* was between Rs 100–Rs 400; a special reward of between Rs 2000-Rs 5000 was offered for works

In translating English works it is necessary particularly, to point out that in almost all cases they must undergo partial alterations to adapt them to the habits and manners of the natives.

In the native languages specified for works, the commonly accepted vernacular dialects [*deshbhasha*] must be used to their *fullest extent* [emphasis in original] to the exclusion of an unnecessary display of any learned tongue: where however, these dialects are deficient in the means of expression, words must be supplied from their cognate languages; Sanskrit for Maratha and Goojaratee, simple Persian for Hindoostanee. The adoption of words from English must necessarily be admitted in cases, where neither the current nor cognate language furnishes them directly or by composition.[54]

Typically for the colonial situation, the decision to fix scripts for Gujarati and Marathi was the result of an official decree in 1826. No doubt, reasons of official convenience and economy had been the paramount consideration. The order declared that, from then on, *balbodh* or the *devnagari* would be the standard script used for Marathi print. This was to be mainly implemented through conferring official recognition upon the ability to read and write *balbodh*; by making these skills a basic pre-qualification for trainee schoolteachers recruited for the government schools being established in the Marathi-speaking areas of the Presidency. From then on, the Native Education Society decided to 'adopt *balbodh* for all their printed books; and also in the written or current hand for letter writing and general business, respectively used in Maharashtra ... '.[55] However, it was impossible to resolve the matter so swiftly and the 1833 edition of *Bodhvachane* used both *balbodh* and *modi* types face-to-face for each page; also, education records show that both *balbodh* and *modi* scripts continued to be taught in the schools, with translation exercises being set to and from English for both Marathi scripts.

---

of a particularly high calibre. See text of circular in G.G. Jambhekar, ed., *MWBJ*, Appendix 2, Vol. 3, pp. 599–602.

[54]Ibid., p. 602.

[55]'Third Report of the Bombay Native Education Society', pp. 15–19 in R.V. Parulekar, ed., *SERB*, Part II, p. 85.

It is quite apparent thus that the conditions under which modern cultural practices were established favoured communities with literate backgrounds. Colonial literacy aimed at producing a new intellectual order, yet this new intelligentsia was mainly drawn from communities with a history of literate skills. Just as the involvement of Christian missionaries in the processes of vernacular standardisation influenced the trajectory of the emerging public discourses, the upper-caste background of native intellectuals had critical implications for the emerging character of the colonial public sphere.

Pandits, *Shastris* and the Making of Early Marathi Print Culture in Bombay

In Western India it was mainly brahmins and some sub-brahmin groups[56] like the *prabhus* and *shenvis* who were among the first to perceive the benefits of the new literate order and respond to the opportunities

[56]A letter from Jervis, Secretary of the Education Society to James Farish, Government Secretary, dated 6 June 1826 gives details of the composition of the four classes in the English School in July 1824. The highest class had 12 boys, of whom 2 were brahmins, 5 *shenvis* and 5 *prabhus*. The second class consisted of 16 boys, including 2 brahmins, 2 *shenvis*, 10 *prabhus* and 2 *shimpis*. One brahmin, 3 *shenvis*, 9 *prabhus*, 2 *shimpis* and one goldsmith made up class three whereas class four had 4 brahmin boys and 2 *shenvis*. 'Extracts from the Bombay Secretarial Records Education Department Files', Vol. 2 of 1826, p. 330 in R.V. Parulekar, ed., *SERB*, Part II, p. 90.

The *shimpis* (tailors) were a well-off community in Bombay, at least from about the time when the British took over the island from the Portuguese in the early eighteenth century. See P.M. Malabari, *Bombay in the Making 1661–1726*, London, 1910, pp. 493–4. Apparently, some enterprising persons from the *shimpi* community had begun to publish a weekly newspaper, *Shimpihitechu*, to voice the interests of the community. The *Bombay Telegraph and Courier* of 20 August 1855 carried the following report: 'We were shown ... the first number of the *Shimpihitechu*. ... The tailor caste of Western India are determined to assert their title to an important place in the community. ... These tailors speak as men, and speak with a sobriety and dignity upon matters of permanent interest'. Quoted in R.K. Lele, *Marathi Vruttpatrancha Itihaas* (henceforth, *MVI*), Pune, 1964, p. 130.

it created. The *prabhus*[57] and the *shenvis*[58] were traditionally trained scribes who had a long and successful history of employment as *karkuns* in different parts of the Peshwa kingdom and in the offices of the colonial trading houses of Bombay. The possession of uncommon literate skills had also allowed the *prabhus* to be closely associated with pre-modern book production.[59] The *prabhu* communities had a long-standing

[57]Malabari refers to the excellent *prabhu* calligraphists, often appointed to copy out important official records, like for example the Minute Book of the Court of Judicature in Bombay in 1726–7. See Malabari, *Bombay in the Making*, p. 435. The Portuguese had also employed *prabhu* scribes, but their harsh proselytising policies had driven the community away from Bombay into mainland areas. However, with the handing over of the island to the British, they returned in large numbers. See *Bombay City Gazetteer*, Vol. 1, Bombay, 1909, p. 241.

Their position as rent collectors and administrative agents under the Portuguese and their access to influential positions at the courts of the Maratha *sardars* made them unpopular with brahmin groups. As an upwardly-mobile group, the *prabhus* tried to adopt *pucca* brahmanical practices like proscribing widow-remarriage within the community to enhance their caste status. This antagonism came to a head after the conquest of Vasai by the Marathas when, around the mid-eighteenth century, local brahmins invoked the judicial powers of the Peshwa's *Nyayadish* at Pune to curb the ritual status of *prabhus*. This summary is drawn from V.D. Rao, 'The Pathare Prabhus: Traditional Origin and History', *Journal of the University Of Bombay*, New Series, Vol. 38, No. 74, 1969, pp. 236–59.

[58]The *shenvis* were a sub-*jati* of the *gaud saraswat* brahmins. They had occupied important positions in the Maratha courts, especially those of Shinde and Holkar. During the reign of Bajirao II, there were attempts to deny brahmanical status to the *shenvis*. The *shenvis* capitalised on their skills as linguistic mediators and translators, first with the Portuguese, and then later, with the British during their negotiations with the Marathas. The *gaud saraswat* brahmins figured as the largest sub-group of brahmins in Bombay in the census of 1780, a position they maintained until 1923, when the last census according to caste was taken. They took to English education and sought employment as clerks in the various commercial houses. In addition, the *shenvis* profited from speculating on the Bombay cotton trade during the boom in the 1860s. In the following years, quite typically for the time, the *shenvi* leadership used associational activity and print to consolidate the caste identity and give it greater visibility. This summary is drawn from N.K. Wagle, 'The History and Social Organisation of the *Gaud Saraswat Brahmins* on the West Coast of India', *Journal of Indian History*, Vol. 48, Part 1, April 1970, pp. 296–333.

[59]Dadoba Pandurang recounts that a prosperous *patane prabhu*, Raghunath

rivalry with the traditionally literate brahmin castes; evidence shows that the pre-colonial Peshwa state was led to intervene in several instances to delimit prabhu claims to twice-born status.[60] However, with the sanction for such restrictions removed under British rule, the *prabhus* were quick to use their literate training to acquire an advantageous position in the emerging world of colonial politics.

Within this overall trend of upper-caste dominance, there were many interesting patterns that showed the diversity of responses to the new literate and political opportunities. Sociological analysis of the response to colonial rule would help pose appropriate questions about the difficulties of creating a standardised cultural order through the agency and design of an alien, colonial state. It could also open up ways of theorising the political choices available to the new intelligentsia as they attempted to negotiate the fraught ideological ground upon which they had to advance their hegemonic aspirations.

Expectedly, it was difficult to proceed with the task of producing and publishing grammars and elementary reading material in Marathi without enlisting the services of native intellectuals. By the early 1820s the Education Society in Bombay had a small group of pandits, *shastris* and *munshis* in its employ to assist in the preparation of the first vernacular grammars and other books through translations into Marathi and Gujarati. We know the identity of the Marathi *shastri mandali* from the names of the contributors to the first Marathi *Shabdakosh* brought out by the Society in 1824. Although sub-brahmin castes like *prabhus* were well represented in the colonial schools, they often left upon acquiring a sufficient training to find clerical employment in one of the colonial offices or in one of the several business houses of the city. It was not surprising to find no *prabhus* or other sub-brahmin castes in the Education Society's *shastri mandali*. Besides the two Englishmen, Captain Molesworth and Major Candy, the group included Ramshastri Janvekar,[61]

Valjeechyabhai of Bombay, was a great lover of books, and maintained a regular workshop that produced manuscripts preserved in elaborately decorated covers. See A.P. Priyolkar, ed., *DPA*. p. 64.

[60]See fn. 57 above.

[61]Janvekar was appointed the Inspector of Marathi schools in and around Bombay in 1830, at a salary of Rs 60 per month, see G.G. Jambhekar, ed., *MWBJ*,

Bapushastri Shukla,[62] Gangadharshastri Phadke,[63] Balshastri Dhagve[64] and Jagannathashastri.[65] Parshuramshastri Godbole appears to have joined later in 1829.[66] These Marathi pandits all came from Konkan, Vasai or the Pune region and, except for the Native Secretary Kashinath Chatre,[67]

Appendix 2, Vol. 3, p. 382. Janvekar had prepared a brief Marathi grammar, which remained unpublished, but continued to be used in manuscript form in the main Society School in Bombay: see A.P. Priyolkar, ed., *DPA,* p. 36. Later, during the Shripat Sheshadri conversion controversy in 1843, Janvekar was associated with the Poona Sanskrit College, from where he helped enlist support for Balshastri Jambhekar. See correspondence between Ramchandrashastri Janvekar and Balshastri in G.G. Jambhekar, ed., *MWBJ*, Appendix 2, Vol. 3, pp. 495–548.

[62]Bapushastri Shukla hailed from Naigaon and had been the *mamledaar* of Haveli *taluka*: see A.P. Priyolkar, *DPA*, p. 35.

[63]Gangadharshastri Phadke of Pune had probably encountered the British during his visits to Bombay as a well-known *puranik* and *gavai* (vocalist). Jagannath Shankarseth was a patron to Gangadharshastri's musical talents. Apparently Phadke lived in Bombay over 1820–1825, being employed by the British for his skills as a learned grammarian. See, 'Life and Character of Prof. Ball Gungadhur Shastree Jambhekar from the autobiography of the late Keshav Shivram Bhavalkar' in G.G. Jambhekar, ed., *MWBJ*, Appendix 3, Vol. 3, p. 20.

[64]An obituary in the *Bombay Durpan* on 22 June 1832 noted that Balshastri Dhagve left the Poona Engineering College and came to Bombay in 1824 to work with the Education Society. See G.G. Jambhekar, ed., *MWBJ*, Vol. 2, p. 43. Apparently, Dhagve was one of the few traditional *shastris* who were not contemptuous of poetic traditions in *prakrit* or the regional languages. See A.P. Priyolkar, ed., *DPA*, p. 52.

[65]Jagannathshastri had accompanied Jervis as his chief pandit and joined the *shastri mandali*. He apparently hailed from the same place as Bapushastri Shukla. See A.P. Priyolkar, *DPA*, p. 35.

[66]Parshurampant Tatya Godbole was invited from Pune, where he worked as a *karkun*, to join the Society because of his reputation as scholar of Marathi poetry. On leaving Bombay, Parshurampant joined the Vernacular Department of the Poona Sanskrit College, where he compiled and helped publish the first official edition of pre-colonial Marathi poetry, *Navneet,* in 1854. See D.P. Potdar, *Marathi Gadyacha Ingrezi Avataar*, p. 53.

[67]Sadashiv Kashinath Chatre (1788–1830), a *konkansth brahmin*, born in Walkeshwar, Bombay, started his career as a scribe in the Engineering Office before being persuaded by Colonel Jervis to become the Native Secretary of the Education Society in 1823. Although he retired before the teaching and bureaucratic arrangements of the education system were formalised, he played a crucial role in bringing together persons who made their mark as the earliest Marathi intellectuals

none had lived in Bombay before their employment in the Society. Though traditionally conservative, brahmins had been counted among the most mobile groups within pre-colonial society and a willingness to travel to secure patronage from those in power had become an intrinsic trait in the brahmin character. Bearing this out, these early brahmin scholars who worked with the Education Society had all travelled to the new capital, specifically through their contact with colonial officials or with the hope of remunerative positions in one of the administrative or missionary establishments. In many cases, the shift to Bombay was made through the mediation of those already in colonial employment.[68] All these men went on to contribute substantially to establishing the bureaucratic infrastructure of the Education Department throughout the Bombay Presidency, often being appointed to important administrative positions after their initial stint in Bombay.[69]

Interestingly enough, despite having worked closely and even supervised the production of the first books through the Education Department, none of the members of the first *shastri mandali,* except perhaps for Kashinath Chatre,[70] seemed to have entertained the idea of becoming print-entrepreneurs themselves. Such initiatives were not uncommon within the Gujarati community in Bombay by this time. Yet these learned brahmins of the *shastri mandali* responded to opportunities for extending the new literacy in a typically traditional fashion. Take the instance, of Kashinath Chatre, one of the most

in the new mould. See D.V. Potdar, *Marathi Gadyacha Ingrezi Avataar*, p. 28 and A.P. Priyolkar, ed., *DPA*, pp. 60–1.

[68]Ramshastri Janvekar was Balshastri Jambhekar's brother-in-law. Apparently, Balshastri's father was a frequent visitor at Sadashiv Chatre's house in Bombay. These links enabled the young Balshastri to live at Chatre's house to acquire the new *Ingrezi vidya.* See A.P. Priyolkar, ed., *DPA*, p. 61.

[69]Encouraged by Chatre, Balshastri went on to play a very important role in the establishment of the Education Department and the Elphinstone College School. For details of Balshastri's career, see chapter three, especially fn. 41.

[70]Kashinath Chatre died before he could carry out his plans to establish a printing press after his retirement. Unlike any of the other *shastris,* Chatre's family had probably lived in Bombay for some time. This factor may have been exceptional in making him more open to the idea of becoming a modern press-man. See A.P. Priyolkar, ed., *DPA*, p. 70.

influential native members of the Education Society,[71] who was greatly praised for his early contribution to the creation of a remarkable and lucid Marathi prose style.[72] Throughout his career and even afterwards he played an important role in bringing together people who were to make a mark as the major intellectuals of the new mould in Marathi. His house was known to have been an informal hostel for bright—of course brahmin—boys from families known to him, so that they could study in Bombay.[73] Chatre was a personal guardian and tutor to both Balshastri Jambhekar and Bhau Mahajan as they completed their education at the Elphinstone School in Bombay in the 1820s and who, among other things, later started and edited the first newspapers and periodicals in Marathi.[74] There were evident tensions between particularistic, brahmanical assumptions about the just ordering of intellectual exchange and the modern principles of open and general access. Clearly, it was beyond the ken and interest of colonial rule to resolve these contradictions and they persisted to affect the intelligentsia's efforts to articulate an anti-colonial hegemonic position. Further examples can be adduced to make this point. Dadoba Pandurang

[71]Chatre earned a monthly salary of Rs 100 as the Society's Native Secretary, with an additional allowance of Rs 75 as the superintendent of Marathi schools in the Southern region. He retired on a pension in 1829. See D.V. Potdar, *Marathi Gadyacha Ingrezi Avataar*, pp. 28–9.

[72]According to Dadoba Pandurang, Kashinath Chatre was among the first to compose Marathi books with correct and pleasing syntax, which led to his reputation as an exemplary stylist and pioneer of Marathi prose. See Dadoba Pandurang's 'Introduction' to *Marathibhasheche Vyakaran*, quoted in D.P. Potdar, *Marathi Gadyacha Ingrezi Avataar*, p. 29. Kashinath Chatre also had a subtle command over English, because of which his translations were much acclaimed and used in the Marathi schools for many years. See A.P. Priyolkar, ed., *DPA*, p. 60.

[73]Apparently, Balshastri recounted how Bapu Chatre had introduced him to many 'advanced' texts and periodicals in English. Bhau Mahajan, the other great figure of the early phase of Marathi journalism, also lived with the Chatre family. Both young men shared the private lessons that Bapu Chatre arranged for his son, Vireshwar Chatre, who also went onto become an editor-publisher. See A.P. Priyolkar, ed., *DPA*, p. 61.

[74]For an account of Jambhekar's pioneering role as the editor of the first Marathi weekly, *Durpan*, see chapter three, pp. 129–35. For details of Bhau Mahajan's important contributions to the vernacular press, see pp. 195–7.

recounted in his autobiography the amused indulgence with which his teacher, Bapudev Shukla, listened to the efforts of *shenvi, prabhu* and *sonar* students as they read in class, often making patronising remarks about the attempts of 'coarse', 'meat-eating' castes to imitate the chaste diction and pronunciation of brahmins.[75] Similarly, Gangadharshastri, one of the contributors to the first Marathi-English *Shabdakosh*, apparently had some reservations about Dadoba Pandurang's Marathi Grammar because the latter, being a *vaishya*, was not supposed to have the moral right to undertake such a scholarly work. These amounted to more than mere individual perceptions and indicated how brahmins generally tended to estimate the intellectual capacities of the 'lesser' castes. Other evidence suggests that the same learned Gangadharshastri showed little curiosity for any of the new knowledges and that his scholarship was mostly confined to the study of grammar.[76]

As against this, the *prabhus* showed a greater inclination towards the professions associated with the modern print trade. As writers working in the English offices and being less likely than the superior castes to harbour a distaste for physical labour, the *prabhus*[77] speedily took to learning the higher professional skills. They figured prominently among the early native editors of newspapers in Bombay. We learn from the title page of one of the earliest English books produced at Bombay in 1803, *An account of the introduction of the cowpox into India*, that its printer came from the *prabhu* community.[78] Of the three editors of the first Marathi weekly, the *Durpan*, Janardhan Vasudevji and Raghunathji Harischandrajee were both *prabhus*.[79] Soon after

[75]See A.P. Priyolkar, ed., *DPA*, pp. 36–7.

[76]One of his students recounts that Gangadharshastri had little patience with the theory of gravity, which often provoked mischievous questions from the class. See Bhavalkar, 'Life and Character of Prof. Ball Gungadhur Shastree Jambhekar' in G.G. Jambhekar, ed., *MWBJ*, Appendix 3, Vol. 3, p. 20.

[77]See fn. 57 above.

[78]This book is in the SOAS Archive. The title page records that it was printed at No. 7, Forbes Street, by Moroba Damoterjee Prabhoo, though the press is not mentioned.

[79]Raghunath Harischandrajee and Janardhan Vasudevji, who assisted Jambhekar in editing the *Bombay Durpan*, were both *prabhus*. Besides working for the *Durpan*, Harischandrajee spent more than thirty years in the important position of the

the *Durpan* closed down in 1840, Janardhan Vasudevji and his brother Vinayak Vasudevji went on to work as editors of the Gujarati newspaper, *Mumbaino Samachar*. Further, as one of the earliest groups to be associated with British rule, it was not surprising that the initiative for the first social organisation with a reformist agenda came from a *pathare prabhu*.[80]

This brings up the all-important question about the financial patronage and support available for early native print initiatives in Marathi. At this point, it is interesting to compare the story of Marathi print with that of Gujarati. In addition to being the first vernacular to appear in print in Bombay, Gujarati had its first native-owned press and its earliest newspaper before Marathi. As is well known, the Parsis

---

Head Accountant of the Grand Arsenal. His obituary described him as a perfect master of English, Sanskrit and the regional dialects. See 'Obituary' in *The Bombay Observer and Deccan Weekly Reporter*, 10 December 1853 quoted in G.G. Jambhekar, ed., *MWBJ*, Appendix 2, Vol. 3, pp. 384–8. Janardhan Vasudevji (1804–1894) was Chief Translator in the Persian Department before going on to become the first native judge at the Bombay High Court in 1864. See A.P. Priyolkar, *DPA*, p. 50. Balaji Sundarji, another *prabhu* student, left school to join the Assistant Commissioner's office as 'Head Prabhu' in 1831. Later, he compiled and published the Krishna-Arjun dialogue as the *Gitabhavchandrika* from Ganpat Krishnaji's Press. See Potdar, *Marathi Gadyacha Ingrezi Avataar*, pp. 12–13.

[80]Ramchandra Balkrishna Jaykar (1820–66) formed the Paramhansa Sabha, one of the earliest associations aimed at opposing *jati* distinctions and idol worship. The Sabha existed in the 1840s. Its members comprised of students of the Elphinstone Institute, including important brahmin and sub-brahmin figures, such as Bhau Mahajan and Dadoba Pandurang. Meetings were held secretly, mainly because of pressure from the *sanatanis*. Although the Sabha had active branches outside Bombay, it did not survive a vicious lampoon in the Bombay press in the late 1850s.

Ramchandra Balkrishna's career saw him moving from the Education Department to a more lucrative position in the Customs Department. He was also the Manger of the Elphinstone Financial Association for some years before his death in 1866. As a reformer, Ramchandra Balkrishna apparently enjoyed the respect of Phule, whose *povada, Raja Shivaji*, published in 1869, was dedicated to him. For more information, see A.P. Priyolkar, *Paramhansa Sabha Va Tiche Adhyaksha Ramchandra Balkrishna*, Bombay, 1966, and J.V. Naik, 'Early Anti-caste Movement in Western India', cited in fn. 25 above.

of the west coast had prospered through their extensive commercial and financial ties with the British and had emerged as major insurance agents, financiers and ship-builders through their involvement with colonial trade. In stark contrast, with the decline of many 'Maharashtrian' banker and trader families after the eclipse of Peshwa rule, the same could hardly be said for the Marathi community in Bombay. There seem to have been only two important Marathi *seths* with major direct dealings with the British, Jagannath Shankarseth, a *sonar*,[81] and Dadaji Dhackjee, a *prabhu*,[82] both of whom were among listed patrons of the Education Society and members of its Managing Committee. Shankarseth took an active interest in the affairs of the Native Education Society, donating money for the first Marathi schools for girls, besides also actively protesting against the government moves in 1847–48 to shift the emphasis in favour of education through English.[83] Crucially, neither of them appeared to have done anything for the promotion of

[81]Babulshet Ganbaseth of Ghodbandar, an ancestor of Jagannath Shankarseth, had moved to Bombay in the second quarter of the eighteenth century, attracted by the trading opportunities under the Company's Government. See Edwardes, *Rise of Bombay: A Retrospect,* Bombay, 1902, p. 163.

As a financier and trader, Shankarseth, was a powerful Marathi *seth*, who used his influence with the British Government to secure a favourable decision for the *sonars* in their caste dispute with the Pune brahmins in 1824. Besides being an active patron of the Education Society, he was also a leading member of the first important political organisation in Western India, the Bombay Association, established in 1851. Jagannath Shankarseth used his contacts with important retired officials and entrepreneurs in England to organise publicity for the demands of the Association in the British Parliament and press.

[82]Dadaji Dhackjee might have been a descendant of Dhackjee, one of the prosperous *prabhu* traders who moved to Bombay from Vasai around the mid-eighteenth century. See Edwardes, *Rise of Bombay: A Retrospect*, p. 163. As another important trader and patron of the Bombay Native Education Society, Dhackjee enjoyed substantial influence with the British administration. See A.P. Priyolkar, ed., *DPA*, pp. 45–7. For Dadajee Dhackjee's role as the leader of the 'orthodox' party that organised the campaign to excommunicate Balshastri on account of his stance in the Shripat Sheshadri conversion case, see G.G. Jambhekar, ed., *MWBJ*, Appendix, 2, Vol. 3, p. 575.

[83]'Minute by Jagannath Shankarseth, dated 1 May 1847 concurred in by Framji Cowasji and Mohammed Ibrahim Mukba' in *RBE for the year 1847–48,* pp. 60–3.

vernacular print. Evidence suggests that Jagannath Shankarseth knew Balshastri Jambhekar, the editor of *Durpan*, quite well, and even supported him in his controversial stance in the Shripat Sheshadri conversion case.[84] On the other hand, Dadaji Dhackjee too was keenly aware of the importance of visibility in the emerging public domain. This is borne out by his major role in organising the conservative campaign[85] against Balshastri on account of the latter's plea that Shripat, an under-age convert to Christianity, be allowed to re-convert to his brahmin *jati* after due *prayaschita*. And yet neither as *seths*, nor in their capacity as prominent public personalities, did either show any interest in the commercial potential for the dissemination of printed material in Marathi or any other languages in the area. Despite being aware of the *Durpan's* serious financial difficulties, Jagannath Shankarseth seems to have done precious little to save the paper from closing down.[86]

In comparison, the substantial Parsi trading community in Bombay was far more receptive to the idea of the publication and circulation of information about various aspects and prospects of the colonial trade. Being a flourishing trading community whose wealth was generated through close links with colonial trade, the Parsis were better predisposed to recognising the advantages and commercial possibilities of independent press initiatives. Fardunji Marzban, a traditional *mullah* from Surat who was trained in Persian, Sanskrit, Hindustani and Gujarati and the Parsi scriptures, and evidently combined these with a keen entrepreneurial mind, became the first Gujarati publisher and the first native editor of a newspaper in Western India. He apparently began life in Bombay as caretaker of Mullah Feroz's *kitabkhana* (book-store) but soon went on to acquire his own book-binding business. By 1812 he had invested in producing a set of Gujarati fonts, with much of

[84]G.G. Jambhekar, ed., *MWBJ*, Appendix 2, Vol. 3, p. 555.

[85]See fns. 111 and 112 below.

[86]Keshav Bhavalkar recalls that the paper closed down because of financial difficulties arising out of a libel case. However, the announcement in the last issue of the *Durpan* dated 26 June 1840 did not mention these details and only announced plans to amalgamate with another native paper, the *United Service Gazette*. See G.G. Jambhekar, ed., *MWBJ*, Appendix 3, Vol. 3, p. 17 and 'The Last Farewell' in *MWBJ*, Vol. 2, p. 142.

the labour for shaping and polishing these types provided by the women of his household. The first books printed by him apparently 'sold in numbers'. In 1814, six years before the first Bengali calendar was printed in Calcutta, he printed the first Hindu *panchang* in Gujarati, sold at two rupees a copy. In 1815 he brought out a Gujarati translation of the *Dabestan*, a history of the sacred literature of the Parsis, priced at fifteen rupees a copy. 1818, the year of the Peshwa defeat in the Deccan, saw him bring out the *Khordeh Avesta*, the Parsi scriptures in Gujarati, along with an accompanying exegesis. This was the first book of its kind both in Gujarati and in the region as a whole.

Marzban's attempts to publish vernacular versions of the sacred texts earned him many opponents but publicity and controversy, no doubt, fed off each other. He bought his own press and issued the prospectus of the *Mumbaino Samachar* on 10 June 1822. Started as a weekly priced at Rs 2 per month, Fardunji went on to edit the paper. Within a few days of the issue of the prospectus, it had apparently attracted a 'hundred and fifty subscribers comprising of 67 Parsis, 14 Europeans, 8 Hindus and 6 Mohammeddans'.[87] Fardunji edited the *Samachar* until 1832 when, apparently forced by pressure from his enemies to leave

[87]Fardunji Marzban was born in a priestly family in 1787. He came to Bombay when he was about eighteen. A propitious order for supplies to the colonial army fetched profits that Fardunji decided to invest in preparing types for Gujarati. After its initial successes, Fardunji's press published many tracts, school books and even a brochure for the government on the advantages of vaccination. He taught himself English in order to understand the new journalistic medium better.

In due course, Fardunji developed active connections with the China trade, even owning a ship, *Hindustan*. Many early native journalist-editors and printers, including Ganpat Krishnaji, trained with him. Fardunji was well acquainted with many important missionaries in Bombay, including John Wilson. He saw himself as a religious reformer, but found himself in the midst of controversy when he published the Parsi scriptures in Gujarati. The fierce discussion that ensued was the first instance of a religious controversy disseminated through the new public medium in Western India. Finding it difficult to continue living in Bombay, he was forced to settle in Goa. This biographical account of Fardunji's life is taken from Marzban Mancherji Marzban, *Leaves from the Life of Khan Bahadur Muncherji Cowasi Murzban with an Introduction Containing the Life Sketch of Fardunji Marzban*, Bombay, 1915.

Bombay, he handed over charge of the paper along with detailed policy guidelines.[88] It is interesting to note that the beginning of print entrepreneurship in Gujarati did not have to wait for an educated readership to emerge from the colonial schools, as was definitely the case with Marathi.

Independent press initiatives in Marathi initially remained subordinate to the production of instructional material and school books, and it was not until Bhau Mahajan's efforts in the 1840s[89] that a small, autonomous reading public emerged in Marathi. There had been some mention of a newspaper in Marathi as a possible channel of communication between the British and the Maratha *sardars*, the erstwhile ruling elite in the Deccan, but the suggestion was apparently given up as risky: it was thought that such a paper might publicise the discontent amongst the disbanded Maratha soldiery.[90] Although there are some references to earlier attempts around 1828 to start a weekly Marathi paper from Bombay, the *Durpan* was the first Marathi newspaper.[91] Interestingly, the money to start the *Durpan* may have come from Parsi *seths*.[92]

Other patterns emerge from the response of various communities to the new print-related professional opportunities. Despite their literate backgrounds and the deep impression that print made upon early

[88]As an editor, Fardunji was greatly exercised by political and ethical concerns. In the first issue of the *Mumbaino Samachar*, he wrote a critical account of the merits of British rule in India, especially the advantages of the press as a public medium that linked the sovereign parliament in England and Indian subjects. He even published editorial guidelines for his successor in the issue of 13 August 1832 on matters of appropriate tone and language policy concerning religious controversies and the publication of correspondence. See ibid.

[89]For details of Bhau Mahajan's life and career, seen fn. 126 below.

[90]R.D. Choksey, *Mountstuart Elphinstone: The Indian Years 1796–1827*, Bombay, 1970, p. 313.

[91]The only available references to this early paper called the *Mumbai Vartman* are in advertisements in the *Bombay Gazette* of 9 July 1828 and the *Bombay Courier* of 5 July 1828, announcing the forthcoming venture. See R.K. Lele, *MVI*, p. 55.

[92]Dadoba Pandurang's autobiography mentions that some wealthy natives decided to invest in an English-Marathi newspaper and appointed Balshastri as the editor. See A.P. Priyolkar, ed., *DPA*, p. 187. The first issues of the *Durpan* were printed by a Cowasji at the Messenger Press, before it was entrusted to Shrikrishna Jagannathjee at the Courier Press. See R.K. Lele, *MVI*, p. 59.

colonial intellectuals, their brahmanical preconceptions about the nature of cultivation and intellectual labour did not allow most high-caste students to overcome their repugnance of the physical labour needed to run a printing press. Despite being rebuked by Balshastri Jambhekar, many brahmin students apparently refused to work the press on the school premises.[93] The staff employed on the first lithographic machines sent out from England in 1824 came from very different backgrounds from those who studied at the Society's schools and who were soon to become proponents of 'general' reform.[94] Similarly, two of the most important figures in the story of Marathi print, well-known for introducing important technical innovations, did not come from upper-caste backgrounds. Ganpat Krishnaji,[95] and later, Javaji Dadaji,[96] worked

[93]As teacher of the Normal School, Balshastri Jambhekar wanted his students to help produce copies of class exercises on the lithograph press. Bhavalkar, who studied at the Normal School in Bombay around 1840, recollects that the otherwise patient Balshastri lost his temper when upper-caste students adamantly refused to 'demean' themselves by operating the school press. See Bhavalkar, 'Life and Character of Prof. Ball Gungadhar Shastree Jambhekar' in G.G. Jambhekar, ed., *MWBJ*, Appendix 3, Vol. 3., p. 7.

[94]The names of native press operators employed under the supervision of Mr Macdowall, the lithographist, are given as Maddoo Bappoo, Abia Nammajee, Rama Ragu and Shaikh Ally. Although these appear to be family names, they point towards persons of non-erudite and, perhaps, humble backgrounds. Whereas the monthly salary of the European superintendent was Rs 350, the head press operator was to get Rs 12 for working on a large press and Rs 8 for the small press and the junior operator in charge of both presses was to get Rs 6 per month. See the 'Bombay Secretariat Records, General Department Files, Vol. 14/70 of 1824', pp. 57–9, quoted in A.P. Priyolkar, *The Printing Press in India*, pp. 92–3.

[95]Little biographical information about Ganpat Krishnaji is available. He was a *koli bhandari* and it is estimated that he was born in about 1800. He apparently began his career as an apprentice at the American Mission press. Having devised his own methods of preparing ink and having set up his own foundry, he prepared the first indigenously manufactured set of Marathi fonts around 1846. Ganpat Krishnaji died in 1860, though his press seems to have been active until 1900. See Govind Narayan Madgaonkar, *Mumbaiche Varnan*, first pub. 1863, 3rd edn., Pune, 1992, pp. 225–6.

[96]Little is known about Javaji Dadaji's early life. He was born around 1830 in a family living in the Umerkhadi area in Bombay, where the Scottish missionaries were active. Javaji's father was an ordinary *sipahi* and their caste is identified as

hard to improve the quality and design of print production in Bombay and ended their careers as successful printer-publishers. However, it is doubtful if either saw themselves as part of the self-professedly reformist elite. There was, thus, a definite tendency for the different types of skills demanded by the new communicative arrangements to be distributed according to social background, with the result that the intellectual/ literary, and technical/entrepreneurial capabilities required for the making of vernacular print culture were often drawn from different social segments. This led to an unfortunate polarisation between ideas of the 'popular' and the 'critical' within the emerging vernacular discourse and, more generally, for native efforts to widen the audience for Marathi print, affecting the possibilities for creating a laicised democratic culture within colonial modernity.

The Possibilities of a 'Popular' Audience for Marathi Print

Given the nature of pre-colonial norms of intellectual exchange and modes of social contestation, it was unlikely that upper-caste groups would rapidly turn into agents of a generally-diffused, laicised knowledge. Lower-caste individuals seem to have been less distrustful of non-exclusive principles of social distribution and perhaps more sympathetic to initiatives for the creation of an egalitarian literate culture. Despite the role of successful print-entrepreneurs like Ganpat Krishnaji and Javaji Dadaji, structural constraints prevented such men from initiating alternative attempts to extend the vernacular reading public. As printer-publishers, they remained dependent on brahmins and other upper-caste groups to compose texts for publication. Paradoxically, the project of colonial literacy theoretically legitimated itself on principles of

---

Maratha. It seems Javaji learnt his trade from Thomas Graham, the well-known printer at the American Mission Press. He worked in several presses before setting up the Nirnayasagar Press in 1864 with a loan from a local *marwadi*. His decision to diversify into the manufacture and selling of Marathi types gave him a virtual monopoly in the trade. The types cut at Javaji's factory were known for their fine quality that helped reduce the quantity of paper required. Barely educated, but wealthy, Javaji did much to assist his fellow caste-men. Upon his death in 1882, all the major papers, including the *Kesari, Subodh Patrika* and the *Dinbandhu*, carried obituaries acknowledging his contribution. This summary is taken from V.K. Dev, *Javaji Dadajiyanche Charitra*, Bombay, 1897.

general access. Nevertheless, being ultimately interested in retaining monopolistic control over the cultural and political spheres, colonial policy reproduced a highly stratified system of admission to social opportunities. In trying to dislodge the severely elitist provisions of colonial education, with little backing either from the government or from upper-caste intellectuals, vernacular publishers faced a difficult task, a pattern well borne out by the career of the first native commercial printer-publisher in Marathi, Ganpat Krishnaji.

Krishnaji's were the earliest attempts to test the market potential for Marathi texts outside the official publications and those intended primarily for pedagogic use. He came from a non-elite caste background but became acquainted with print as a technical apprentice in the American Mission Press. However, like Javaji Dadaji later, he had little formal schooling and whatever familiarity he may have had with English and modern ideas of literacy were imbibed through his association with missionaries. For his first job, a Marathi almanac which came out around 1835, he used stone types that he had cut on his own, and an iron press he had managed to construct.[97] As the only independent Marathi publisher until Bhau Mahajan established his press in about 1843, Krishnaji's establishment was the sole printing outlet for any Marathi material that fell beyond the scope or capacity of the government or missionary presses. Thus, when the Education Society refused to sponsor the publication of Dadoba Pandurang's *Marathi Bhasheche Vyakaran*, he had it published from the Ganpat Krishnaji press in 1836.[98] The first Marathi periodical brought out by Balshastri, *Digdarshan,* appeared, in 1840 and was initially issued from Ganpat Krishnaji's press, as did the early numbers of Bhau Mahajan's important weekly paper, *Prabhakar*, established in October 1841.[99]

Nevertheless, as a commercial publisher Krishnaji could not limit

[97]Govind Narayan Madganokar, *Mumbaiche Varnan*, p. 225.

[98]The Education Society refused Dadoba's petition for official patronage for his Marathi Grammar. Eventually, he had it printed at his own expense from Ganpat Krishnaji's press in December 1836. See G.G. Jambhekar, ed., *MWBJ*, Appendix 2, Vol. 3. p. 413.

[99]The *Prabhakar* of 21 November 1841 carried a notice stating that contributions ought to be sent to the Ganpat Krishnaji press. However, within a few months

his output to the literary and journalistic endeavours of the reformed, English-educated elite. As a devout, 'unreformed' Hindu who shared the worldview of many potential vernacular readers, he aspired to use the new medium to publish religious materials which, until then, had been limited to oral transmission. Besides his admirable technical ingenuity, Krishnaji's major contribution lay in pioneering efforts to bring out compositions familiar to a Marathi-knowing, unschooled, 'neo-Hindu' audience.[100] In this respect, his first choice was to bring a printed version of the well-known dialogue between Arjun and Krishna in 1839, along with a simplified prose exegesis entitled *Bhavachandrika-Shrikrishnaarjun Samwaad.*[101] This was followed by the publication of the second Marathi periodical, *Dnyanchandrodaya*, from the Krishnaji Press.[102]

---

of commencing publication, the *Prabhakar* had its own press. See R.K. Lele, *MVI*, pp. 72–5.

[100]The 1850s saw a series of native Marathi publications launched to 'defend' Hindu beliefs, often by highlighting the inconsistencies within Christian theology, and through allusions to radical rationalists like Paine and Voltaire. Morobhat Dandekar's *Updeshchandrika*, started in 1844 in the aftermath of the Sheshadri affair, was one such short-lived venture of the 1840s that had the support of Jambhekar and Bhau Mahajan. The liberal Poona weekly, *Dnyanprakash,* also occasionally advised potential converts to read Western authors like Newman and Carlyle to get a true perspective on the Christian religion. Known for its balanced reporting, the *Vartmandeepika*, which appeared in 1853, was published from the Krishnaji press. Thus, there were discernible continuities between liberal and revivalist arguments. But increasingly through the 1850s, as the discursive gap between the vernacular and English spheres widened, the popular defence of the Hindu faith was taken up by men like Visbhnubuwa Brahmachari, the itinerant preacher, who had little knowledge of English, but drew huge crowds through his pugnacious, rhetorical style. Often criticised by the reformist press, Vishnubuwa's discourses drew favourable comment from publications like the *Saddharmadeepika*, which appeared from Bombay from 1854 with the explicit aim of combating missionary discourse. See R.K. Lele, *MVI*, pp. 119–25. For more information on Morobhat Dandekar's *Updeschandrika,* see G.G. Jambhekar, ed., *MWBJ*, Appendix 3, Vol. 3, pp. 92–5.

[101]This was published by Balaji Sundarji Prabhu, see D.V. Potdar, *Marathi Gadyacha Ingrezi Avataar*, p. 12.

[102]*Dnyanchandrodaya* was edited by Pravaskar. Dadoba Pandurang mentions Pavaskar as the much-loved, nimble-minded teacher at the vernacular school in Bombay, because of whose efforts the Marathi students were much better-trained

Aiming to print versions of traditional pre-colonial Marathi poetic texts, the *Dnyanchandrodaya* was the first Marathi newspaper to differ from reformist publications like the *Digdarshan* and the *Prabhakar*. It seems that Krishnaji's interest in bringing out the *Dnyanchandrodaya* exceeded merely printing it; evidence suggests that he also helped manage its circulation and subscriptions.[103] Priced at eight annas per issue, the journal published the *Krishnalilamrut* and a collated version of the Gita containing *shlokas* in both Sanskrit and Prakrit along with *abhangs* from the *Dynaneshwari* and corresponding vernacular compositions from Moropant, Tulsidas and Mukteshwar. Although the journal itself did not last long, the idea of making available traditional textual traditions through print soon acquired a following—initially perhaps, the interest came mostly from the new intellectuals linked with the colonial establishment.[104]

In publishing vernacular texts outside the strict realm of the colonial curriculum, Krishnaji was exploring the commercial possibilities of the new communicative medium. His choices suggest he tried to broaden the range of vernacular texts available for dissemination though print, even as he tried to enlarge the audience for vernacular print by drawing upon pre-colonial cultural resources. The importance of Krishnaji's efforts to develop a Marathi textual corpus became apparent when the official Vernacular Department at Poona College followed suit with an anthology of pre-colonial poetic works, *Navneet*, compiled by Parshuram Tatya Godbole in 1854.[105] This anthology became something of a

---

in mathematics than their counterparts in the English school. Pavaskar's name also figures as the publisher-printer for the *Prabhakar* between 1842 and 1855. See A.P. Priyolkar, ed., *DPA*, pp. 37–8.

[103]Information printed alongside the title in the inaugural issue, quoted in G.G. Jambhekar, ed., *MWBJ*, Appendix 3, Vol. 3, p. 43.

[104]Letter dated 13 August 1841 from the *Jyotishguru* Elect of Poona College, Narasimha Joshi to Parshurampant Godbole reprinted in G.G. Jambhekar, ed., *MWBJ*, Appendix 2, Vol. 3, pp. 460–1. Writing from Bombay while training to take up his position at the Poona College, Narasimha Joshi alluded to the recently started *Dnyanchandrodaya*, which had been publishing Sanskrit *shlokas* of the Gita along with Vaman's *prakrit* verses, Moropant's *aryas*, Tulsidas's *dohas*, Mukteshwar's *ovis* and Dnyaneshwar's *abhangs*.

[105]D.V. Potdar, *Marathi Gadyacha Ingrezi Avataar*, p. 54.

classic and, although it underwent changes in subsequent editions, it represented the beginning of the efforts to canonise pre-colonial poetic traditions as part of the 'literary' past of modern Marathi.

Krishnaji's pioneering efforts to publish sacred and 'popular' pre-colonial poetic texts illustrated many trends that were to characterise the emerging sphere of vernacular production. As Ranade noted in his *Report on Vernacular Literature*, compiled in 1864, for one reason or another, vernacular authors and publishers were mostly individuals who had not passed through the rigours of a full English education or were school dropouts.[106] The transfer of pre-colonial textual idioms into forms consonant with ideas of modern publicity and standards of general circulation involved complex shifts and required the negotiation of many difficult ideological questions. It was a tragic paradox of colonial modernity that those who played a crucial role in shaping these processes were often not among the best-trained minds of their period. Though the standardisation of the vernaculars had been crucial to the elaboration of colonial ideology, official interest in the emerging vernacular sphere was subject to obvious limits. Given the secondary status of the vernacular sphere within the emerging hierarchy, it was unlikely that the administration would take initiatives to ensure that these processes would receive due collective deliberation. Instead, these processes were more likely to come about through serendipitous impulses at the margins of the emerging public sphere. Intellectuals like Balshastri Jambhekar and Bhau Mahajan were keenly aware of the importance of widening the base of the vernacular literate public. Despite their deep regard for the mother tongue and their resentment of official attempts to regulate Marathi style, as critical rationalists it was unlikely that they were favourably inclined towards incorporating pre-colonial textual traditions. Ironically, it was also unlikely that a subaltern intellectual like Phule would undertake such a task of recovering pre-modern vernacular texts in the new discursive medium. For, in wishing to create a lower-caste counter-discourse according to modern principles, Phule's writings wanted to highlight the *complete* alienation of non-

[106]M.G. Ranade, 'A Note on the Growth of Marathi Literature, *Royal Asiatic Society Bulletin*, Vol. 20, 1902, pp. 78–105.

brahmin castes from the pre-colonial textual corpus. Efforts to draw upon pre-colonial textual elements in order to create a literate audience beyond the small circle of reformist opinion thus apparently conflicted with aspirations to establish a critical vernacular discourse based on principles of equal exchange.

With the possibilities for publicity open to both reformist and 'unreformed' segments, it was inevitable that the vision of progressive, 'high', colonial intellectuals like Balshastri and Bhau Mahajan would be at odds with directions taken by other efforts to influence the new public domain. For, apart from the missionary presence in the emerging public arenas, it was evident that the new regime had also created openings for the renewal of older rivalries between brahmins and upwardly-mobile castes like the *sonars*[107] and *prabhus*. Quick to respond to the opportunities for mobility through colonial literacy, the latter were also at the forefront of attempts to organise *sabhas*[108] to consider the value of traditional disciplines like *vedanta, nyaya* and *vyakaran*—attended by *shastris* of the Poona College along with others exposed to Western knowledge. Such gatherings received added publicity through newspaper reports, and these only highlighted the complex and irreconcilable tensions between pre-modern social values and cultural practices that existed side by side with modern political values. Similar tensions were evoked through publicity for the Shripat Sheshadri reconversion case,[109] which polarised opinion within the Hindu com-

[107]For an account of how early colonial courts tried to arbitrate between conflicting claims over rank and ritual privilege between rival *jati* groups, see Narendra Wagle, 'A dispute between the *pancal devajana sonars* and the brahmins of Pune regarding social rank and ritual privileges: a case-study of the British administration of *jati* laws in Maharashtra, 1822–25', in N.K. Wagle, *Images of Maharashtra: A Regional Profile of India*, London, 1980.

[108]The *Bombay Durpan* of 20 January 1832 alludes to one such *sabha* held at Raghunathjee's house earlier that month. See *Durpan* files, Vol. 1, held at the Bombay State Archives.

[109]Missionary activity was one of principal challenges confronting the early colonial intelligentsia. One of the early controversies involved the Shripat Sheshadri conversion episode of 1843–4. Shripat's conversion had been revoked by the colonial court through an order passed on 8 November 1843. The point of contention was whether Shripat ought to be re-admitted to his high-caste

munity. Balshastri and Bhau Mahajan were aware of the need to counter the missionary critique, but felt that this had to be balanced with the important objective of creating a rational, self-reflexive discourse through the vernacular, for this alone could help maintain brahmanical claims to moral leadership.

Their stance in the Shripat Sheshadri case exemplified this belief. The controversy centred around the status of Shripat, a brahmin boy whose conversion to Christianity at the Bombay Scottish Mission had been invalidated by the High Court on the grounds that he was below the age of legal consent. Progressive, English-educated Marathi intellectuals like Balshastri and Mahajan were of the opinion that if Hindu *samaj* was to effectively contend with missionary propaganda, it would need to be willing to re-admit the boy to brahmin status after due *prayaschita* (ritual atonement). Balshastri spent much time enlisting public support for his arguments from the *shastris* at the Poona College and from pandits from far off places like Nasik, Kolhapur and even Benares.[110] The correspondence between them drew comments and publicity in the Marathi native papers, which was not always as favourable as the positions taken by Mahajan's *Prabhakar*. Opinion was polarised between reformed brahmins like Balshastri, Mahajan and their associates in the Poona College and the anti-reformist lobby consisting of 'lower' brahmin orders like the *bhats, puraniks* and the sub-brahmin castes like the *prabhus* and the *shenvis*.[111] Dadaji Dhackjee,

status. Balshastri argued that re-admitting Shripat after due *prayaschita* would be the optimal strategy if Hindu *samaj* was to accommodate the threat posed by missionary critique. Clearly, Balshastri realised the threat to brahmanical hegemony from missionary critique and colonial law. In a move that anticipated the more pronounced accommodation of 'orthodox' opinion in the latter half of the nineteenth century, he strove hard to canvass for support among *shastris* and other prominent persons in the Hindu theological hierarchy from places as far as Kashi. For details of the Sheshadri controversy, see Murray Mitchell, *A Memoir to the Reverend Robert Nesbit*, London, 1858, pp. 215–40. For details of Balshastri's efforts to mobilise support for his case in Pune, Benares and in the native press and the campaign against the 'progressive' brahmins, see G.G. Jambhekar, ed., *MWBJ*, Vol. 3.

[110]G.G. Jambhekar, ed., *MWBJ*, Vol. 3, pp. 486–579.

[111]There were reports in the native press of a 'schism' among the brahmins of

the *prabhu seth*,[112] played a prominent role in organising the anti-reformist campaign to excommunicate Balshastri and Bhau Mahajan for their unorthodox arguments. Faced with the challenge from the 'orthodox' quarter, Balshastri decided to accede to public pressure and undertook *prayaschita*, though Mahajan remained unrelenting.[113]

Progressive intellectuals like Bhau Mahajan and Balshastri argued for the need for a vernacular discourse based on principles of individual autonomy and rational social exchange. However, the elitist dimensions of colonial literacy prevented such perspectives from becoming popular commonsense. In comparison, the less critical 'indigenist' arguments against the missionary critique had more in common with 'popular' opinion of the larger 'unschooled public'. Given his keenness to print traditional 'popular' Hindu religious texts, Ganpat Krishnaji's interest in the dissemination of an anti-missionary discourse was hardly surprising, thus pointing once again to the faultlines emerging between high and low varieties of the emerging vernacular discourse. The Ganpat Krishnaji Press published the *Digdarshan* and the *Prabhakar* until Bhau Mahajan established the Prabhakar Press in 1842, after which the latter seems to have emerged as the choice for pro-reform publications.[114] Not only did the *Digdarshan* and the

Bombay and deep divisions between brahmins and *prabhus*. See reports from *Prabhakar* and *Dnyansindhu* quoted in G.G. Jambhekar, ed., *MWBJ*, Appendix 2, Vol. 3. pp. 549–9.

[112]In subsequent years, Dadaji's Dhackjee's support for revivalist discourse became even more explicit, as he played host to Vishnubuwa Brahmachari, the 'unreformed' itinerant preacher who drew huge crowds on Chowpatty Beach in Bombay during 1857–8. Dhackjee financed the building of an ostentatious temple at Thakurdwar, which became the venue for many revivalist Hindu meetings. See 'Preface', George Bowen, *Discussions by the Seaside*, Bombay, 1857.

[113]G.G. Jambhekar, ed., *MWBJ*, Appendix 2, Vol. 3, pp. 572–7.

[114]Jambhekar wrote for the *Updeshchandrika*, see G.G. Jambhekar, ed., *MWBJ*, Appendix 3, Vol. 3, p. 16. Further, the *Durpan* of 13 April 1832 carried a favourable report about Morobhat's response to Wilson's attack on the Hindu religion. Keenly aware of the politics of print, Jambhekar helped publish the *Updeshchandrika* from the Prabhakar Press as a 'progressive' response to missionary propaganda. For more information on Morobhat Dandekar's *Updeshchandrika*, see *MWBJ*, Appendix 3, Vol. 3, pp. 92–5. See also fn. 100 above.

Prabhakar switch to the Prabhakar press, another 'rationalist' periodical, Morobhat Dandekar's[115] *Updeshchandrika*,[116]—explicitly brought out to counter missionary propaganda—also commenced publication from the latter establishment in 1844. On the other hand, the Ganpat Krishnaji Press emerged as the preferred site for the publication of an increasingly revivalist discourse. The *Prabhakar* had opposed missionary attacks on native religious practices but had been equally forthright in its critique of chauvinistic 'indigenist' arguments that defended the Hindu faith by ranting against 'foreign attacks'. A new cheaply-priced weekly, the *Vartmandeepika*,[117] sold at Rs 5 per annum, was started from the Ganpat Krishnaji Press in 1853, announcing its intention to simultaneously contest the reformist and missionary discourses.[118] As

[115]Morobhat Dandekar was Jambhekar's senior by about 15–20 years. This self-styled defendant of Hindu religion was a *shakta* who came to Bombay from Nagpur. He knew no English and relied for his knowledge of Christian texts on missionary translations into Marathi and on explanations he received from his associates. See Baba Padmanji's reference to Morobhat Dandekar in his autobiographical account, *Arunodaya*, Bombay, 1888, p. 125.

[116]The *Updeshchandrika*, a monthly publication, was priced at an affordable four annas per issue. In its Introduction, the weekly addressed its readers as *majhe deshche lok*, one of the earliest instances in Marathi of the reading audience being identified as 'compatriots'. Hitherto, the native press had used more tentative and general terms like *'ettedeshiya lok'* (the people living here), *'native'* or *'ya deshant rahanare lok'* (the people living in this region): the task of collectively defending one's identity through the press highlighted the overlap between the emerging modern 'patriotic' and 'religious' community.

Emphasising that missionary propaganda *(sanchar)* had been particularly effective because of its use of the printed medium, the introduction stressed that a defence of the *hindudharma* needed to be carried out through a regular publication. Dandekar's introduction shows a similarity with Baba Padmanji's critique of the Hindu faith. Both identified the 'lack' of an easily identifiable set of core beliefs as a major 'weakness' of the Hindu religion. Dandekar also underlined the point that the journal would not accept letters from missionaries. See 'Introduction' to the *Updeshchandrika*, reproduced in G.G. Jambhekar, ed., *MWBJ*, Appendix 3, Vol. 3, p. 96.

[117]The annual subscription to the *Vartmandeepika* was Rs 5, while its chief rival, *Prabhakar*, sold at Rs 12 per annum.

[118]It is not entirely clear who the editors of the *Vartmandeepika* were. From the conflicting references available, Keshavshastri Gadgil and Laxmanshastri Halbe emerge as the likely candidates.

a print-entrepreneur guided by the commercial logic of the publishing trade, Krishnaji continued to publish materials representing various ideological positions, including reformist texts. However, this would not negate the general point proposed here that the disjunctions between critical and popular impulses crucially affected the trajectory of the vernacular sphere, as a result of which uneducated but successful publishers like Krishnaji remained dependent upon the output of upper-caste intellectuals.

Clearly, the situation of the colonial intellectual elite was determined by complexity and contradiction. The intelligentsia was meant to aid the transformation of a particularised public domain to a public sphere based on universalistic norms. Their proximity and direct links with colonial power put them in a greatly privileged position. And yet, as a subordinate, numerically marginal elite, they found their position constrained. As the primary instrument of publicity and political communication between the colonial state and native society, the press became an obvious site where the intelligentsia tried to come to terms with its paradoxical position of simultaneous influence and marginality. It is important, therefore, to consider examples from the intelligentsia's efforts to establish a sphere of critical discussion though the vernacular newspaper press.

Re-inventing the Public Terrain: The Early Marathi Press and a Critical Vernacular Sphere

The press represents the most suitable site to analyse the structure of exchanges and meanings of publicity that were established through print. Unlike in the West, vernacular press initiatives emerged concurrently with official attempts to institute a programme of 'general' education and preceded the emergence of a modern 'literary' discourse in the vernacular. These initiatives to sustain a native press thus have a strong claim to being a key and sensitive domain in which we may monitor shifts in the intelligentsia's self-perceptions as they advance their status as spokespersons of a hegemonic discourse. It was through the press that the intelligentsia first confronted questions about the identity, size and location of their audience and their relation to a potentially infinite, literate community—in reality an exclusive, internally-stratified and subordinate elite. Native press initiatives in the Bombay-Pune region show the intelligentsia's attempts to deal with the divisions implicit in the colonial bilingual relation, although in different ways, both before and after 1857.

In choosing a symmetrically bilingual structure, the *Bombay Durpan* was concerned that the benefits of the new discourses ought not to remain restricted to those who knew English. However, in adopting a bilingual structure, Balshastri was also trying to play down the political differences between English and Marathi and the lack of homology between the interests, size and identity of the colonial English and vernacular reading communities. Realising that English represented the language of access to the discourses of modern rationality in addition to being the language of government, he knew English was indispensable. Equally, a native paper had to be a bridge between the government and its native subjects, and hence the vernacular could not be ignored either. Although meant as a channel of 'native improvement', given the small size of the vernacular reading public the English columns were also a way to widen its readership to include, perhaps, a small number of subscribers from official circles. Nevertheless, the symmetrical relation between English and Marathi that Balshastri sought to posit was not sustainable and the paper could not keep up its bilingual design, especially in its latter years, before folding up eventually in 1842.

However, the *Durpan* was noteworthy not only for the bilingual relation it proposed but also for its attempts to assume a critical stance *vis-à-vis* both native society and the colonial government.[119] An editorial column that appeared in its issue of 4 May 1832 exemplifies its aspiration to create a space for a modern rationalist discourse about native society. Asserting its ambition not to identify with the opinions expressed in its columns, the editor spoke of the *Durpan's* wish to follow a policy that transcended particularistic loyalties:

> We do not consider it our duty to obtrude our opinions on any religious question whatever, whether relating to Hindu, or any other creed,

[119]See chapter three, esp. pp. 131–3, for details on the critical position that the *Durpan* took *vis-à-vis* the English papers and the colonial administration.

which our correspondents may choose to discuss, and both sides of which are given in our paper. We do not think our opinions on the particular subject alluded to will throw any light on the question and we are anxious to avoid the imputation of prejudice or partiality which we might incur if we were to side with either party.[120]

Such views indicate the seriousness of Balshastri's efforts to apply the new critical perspectives through a symmetrically bilingual, rationalist discourse. The importance of such efforts to establish a liberal discursive sphere of impartial exchange became apparent when, not long after, by the late 1840s, there were signs of change in the aims of the native press. Whereas *Durpan* had consistently preferred to identify its community of readers through religiously neutral terms such as *'ettedeshiye lok'* (people of this region), increasingly, non-particularistic terms such as *'hindu lok'* were soon used interchangeably with more general terms to denote the native 'public' in the vernacular press. The great distance between the language of government and the lives of its ordinary subjects was brought out poignantly by a public letter published in the bilingual columns in the *Durpan* of 13 July 1832. Ostensibly received from the ryots of Pune, the letter conveyed the dissatisfaction of a large number of peasants with the recently completed revenue assessment which would benefit only a small minority of wealthy cultivators: 'After compliments, we the ryots of Poona, beg to acquaint you that the Governor Saheb having appointed Major Robertson in to the situation of the Collector of Poona, we are very happy; for he is well acquainted with the inhabitants of the city, and his conduct has always been just and good towards us.'[121] Encountering the ryots' grievances thus expressed through the first person in formal Victorian diction jarringly brings home the incongruities of the colonial bilingual situation and the extreme

[120] 4 May 1832, *Durpan* files, Bombay State Archives, Vol. 1, p. 110.

[121] 13 July 1832, *Durpan* files, Bombay State Archives, Vol. 1, p. 178. An editorial comment explained that the paper had initially hesitated to publish the letter as it had arrived without the necessary signatures. However, asserting that the writers had not attached their signatures only because they had not realised the importance of such a step, the editors decided to print the letter. The editors claimed they could vouch for its contents from their personal knowledge of the state of affairs around Pune.

unlikeliness of the ryots actually speaking through the medium of the press using English. These difficulties could not be resolved simply through the *Durpan's* bilingual structure and it is significant that the series of subsequent native newspaper ventures for 'Marathi' audiences were monolingual: the *Prabhakar, Dhumketu* and *Dnyanprakash*. By the time the *Durpan* ceased publication, announcing its plans to amalgamate with another native paper, the *United Service Gazette*, the proprietors of the *Gazette* decided to simultaneously bring out a separate Marathi weekly, the *Mumbai Akhbar*. The *Mumbai Akhbar* announced in its inaugural issue that it would not be able to keep up the bilingual policy followed by the *Durpan*. Explaining that certain constraints had made the *Durpan's* bilingual structure unsustainable, the introduction went on to elaborate its own strategy to straddle the divide:

> *because it [the Durpan] carried insufficient news about Maharashtra readers, it was unable to fulfil their aspirations,* and therefore this announcement of its closure henceforth. However, all those issues concerning the welfare of this land that need to be communicated to the government and the officials will be announced through a new English newspaper, the 'United Service Gazette'. Since the *Durpan*, many natives have developed a taste for reading newspapers, and it is the wish of many that there ought to be a paper in Marathi that publicises all that is new and important all around the world. And for that purpose it has been decided to publish a paper in the Marathi language not *containing any English print* that will come out each Saturday.[122] (emphasis added)

Requesting the support of all those who had patronised the *Durpan*, the editors of the *Mumbai Akhbar*, the first paper entirely in Marathi, reiterated their intention to observe neutrality and a strict faithfulness to fact in reporting all matters generally useful, and also promised to publish matters concerning the welfare of peasants. Such claims to report on the problems of the peasantry would count as the earliest instances of the Marathi intelligentsia's public acknowledgement of their representative role. This was a crucial step, for to speak on behalf

[122]Translated from Marathi, Prospectus of the *Marathi Akhbar*, published in the first issue of 4 July 1840, quoted in R. K. Lele, *MVI*, pp. 71–2.

of the peasants and others not conversant with English was also to implicitly admit the reality of the bilingual divide. Among the 'lessons' that the intelligentsia was internalising was the realisation that their unique importance lay in their ability to straddle the two ends of the political hierarchy. Somewhat paradoxically, as the intelligentsia began to recognise the dual nature of their ideological task, they also realised the political asymmetry of the colonial linguistic hierarchy and became increasingly aware of the representative possibilities of their position. They could do little to reduce the severity of the political divide, but they could try and work out ways to span the linguistic hierarchy by, somewhat awkwardly, using the vernacular to address the native community and adopting English for the parallel representation of subaltern interests to the *Ingrezi* government: 'Matters that would result in the welfare of the poor and the needy brought to the attention of the government would be rendered into English and publicised through the English paper ... the paper will contain news from China, Bengal, Madras and Delhi among other places too'.[123]

The *Mumbai Akbhar* proved to be the first of a series of Marathi newspapers that emerged in the Bombay–Pune region. By 1845, according to a report in the missionary weekly, *Dnyanodaya*, there were four or five Marathi newspapers and six Gujarati newspapers in the Presidency.[124] The 1850s saw the first Marathi newspapers being published from outlying towns and cities like Kolhapur, Jamkhandi, Satara and Ahmadnagar.[125] Of the papers started in the 1840s and 1850s, the most remarkable were those edited by Bhau Mahajan[126]

[123]Ibid., p. 71.

[124]Quoted in R.K. Lele, *MVI*, p. 82.

[125]Ibid., pp. 131–3.

[126]Bhau Mahajan alias Govind Vitthal Kunte (1815–90), Balshastri's classmate and friend, had the reputation of being a fearless and independent intellectual. At Elphinstone, he was known as an avid and receptive student who paid little heed to the disciplinary regime of examinations and restrictive classroom practices. Bhau Mahajan resolutely stayed away from government service. Also, unlike Balshastri, Bhau stubbornly refused to undertake the *prayaschita* demanded in the *shastric* sentence passed against them in the Sheshadri case. He turned down an invitation to participate in the official project to prepare Marathi schoolbooks under Major Candy's superintendence. As the first full-time professional editor

from Bombay, the *Prabhakar* and the *Dhumketu*. These were established in 1841 and 1853 respectively, and continued until Mahajan finally left Bombay in 1862. It is not easy to establish reliable circulation figures for any of these papers, but the evidence suggests that the readership was far from alarmingly large. A reference in a contemporary newspaper had estimated that, after a year of its existence, the *Durpan* had about 250 subscribers, at least some of whom were from places away from Bombay.[127] Nevertheless, despite its limited circulation, the vernacular press was emerging as an important means for the dissemination of information that helped strengthen the ideological bonds between colonial intellectuals who shared a similar training and interests. We know that the important paper, *Prabhakar*, edited by Bhau Mahajan, had subscribers in the provincial town of Junnar[128] and was also read in Belgaum.[129] Further, the fact that from 1848 onwards Gopal Hari Deshmukh from Pune chose to publish his important *Shatapatre* (a hundred letters) in the *Prabhakar* instead of in the more sedate and well-known weekly, *Dnyanprakash*, shows that the Bombay paper had established a considerable reputation for itself.

Like Balshastri Jambhekar, Bhau Mahajan's contribution to the vernacular press was many-sided. He showed remarkable qualities of enterprise as the manager and publisher of the *Prabhakar* and the *Dhumketu*. More importantly, not only did these papers constantly reiterate the need for channels that allowed the free public exchange of 'all' points of view, time and again they showed their commitment

---

and journalist in Marathi, and independent publisher, he successfully edited two weeklies and a periodical, *Dnyansindhu*, until he left Bombay in 1862. He was widely respected as a learned scholar of both English and Sanskrit and for his lucid and critical Marathi style. Bhau Mahajan's balanced and unorthodox editorial style was an impressive achievement; his *Dhumketu* was also the least expensive Marathi weekly until then. That hardly anything is known of his life after he left Bombay to live in Nagpur is indicative of the changed political temper after 1857.

[127] *Oriental Christian Spectator*, March 1833 quoted in, *MWBJ*, Appendix 2, Volume 3, p. 586.

[128] Bhavani Shankar Sridhar Pandit, ed., *Raosaheb Keshav Shivram Bhavalkaryanche Atmavritta*, p. 76.

[129] Baba Padmanji, *Arunodaya*, Bombay, 1888, pp. 159–60.

to sustaining a rational social discourse. Aiming to establish a vernacular arena based on the 'common good' according to principles of modern social rationality,[130] the two papers did not refrain from sharply criticising the colonial government.[131] Neither were revivalist voices, like that of Vishnubuwa Brahmachari[132]—such voices had already begun to be heard in the colonial public sphere in Bombay—spared. More importantly, as editor Bhau Mahajan tried to ensure that the criticism was always reasonable. Thus, although the *Prabhakar* often criticised the activities of Christian missionaries, this did not prevent it allowing a prominent native convert like Baba Padmanji[133] from publicising his opinions within its pages. Similarly, as part of their engagement to critically reflect upon changes introduced through colonial rule, the columns of Bhau Mahajan's papers provide us with some of the most telling and incisive commentary on the implications of the bilingual divide in colonial society.[134]

By the late 1840s and early 1850s the price of the Marathi papers had fallen significantly since the time of the *Durpan*. The *Durpan* had been available to subscribers at Rs 24 per year or at the rate of Rs 6 per

[130]The *Prabhakar* of 5 July 1852 carried a report, sharply critical of the hypocrisy of *shastris* who claimed exclusive access to Sanskrit texts. For, it was quite common for many *shastris* and *vydicks* in Bombay to visit persons from affluent communities and teach them the *Vedas*. Besides, these *shastris* were not averse to teaching the Hindu texts even to Englishmen. The report questioned how it could then be wrong for others related by closer ties of locality (*desh*) and religion (*dharma*) to read the Sanskrit texts. Summarised from excerpt quoted in R.K. Lele, *MVI*, p. 78.

[131]A report in the *Prabhakar* (date not mentioned) was bitterly critical of the economic drain caused by British rule, and pointed out that this dismal state of affairs was aggravated by the corruption among British officials. See ibid., p. 77.

[132]The *Dhumketu* was sharply critical of both Vishnubuwa Brahmachari and missionary propaganda. See ibid.

[133]Baba Padmanji, who converted to Christianity, refers warmly to Bhau Mahajan in his autobiography, *Arunodaya*. Apparently, Bhau was of the opinion that Christianity had much to teach about how religion could be combined with a social conscience. Padmanji published an account of his reasons for converting in the *Prabhakar*: see *Arunodaya*, Bombay, 1888, p. 88.

[134]See extracts from *Prabhakar* of 12 December 1841 and 8 May 1842, quoted in R.K. Lele, *MVI*, pp. 77–8.

quarter.[135] The *Mumbai Akhbar* was priced at Rs 5 per quarter and a discounted price of Rs 4 if paid for in advance.[136] Besides his contribution to the making of rationalist vernacular discourse, Bhau Mahajan was the first publisher-editor who was able to bring the prices of Marathi papers to a more accessible level. Proving himself a shrewd and capable entrepreneur, he priced the *Prabhakar* at Rs 12 a year whereas the *Dhumketu* sold at an incredible annual cost of Rs 4.[137] The *Dnyanprakash* published from Pune was priced at Rs 10 per year, with a half-yearly rate of Rs 6.[138] Even so, with the spread of the new standardised vernacular idiom severely limited by the under-funded network of colonial schools,[139] short-lived publishing ventures or pleas for increased patronage were quite common.[140] Thus, despite attempts to establish a sphere of critical opinion through the Marathi press, the vernacular sphere could hardly hope to exist independently of its English counterpart. With Elphinstone College School and Pune College being the two main centres of English instruction until the mid 1850s, a sizeable native readership in English was hardly a strong-enough possibility to render the idea of a native newspaper in English viable.

This also meant that native communities had to resort to Anglo-Indian papers to communicate information to the notice of the colonial

[135]Ibid., p. 59.

[136]Ibid., p. 71.

[137]Ibid., p. 121.

[138]Ibid., p. 95.

[139]For an estimate of the numbers enrolled in the English and Vernacular Schools between 1826 and 1842, see chapter three, pp. 137–9.

[140]The *Digdarshan* of November 1840 carried an announcement for a forthcoming weekly, the *Vartmanpadavi*, which hoped to sell at a low price to attract more subscribers. However, the advertisement also admitted that the weekly would only begin publication if it attracted an adequate number of subscribers in advance. See R.K. Lele, *MVI*, p. 61.

Vireshwar Chatre, son of Sadashiv Kashinath Chatre, was the publisher-editor of several Marathi weeklies started in Bombay and Pune in the 1840s, such as the *Dnyansindhu, Mitrodaya, Arunodaya, Dnyanbodhak*, each of which lasted for a few years. See R.K. Lele, *MVI*, pp. 84–7. The *Dnyanodaya* of 15 April 1853 mentions a paper called the *Shukrodaya* that ceased publication after only three issues. See R.K. Lele, *MVI*, p. 119.

government, or to fellow natives who were unlikely to follow the Marathi papers. Surely that was why plans for the second—and one of the longest surviving—Marathi newspaper from Pune, the *Dnyanprakash*, were announced in the English *Telegraph and Courier* of 6 January 1849:

> Krishnaji Trimbuck Ranade inhabitant of Poona intends to *publish a Newspaper in the Marathi Language* with a view of affording useful information on every topic of local interest. It will be open for free discussion on subjects of general utility, scientific investigation and the speculations connected with the antiquities, statistics, curiosities, history and geography of the country and of the Deccan especially ... the patronage and support of all interested in the diffusion of knowledge and Welfare of the People is earnestly solicited.[141]

However, the way the *Dnyanprakash* introduced itself to its Marathi audience diverged significantly from the tone and substance of the English announcement quoted above. Unlike the clipped tones of the brief English statement, the Marathi version was a more detailed elaboration of the paper's objectives. It pointed out that inadequate channels for the communication of news among natives often resulted in the poor dissemination of news even within the country (*desh*). On the other hand, the English press enjoyed the advantages of various facilities like the posts and the telegraph set up by the *ingrez lok* (Englishmen), which enabled them to circulate both local and overseas information far more efficiently. This admitted the discrepancy in the status of the vernacular and English spheres, because of which vernacular papers had to depend on their 'superior' English counterparts for information. The *Dnyanprakash* hoped to alleviate this situation and promised to translate and publish all useful items from the English press:

> but also, as people who find it strange [that] the English rule here, and therefore unless the former are familiarised with ways [*riti*] of the [English] nation [*desh*], there will be no way to work out ways to ensure the welfare of the peasants [ryot]. ... As such, after deliberately considering

[141]'Prospectus' signed by Krishnaji Trimbuck Ranade, issued in *Bombay Telegraph and Courier* of 6 January 1849, quoted in R.K. Lele, *MVI*, p. 91.

all these benefits, the general public [*sarv lok*], *sowkars, sardars* and gentlemen [*grahasth lok*] ought to patronise the paper and unstintingly help in the above cause.[142]

Like many other ventures of this period, it proved difficult to manage the *Dnyanprakash* as a self-sustaining, financial proposition. Yet it lasted until 1950, indicating that it fulfilled some definite ideological and political functions. In surviving for such an impressive length of time the *Dnyanprakash* shared certain characteristics of the next generation of very influential native papers started in Bombay in the 1860s.[143] Like the *Indu Prakash*[144] and the *Native Opinion*[145] started from Bombay in the 1860s, and the *Subodh Patrika*[146] established in

[142]Translated from Marathi, *'Prastavana', Dnyanprakash,* 1st February 1849, quoted in R.K. Lele, *MVI*, p. 91.

[143]For a further discussion on the politics of bilingualism as represented in the post-1860 native press, see chapter five, esp. pp. 219–23.

[144]*Indu Prakash* first came out on 2 January 1862 and it continued to appear until 1924. It remained a weekly until 1902, after which it appeared as a daily. It adopted the bilingual mode from the beginning. Among the most consistently pre-reform native papers in Bombay, its contributors included many prominent Marathi intellectuals, like Gopal Hari Deshmukh, Sakharam Gadgil, Bhandarkar, Mahadev Ranade, Vishnushastri Pandit, Keshavshastri Gadgil and Halbe.

[145]The brainchild of Narayan Mandlik, one of the most influential public figures of his time, *Native Opinion* was launched on 4 January 1864. Mandlik had personally invested in the *Native Opinion* and played a major role in deciding its general editorial policy until he sold the paper and the press in 1870. Mandlik frequently wrote for the paper, especially for its English pages. Although the paper ran up substantial losses, it had sufficient funds to employ an editorial staff on a regular salary. The *Native Opinion* was published as an English paper for the first two years, but from 1st July 1866 it became a bilingual publication, using both English and Marathi. The paper survived until 1908. To begin with, its annual subscription was Rs 15, but this was reduced to Rs 12 to gain more readers. For a biographical account of Mandlik and his role in the *Native Opinion*, see G.R. Hawalder, *Raosaheb Mandlik Yanche Charitra,* Bombay, 1927.

[146]The *Subodh Patrika* was formally managed through the Bombay Theistic Association, a body closely linked to the Prarthana Samaj. The Samaj was established in 1868, but the paper emerged much later on 4 May 1873. It first appeared as separate Gujarati and Marathi editions. It was priced at a highly subsidised rate of 12 annas per year. Under the editorship of Palekar, the *Patrika* assumed its bilingual

1873, the *Dnyanprakash* also survived well into the next century. More crucially, unlike the previous generation of native newspapers of the 1840s, the three major weeklies that appeared through the 1860s and the 1870s were all bilingual ventures. This marked a clear shift in the pattern of native press initiatives. Besides differences in the way they were managed, the structure of the bilingual relation proposed in this set of post-1857 papers also differed significantly from the bilingualism of the *Durpan*.

The next chapter will elaborate more fully the nature and underlying causes of these shifts, arising out of the divisive effects of educational policy in the late 1850s. However, what can be emphasised here is that the *Dnyanprakash*, started in 1849, also resorted to the bilingual mode from 1863,[147] a fact that will only reinforce the point that these shifts signified an important juncture in the intelligentsia's self-perceptions. In adopting the bilingual mode, these papers signalled their intention to span political and linguistic divisions, but unlike the *Durpan* they could not posit a relation of equivalence between English and the vernacular. This then brings up questions about whether such shifts also saw accompanying changes in the ideological orientations of the intelligentsia as they 'progressed' towards a potentially hegemonic, anti-colonial position.

---

form that included both English and Marathi columns. See R.K. Lele, *MVI*, p. 168.

[147]R.K. Lele, *MVI*, p. 96.

5

Bilingualism, Hegemony and the 'Swing to Orthodoxy'

The Shaping of the Political Sphere (1860–1881)

Introduction

Until now we have discussed how colonial education and native press initiatives were important in establishing the structure of state–society relations and the arenas of political contestation.[1] Emphasising the artificiality of the view that sees developments in the colony as a 'later' aberration of Western ideals, our discussion has sought to analyse the specific nature of India's modernity, especially as it was shaped by the interaction between colonial policy and native initiatives. In doing this, the sequence and constituent elements of Western modernity have been invoked in so far as they provide historical and analytic points of reference, rather than as normative or political ideals.

Colonialism attempted to encapsulate the discourses of Western

[1]Colonial rule did not *replicate* the relation between the centralised modern state and its subjects as it evolved in the West. The term 'state-society relations' is used here to stress the difference through which modern political practices were disseminated within colonial society, resulting in a governmental structure that was, at once, alien and deeply intrusive. In describing the new political arrangements, vernacular discourse was forced to adapt and redefine analogous pre-colonial terms like *raja* (rulers) and *praja* (ruled): see pp. 242–4 below.

modernity into a pedagogic prototype. If colonial *liberalism* represented a dislodged and asymmetrical version of the metropolitan original, the rule of colonial *difference* applied equally to the emerging space for hegemonic articulation in India. In extending modern principles pedagogically, colonial power was not particularly interested in finding ways to *mediate* the contradictions it created. Its aims ultimately rested on pragmatic calculations to *prevail* over the disjunctures it had introduced by monopolising authority over regulatory norms. Thus, even while introducing irrevocable institutional shifts, the colonial-modern political order had restricted possibilities towards engendering a hegemonic discourse. This, in turn, limited the range of political options open to the local intelligentsia. Overdetermined by their proximity to the state and their minority status within society, their position was unlikely to be sufficiently hegemonic. And yet, as the preceding discussion on the possibilities for laicisation and the story of the native press initiatives has shown, neither the paradigm of dominance[2] nor of collaboration[3] adequately describes the complexity of the position of intellectuals and their political efforts. Thus, in speaking of the efforts of the intelligentsia to secure ideological influence, the terms hegemony/ hegemonic cannot be used in the strict Gramscian sense; allowance needs to be made for colonial difference, and this also fruitfully allows

[2]I refer here mainly to Ranajit Guha's thesis that colonialism in South Asia ruled through dominance without hegemony. In making his passionate, polemical response to the Cambridge School historians who sought to explain the colonial project as a collaborationist enterprise, Guha was, quite rightly, seeking to preserve the central charge of the illegitimacy of the colonial enterprise. But surely, one of the most tragic dimensions of the colonial encounter was the fact that Western imperial power was able to irrevocably reconstitute political hierarchies across many dissimilar social worlds, even while remaining aloof from their internal dynamic. The abiding ways in which colonial rule reinscribed political structures and norms on the subcontinent and their apparent capacity to outlast their colonial imposition requires us to re-examine questions about colonial hegemony. See Ranajit Guha, *Dominance without Hegemony and its Historiography*, Cambridge, Mass., 1999.

[3]Anil Seal, *The Emergence of Indian Nationalism: Competition and Collaboration in the Late Nineteenth Century*, Cambridge, 1968; John Gallagher, *Locality, Province and Nation: Essays in Indian Politics 1870–1940*, Cambridge, 1973.

the terms to be interrogated from the perspective of alternative, non-Western modernities. The use of these terms here is for the purpose of describing the ambitions of a group which, admittedly, did not enjoy political dominance, yet could use its closeness to authority to achieve a hegemonic position.

In proposing such a connection between the structure of colonial literate arrangements and the emerging pattern of political articulation in Western India, I admit the usefulness of the Habermasian idea of links between aesthetic norms and cultivated audiences through the bourgeois literary sphere and the liberal political sphere.[4] In Habermas' own work, however, there are suggestions about the limits of the emancipatory potential of the liberal public sphere, and on the extent to which this ideal conception of critical liberalism remained historically unattained even in the West.[5] Moreover, an important body of critical opinion[6] has pointed out that a significant flaw in Habermas' conception of the liberal public sphere is its unwillingness to admit the role of the bourgeois public in appropriating and marginalising more radical and inclusive notions of public participation and deliberation current in eighteenth-century Western Europe. In other words, a justified criticism of Habermas' notion of the public sphere admits its core theoretical value but expresses dissatisfaction with its readiness to abstract an ideal notion of the public at the expense of historical sensitivity.[7]

The colonial context provides yet another perspective on Habermas' valorisation of liberal communicative norms as a critical ideal. If, in keeping with the claims of the Enlightenment, bourgeois liberalism is to be understood as having established the possibilities of rational and consensual social communication in the West, surely its extension as colonial rationality profoundly challenged what is meant by a hegemonic ruling culture based on consensual reasoning. Arguably,

[4]See Jurgen Habermas, *The Structural Transformation of the Public Sphere: An Inquiry into a Category of Bourgeois Society*.

[5]Jurgen Habermas, 'The Public Sphere', *New German Critique*, Vol. 3, No. 49, 1974.

[6]See Craig Calhoun, ed., *Habermas and the Public Sphere*, Cambridge, 1993.

[7]See George Eley, 'Nations, Publics and Political Culture: Placing Habermas in the Nineteenth Century' in Craig Calhoun, ed., *Habermas and the Public Sphere*.

Habermas could posit the bourgeois public sphere as a normative ideal largely because, despite his concern with modern political processes, his work shows little interest in the structures of domination, marginality and contestation. Students of colonialism are hard put to ignore such questions of hierarchy when dealing with the history of ideas and political processes. Powerful representations that define entire societies and their cultural pasts as marginal were only too important to the sphere of colonial ideology and the transfer of modernity outside the West.

Foucault's work[8] has taught us much about complex contradictions between the principles of modern political rationality and their institutional effects in the West. If anything, the incongruity is more sharply borne out in colonial contexts where modern political discourses established themselves mainly through radical bureaucratic intervention. The colonial situation thus exemplifies the disjunction between bourgeois liberal principles and the ideological apparatuses that these have helped engender. Quite at variance with liberal claims, the formation of the colonial public sphere was premised on the ability of colonial power to devise permanent discursive and institutional shifts affecting the lives of whole populations in the territories it controlled, even while it engaged itself with very small groups within these societies. The construction of colonial power came about through its appropriation of the authority to alter the universe of ideas and social 'commonsense' on the subcontinent without needing 'consent'.[9] The durability of liberal ideology in the colonial situation thus owed

[8]Michel Foucault, *The Order of Things: An Archaeology of the Human Sciences*.

[9]Keeping in mind the role of colonialism in transferring political vocabularies current in most parts of the non-Western world, we have to admit the theoretical possibility that 'consent', in the full sense of the term, was secondary to the making of alternative modernities. If colonialism was an encounter between diverse and incommensurable social rationalities, it would be illogical to apply the criterion of consent to the 'acceptance' of colonial rule. It could not have been a question of consent by pre-existing individuals, for, characteristically, colonial power operated through imposing its own normative criteria, conceding little to the internal logic of the disparate social worlds it encountered and sought to penetrate. If the very procedures to create 'individuals' were part of the institutional arrangements of colonial power, the issue of consent could hardly have an analogous significance to its place within Western modernity.

more to the efficacy of the modern Western imagination to institute mechanisms that monopolised normative authority over cultural and political spheres, rather than to the 'innate' rationality of liberal political reasoning or its consensual communicative strategies. The crucial question, therefore, when interrogating Habermas from the perspective of post-colonial theory would be the apparent ability of the political logic of modernity to accommodate and survive in contexts inimical to the principles of liberal communicative reasoning.

The crucial role of colonial education in creating India's modernity also suggests the nature of relations between the structures of modern power and knowledge. Thanks to the enlargement of communicative networks alongside the growth of the market since the early modern period in Europe, the power to regulate the production and flow of communication acquired added political significance. With political authority no longer legitimated through ideas of divine sanction or privilege, ruling elites derived their status with reference to norms of general circulation and a self-reflexive social rationality. If modern knowledges based on 'superior' reasoning claimed to furnish general social truths, political modernity drew upon these to claim the advantages of general circulation and dissemination, especially for the purpose of establishing better-informed procedures of policy-making and control over subject populations. Discourses of individual improvement which, historically speaking, have been so vital to both modern subjectivity and capitalistic/political rationality, were only the obverse side of such values of general circulation. The Western bourgeoisie's claims to social leadership were thus built upon their overlapping ambitions to regulate the domains of cognition and culture, and their desire to control subjectivity through an ideology of improvement. Such tensions between actual control and a promise of betterment were intrinsic to the universalistic logic of liberalism, and to the internal differentiation of its economic, political, social and ideological domains. Implicit within modern political reason is this link between pedagogy and control, manifest in its most contradictory form within the colonial context.

If the dialectic between control and improvement was one characteristic of liberal ideology, another mark of the bourgeois character was the inverse relation between its support of egalitarian principles of general access and its control over the mechanisms of social and political power. The bourgeois classes showed an uncanny ability to forsake their advocacy of egalitarianism as they advanced in their quest for greater social and political influence. The swing in favour of greater social and political orthodoxy as liberal intellectuals assumed representative or nationalistic positions was not peculiar to the colonial context. However, within Western modernity, the emergence of egalitarian discourses in the last decades of the eighteenth century were founded upon developments that had yielded a secularised political structure over the previous two hundred years—these conditions were remarkably absent within colonial modernity. Shifts in the ideological positions of the colonial intelligentsia thus have to be theorised somewhat differently and understood in terms of the dilemmas and constraints that characterised their contexts.

Colonial Intellectuals, Hegemony and Orthodoxy

The trajectory of changes resulting from the colonial impact has been frequently described in terms of an 'initial' phase of *social reform,* followed by a period when efforts to organise an anti-colonial resistance led to the more 'mature' phase of *political reform* in the latter half of the nineteenth century. Granting that a distinction needs to be made between the early and later phases of anti-colonial consciousness, to mark these differences in this way is to accede to the gloss that nationalist discourse wishes to place upon its own pre-history. Evidence suggests that the actual response was far more complex than is suggested by such a binary division between a social phase followed by a more political one. Early local intellectuals did not see themselves as proto-nationalists, but that is not to say that their engagement with colonial rule did not show serious political concerns. To imply that political awareness about colonial rule emerged only with nationalism is a claim internal to nationalist self-narratives and needs to be questioned in reconstructions of the intelligentsia's attempts to assume a potentially hegemonic position. In the first few decades of colonial rule the intelligentsia were yet to contest the legitimacy of the colonial state and make concerted demands for a share in administration. Nevertheless, these intellectuals were driven to introspection by at least three aspects of the new political arrangements, namely (1) the provisions for publicity and standardised laws through which colonial power legitimated itself; (2) the political pre-eminence of the West arising from the expansion of knowledge from the early modern period onwards; and (3) missionary critiques of inequalities within the native social order. These areas suggested a discernible engagement with the *political* dynamic of the colonial encounter.

The Rebellion of 1857[10] precipitated shifts in the attitude of the colonial regime towards native society. Post-1857 major changes included the extension of the education project into a system of higher learning, which affected the position of the intelligentsia and the range of options open to them in negotiating the structure of colonial power. Recognising this and mindful of the general argument presented here about interlinkages between the cultural and political spheres, it seems pertinent to juxtapose this ideological shift (which accompanied the so-called 'transition' to the phase of political reform) with two other contemporaneous trends with which this is not usually correlated. The shift towards orthodoxy as 'political' activity gained precedence over 'social' reform also coincided with shifts towards conservatism discernible in the vernacular sphere, particularly at the point when vernacular literary forms approached their 'renaissance' from the late 1860s onwards. Indeed, if such shifts were a necessary prelude to an incipient nationalism, then the underlying constraints and political considerations that made an ostensibly 'mature' intelligentsia adopt more conservative social positions need to be probed. As these changes in the post-1857 period overlapped with the intelligentsia's attempts to claim a more representative position, it would be worthwhile to ask what bearing some of the internal divisions within society may have had upon the collective choices that intellectuals were making.

[10]While it was true that colonial intellectuals generally did little to show their disapproval of the administration's brutal repression of the insurgency, we need to know more about regional differences in the responses to the Rebellion. For references to an editorial about the rebel leader Tatya Tope by Bhavalkar in the Pune weekly, *Dnyanprakash*, see editor's Introduction in Bhavani Shankar Sridhar Pandit, ed., *Raosaheb Keshav Shivram Bhavalkaryanche Atmavritta*, p. 2.

A key element of this turn to orthodoxy from the 1860s was the intelligentsia's increasing reluctance to admit a commitment towards egalitarianism, especially in their critique of native social structures and practices. Having noted the difficulties in the creation of 'popular' literature in vernacular print culture, we need to probe the links between the internal discontinuities of the elitist project of colonial literacy, the intelligentsia's diminishing interest in egalitarian possibilities, and the emergence of a strong orthodox strain within native discourse from the mid-1860s.

The divisions created by colonial bilingualism affected the trajectory of the emerging reading publics, complicating the fissured ideological ground available to the colonial intelligentsia. But as local intellectuals became increasingly confident of the uniqueness of their position in negotiating the linguistic divide, their discourse gradually forsook even the minimal support it had shown to the principles of equal and universal access. We saw earlier that the bilingual relation, especially the intelligentsia's perception of it, had altered quite substantially from its representation in the first bilingual English-Marathi paper, *Bombay Durpan*. The press was not the only site where the intelligentsia's efforts to negotiate the linguistic divide became evident; the discontinuity between the English and vernacular spheres also affected their attempts, from the 1860s, to develop a regional network of political associations. Voluntary associations were first deployed to forge internal links between intellectuals, and then from the late 1860s they proved useful as a network of provincial *sabhas* to influence the course of colonial policy. The formation of the Sarvajanik Sabha in Pune in 1871, considered one of the important antecedents of nationalist consciousness in the Bombay–Pune region, showed that the political centre had shifted away from the Presidency capital to the 'vernacular' capital, Pune, by the 1870s. This indicates the importance of the vernacular sphere within a political structure based on quasi-representative principles. Our discussion will focus mainly on a hitherto little-known monthly Marathi journal published by the Sabha called the *Pune Sarvajanik Sabheche Masik Pustak,*[11] evidently started

[11]To the best of my knowledge, there are no references to the Marathi journal of the Sarvajanik Sabha in any of the existing writings on the political history of

to reach larger native audiences than its quarterly English counterpart could hope to. The publication of the English and the Marathi versions of the Sabha's journal as separate editions foreshadowed the logic that the launching of Tilak's *Kesari* and *Maratha* was to demonstrate more clearly—namely, the existence by around 1880 of two distinct, almost discrete reading publics in English and in the vernacular, neither of which could be ignored. Finally, some of Vishnushastri Chiplunkar's[12] writings from the 1870s, which are generally taken to mark the coming of age of Marathi prose and, as such, can be regarded as crucial to ideological consolidation within the vernacular sphere, will be examined. Some important essays in Chiplunkar's *Nibandhmala* indicate the vernacular intelligentsia's perception of the relation between English and Marathi at this crucial point within the development of anti-colonial consciousness.

In discussing Chiplunkar's work, my aim will also be to trace the

colonial Western India. The only journal alluded to is the *Quarterly Journal of the Pune Sarvajanik Sabha*, published from 1877 onwards, about six years after the Sabha was formed. Given its location in Pune and its evident intentions to mobilise wide support, it would be curious to assume that the Sabha did not consider publishing a Marathi journal. The Marathi journal was apparently started in September 1881: see announcement entitled '*jahiraat*', dated 1 September 1881, signed by the secretaries of the Sabha, back cover of the *Pune Sarvajanik Sabhache Marathi Pustak,* Vol. 1, No. 2, October 1881.

[12]Vishnushastri Chiplunkar's (1850–82) most important contribution to the making of modern Marathi discourse lay in his work as editor and writer for the important literary journal *Nibandhmala* that he published from Pune between 1874 and 1881. Known to have been an indifferent student, he completed his BA in English, Sanskrit and History from Deccan College in 1872 with some difficulty. In 1874, he began teaching at the Poona High School, but was not happy doing that. Before starting the *Nibandhmala*, Vishnushastri had contributed to the *Dnyanprakash* and the *Shalapatrak*, edited by his father, Krishnashastri Chiplunkar. In 1877, he established the Chitrashala Press to bring out inexpensive chromolithographs of historical and mythological images. The Aryabhushan Press opened in October 1880, from where the *Kesari* and the *Maratha* were published and he was a founding member of the Deccan Education Society, established around the same time. This summary is taken from the obituary that appeared in the *Maratha*: see 'The late Vishnushastri Chiplunkar: In Memoriam', *Maratha*, 19 March 1882.

political equations underlying the ideology of the 'mature' vernacular intelligentsia in the 1870s. There were ideological continuities between the literary politics of *Nibandhmala* and the next landmark in the story of the bilingual divide in the Bombay-Poona region—namely, the joint and simultaneous launching of the *Kesari* and the *Maratha* by Tilak and Agarkar in January 1881. Not the least of these links was the fact that these three men had been classmates and were, by then, close associates in these and related projects. *Kesari* was the first Marathi paper to reach anything like a mass audience,[13] and it echoed the ideological stances of *Nibandhmala*. This was particularly evident in two ways. Both *Kesari* and *Nibandhmala* showed that, given the difficulties within colonial modernity in forging mediatory links 'on the ground' through a network of *sabhas* and political associations, their editors realised the particular advantages of the press. That was one of the important reasons for both publications keeping up a virulent anti-lower-caste discourse. The *Kesari* and the *Maratha* reveal some of the divisions within the colonial public domain in Western India at a juncture which also saw the emergence of full-fleged nationalism.

Colonial Bilingualism, the Native Press and Questions of Hegemony After 1857

Once an arena of colonial publicity had been established, it was clear that it would be negotiated by native elites and be vulnerable to the logic of its own operation. In a little over a decade, officially sponsored attempts to involve a handful of native pandits and *shastris* in a collaborative project had already led to the first native initiatives to found vernacular newspapers. The size of the audiences for the new discourses

[13]In less than two years after it appeared, the *Kesari* put its circulation figure as 3500. Notwithstanding the fact that these figures cannot be taken as reliable estimates, the aggressive brand of journalism *Kesari* adopted gave it an edge and it enjoyed a larger reach than any other Marathi newspaper at the time. In the years leading to the textile strike of 1908, the *Kesari* claimed a circulation of 22,000, while the corresponding figure for *Maratha* was put at 11,000. See 'The Labour Movement and Development of Freedom Struggle' in I.M. Reisner and N.M. Goldberg, *Tilak and the Struggle for Indian Freedom*, Bombay, 1966, p. 435. See also fn. 105 below.

was a crucial concern. The main advantage that the vernacular sphere enjoyed over the dominant English sphere was its great numerical strength, which made it an important consideration within the calculations of the colonial state and, subsequently, in the making of an anti-colonial discourse. The intelligentsia's perceptions of the bilingual relation, especially prior to their self-consciously nationalist phase in the early 1880s, is thus an important means to analyse their attempts to acquire hegemony.

Dissemination vs. Representation: Colonial Intellectuals and Vernacular Production

To establish hegemonic influence within the colonial-modern political arena, the new intelligentsia needed to demonstrate their capacity to authoritatively represent collective opinions and identities. Dominance over the vernacular sphere was crucial to any such representational claims. If the intelligentsia forsook their earlier commitment to egalitarian norms as they moved closer to articulating a hegemonic anti-colonial discourse, this shift occurred in the context of their growing awareness of the importance of the vernacular sphere. The shift towards orthodoxy was most strongly reflected by the dominant strands within vernacular discourse which showed signs of intolerance as it entered its more 'mature' guise in the latter half of the nineteenth century. To attribute signs of narrow-minded anxiety to later vernacular discourse exactly at a point when it is supposed to have truly come into own would paradoxically seem to contradict its self-narrative. It would also challenge the accepted commonsense within nationalist historiography, where this period is usually described as the 'renaissance' of vernacular literatures. If the intelligentsia's earlier commitment to ideas of general access was demonstrated by their initiatives to extend reformist discourses, the shift to orthodoxy showed that they were less than eager to back non-hierarchical social principles as they moved closer to assuming a representative position. The difference in the intelligentsia's orientation before 1857 and after is a shift in their self-perceptions. In other words, this paradox could be more sharply expressed as the tension between the logic of dissemination and that of representation: the pre-1857 intelligentsia saw its main function as dissemination, a perception that receded as it grew more aware of its representative potential.

The first generation of pre-Rebellion intellectuals was much better placed when balancing its cultural pride with conceding the need for Marathi to 'learn' from English. Though troubled by the loss of sovereignty and by the 'immaturity' of Marathi in comparison with the European vernacular forms, the writings of the generation of Balshastri and Bhau Mahajan showed greater self-assurance in assessing the relative positions of the vernacular and English spheres. Two interrelated explanations come to mind. Firstly, in the early years of colonial rule the subordination of the vernacular sphere had not acquired the fixity of an irrevocable social hierarchy. The small public of 'reformed' individuals from colonial schools was still not differentiated into English and vernacular segments, as was to happen once the bilingual hierarchy was firmly embedded into the education system from the late 1850s. In other words the intelligentsia was not yet entirely aware of the full implications of internal fissures within their small numbers in relation to their position as political intermediaries and champions of reform. Secondly, although aware of their function as ideological links, the pre-1857 intelligentsia seemed less perturbed than its successors in later decades by the political consequences of their isolation. When early colonial intellectuals spoke of '*dnyanprasar*' (spreading enlightenment), they spoke from a position of assumed leadership. They could not have been unaware that they were writing for a small-sized literate vernacular public—of around a couple of hundred people at most[14]—or their

[14]In 1840, the total number of students in the Bombay Presidency enrolled in the vernacular schools was put at over 10,000, but that figure included students in the Marathi, Gujarati and Kannada classes. However, the number of persons who regularly read the weekly papers, or those who actually subscribed to one or more of the papers, would have been only a small percentage of this figure. For estimates of the circulation of the *Durpan* and Balshastri's periodical, *Digdarshan*, see chapter four, p. 195 and chapter three, fn. 52.

Complaints about the scarcity of readers and subscribers remained common in the press even until the end of the century. An article entitled 'Censorship of the Vernacular Press' in the *Quarterly Journal of the Pune Sarvajanik Sabha*, Vol. 1, July 1878, made the following observations on the limited influence of the vernacular press: 'The reading portion of the people form, it may safely be said,

own dependence on government; even so, their isolated position was not yet further complicated, as it was soon to be, by the need to actively 'back up' the legitimacy of their leadership claims through establishing the *representativeness* of their discourse.

Take for instance the case of the *Durpan*. Its avowed objective was to nurture native minds through the dissemination of 'useful' information, Western knowledge, and reports on significant developments in different parts of the world in order to promote habits of impartial, independent inquiry. Yet in its prospectus the *Durpan* did not actually emphasise its role as an intermediary which *represented* the general opinions of native society to government. The paper's linguistic policy showed it was not keen to foreground the linguistic asymmetry between English and Marathi or the fact that the two 'publics' it hoped to address were, in reality, largely discrete. In doing this, Jambhekar was underplaying the paper's status as an intermediary within the asymmetric colonial political hierarchy, for to admit this would have been to acknowledge the cultural and political subordination of the vernacular sphere and native society.

Thus, this generation of intellectuals saw their primary function as *dissemination*. They had not yet become aware of the political benefits that they, as a social class, stood to derive from their position as intermediaries. Being thus less concerned with foregrounding its representative position, early anti-colonial consciousness was less guided by instrumentalist political considerations in its advocacy of vernacular discourse. Early arguments for the 'cultivation' of the vernaculars show a greater disinterestedness, a lack of calculation about the importance of vernacular discourse. Soon, their self-conceptions about their political function began to alter: from seeing themselves as agents of dissemination to being representative spokesmen. A good example of this in the mid-nineteenth century is the introduction offered in the first issue of the *Dnyanprakash*, the important Pune weekly. Explaining the rationale underlying its publication, the *Dnyanprakash* said: 'Newspapers are not only the way to create bonds, but of conveying

an infinitesimal part of the ignorant and unenlightened masses, and of this reading portion, an infinitesimal part possesses any taste for newspaper reading.'

opinions among each other, of communicating information to the government, of uniting people for a common project (*udyog*) ...'[15]

Even while thus foregrounding its intermediary and representative role, the *Dnyanprakash* acknowledged its dependence on the English sphere by admitting it would need to gather most of its news from the English papers. In doing this, the contingency and derivativeness of vernacular discourse was being conceded in ways quite different from those in the *Durpan,* or in the later monolingual weekly *Prabhakar.* That is, having advanced their political claims by foregrounding their representative character over disparate and underprivileged groups, it seemed that the intelligentsia could now afford to admit the subordination of the vernacular sphere more openly. Curiously, they could do this even while deceptively giving vernacular initiatives a more 'autonomous' appearance by readily accepting the difficulty of sustaining a bilingual discourse. The *prastavana* also emphasised another aspect that was to became more evident in the coming decades, i.e. the intelligentsia's awareness of the relative weakness of other sites, such as voluntary associations and the market, for strengthening links to form impersonal social networks. On account of the limited scope of these, intellectuals had to rely largely on the press for social alliances, a point emphasized via Tilak's political project through the *Kesari* and the *Maratha.* By the 1850s, the press was no longer regarded simply as an instrument of *dnyanprasar.* Rather, it was already the instrument through which the results of the dissemination hitherto undertaken needed to be consolidated by accommodating and representing heterogeneous interests to the government. As the intelligentsia began to consider possible alliances towards hegemonic influence, they showed an increasing lack of enthusiasm for widening the discursive scope of the new *vidya.*

By the time vernacular discourse became preoccupied with developing a modern, literary aesthetic, the grounds for the arguments in favour of cultivating modern Marathi forms had altered from the concerns emphasised within early native discourse. An emphasis in the earlier

[15]Translated from Marathi, '*Prastavana*', *Dnyanprakash*, 1 February 1849, quoted in R.K. Lele, *MVI*, p. 91.

arguments had been upon developing vernacular vocabularies that would help the extension of a modern, socially self-reflexive, rationalist discourse. After the 1860s, the emphasis was on defining the norms for a 'high' vernacular literary canon of Marathi writing and its past. Such attempts to articulate a collective self-identity of the Marathi people were part of the vernacular intelligentsia's ambitions to *exclusively* assert its right to speak on behalf of the modern Marathi literate community. Efforts to define a relatively homogeneous, vernacular literary/cultural identity were part of the larger assertions of a predominantly upper-caste intelligentsia's representative claims over a numerically significant, non-English educated 'public'. Only by thematising the politics of bilingualism and the intelligentsia's attempts to span the linguistic divide to articulate a counter-hegemonic position, therefore, can the increasing orthodoxy of post-1857 native discourse be properly analysed.

The Making of an Anti-Colonial Alliance After 1857

Quite justifiably, 1857 is seen as a watershed in state-society relations. The provocations for the Rebellion of 1857 were complex and regionally diverse, but could at one level all be seen as a single political convulsion against the changes precipitated to serve colonial economic interests. After 1857 the regime decisively shed some of its earlier 'liberalism', adopting a stringent and increasingly centralised pattern in its policy on all fronts, including the areas of revenue, education and the press. The years after 1857 also saw a big increase in the investment of metropolitan capital in various fields. With Bombay emerging as a leading commercial city, a significant proportion of this was directed towards the Presidency capital.[16] However, it has been shown that by

[16]The mid-nineteenth century saw a rapid rise in the commercial traffic through Bombay. This was partly due to some of the foreign trade from Calcutta now being diverted to Bombay. The boom in the cotton market in the early 1860s also contributed to this increase. With cotton being paid for in bullion, the period saw speculative activity in the city reach a frenetic pace. Ambitious proposals for urban development schemes, such as those financed by the Backbay Reclamation Company and others to develop transport and communication networks, were taken up. For an account of the economic activity in the period, see the introductory chapters of Raj Chandavarkar, *The Origins of Industrial*

this time there were also signs of a small section of the native *seths* in Bombay reacting against the discriminatory constraints they faced in the export trade: they diversified into manufacturing for the indigenous market, notably the spinning of raw cotton.[17] The interests of this emerging lobby of indigenous entrepreneurs conflicted with the aims of colonial policy, which was to safeguard the interests of metropolitan capital.

Such shifts in the economic sphere coincided with changes in ideology which related to the establishment of the University of Bombay. The defeat of the rebel forces ended hopes for a resistance built around pre-colonial modes of political organisation and leadership. Although the intelligentsia's response to the Rebellion had been mainly one of silence or denunciation,[18] even when there had been implicit sympathy for the rebel cause there was little possibility of an identification of interests between intellectual elites and rebel leaders. By then the redefinition of the rural–urban divide under colonial rule had signif-

---

Capitalism in India: Business Strategies and the Working Classes in Bombay 1900–1940, Cambridge, 1994. See also S.D. Mehta, *The Cotton Mills of India: 1854–1954*, Bombay, 1954; M.D. Morris, *The Emergence of an Industrial Labour Force in India: A Study of the Bombay Cotton Mills, 1854–1947*, California, 1965; K.N. Chaudhuri and Clive Dewey, eds, *Economy and Society: Essays in Indian Economic and Social History*, Delhi, 1979.

[17]The first cotton mill in Bombay was established in 1854 as a joint stock company, with equipment imported from Manchester. This was the Bombay Spinning and Weaving Company floated by Cowasjee Davar, Maneckjee Petit and James London. The shareholders' agreement, dated 7 July 1854, was in Gujarati and was signed by more than fifty leading traders, most of them Parsis. The second cotton mill, the Oriental Spinning and Weaving Company, was floated in 1854 by a group comprising some of the leading Parsi, Jewish and *bania* magnates of the city. By 1865, there were ten cotton mills in the city, with many of them also producing yarn for handloom weavers. This summary is drawn from Raj Chandavarkar, *The Origins of Industrial Capitalism in India* and S.D. Mehta, *The Cotton Mills of India*.

[18]By the 1850s, many English papers in Bombay were partly owned by Parsis. One such paper was *The Bombay Times*, whose editor, a Scotsman, was forced to resign because of pressure from native shareholders over his writings on the events of 1857. Dinshaw Wacha, *Shells from the Sands of Bombay: My Recollection and Reminiscences 1860–75*, Bombay, 1920, p. 198. See also fn. 10 above.

icantly corroded previously existing ideological links between town and country, between pre-colonial urban and provincial intellectuals. As it became obvious that the colonial intelligentsia shared little common ground with the rebels of 1857, the situation seemed ripe for a restructuring of relations between the colonial state and the native intelligentsia, which in turn brought to the fore questions about the intelligentsia's own hegemonic aspirations.

Some efforts had been afoot in 1853 to organise a 'popular' political forum led by the formerly powerful *sardar* families of the Deccan.[19] Similar intentions to bring together the wealthy *seths* and colonial-educated intellectuals of the provincial capital in a common forum had resulted in the Bombay Association, established in August 1852. Although the Association had organised petitions to the British Parliament, the alliance was fraught with tensions, and the intelligentsia had to remain content with a subordinate position.[20] But with the reconfiguration of relations between the administration and native society after 1857 and the investment of native capital in industrial production, the possibilities seemed favourable for a rapprochement between indigenous entrepreneurial interests and the aspirations of the bureaucratic intelligentsia. When attempts were made to revive the Bombay Association in 1860, the executive committee was still dominated by *sethia* elements, but it was also clear that, on account of their legal expertise, the intelligentsia now enjoyed greater weight and influence as intermediaries and their claims could no longer be as easily dismissed.

The collapse of the cotton market in 1865 saw a steep increase in food prices and rent, leading to rising discontent among the lower and intermediate ranks of the bureaucracy. As a containment strategy, the government announced reform measures to re-organise the Bench of Justices, the body in charge of the city's administration, into the new Municipal Corporation. The intelligentsia used this opportunity to mount a press campaign to publicise their demands for more substantial

[19]N.R. Phatak, *Nyayamurti Ranadeyanche Charitra*, Bombay, 1924, p. 185.

[20]See Christine Dobbin, *Urban Leadership in Western India: Politics and Communities in Bombay City 1840–1885*, London, 1972, pp. 79–86.

political reform and an equitable tax structure. They employed their familiarity with colonial administrative and legal structures to demonstrate their clout and demand a greater influence on political fora. As a result, by the late 1860s the managing committee of the Bombay Association included a significant number of law graduates like V.N. Mandlik, B.M. Wagle and other university-educated figures like Ranade and Bhandarkar.[21] There had emerged an elite sub-section of the colonial intelligentsia consisting of lawyers, pleaders and other administrative personnel who, over the previous two or three decades, had worked their way into senior bureaucratic positions. Enjoying a privileged stability, this budding class of professionals also capitalised on financial opportunities in the stock market boom of the early 1860s.[22] The events of 1857 had shown that colonial authority would have to be challenged on its own ground, through a use of the political vocabularies of liberalism. Realising this, the post-1857 intelligentsia showed its 'maturity' through an increasing willingness to regard the emerging class of native capitalist entrepreneurs as potential allies in the ideological struggle to contest the legitimacy of the state. But, given the absence of representative channels, this challenge needed to be symbolically staged through available public arenas like the press.

[21]'Proceedings of the First Annual General Meeting of the Bombay Association, 1869', p. 8; 'Minutes of Proceedings of the Third Annual General Meeting of the Bombay Association, 5 October 1871', p. 10, cited in Dobbin, *Urban Leadership in Western India*, p. 89.

[22]Bhau Daji Lad's (1822–74) career is a good example of the profile of this generation of colonial intellectuals. Born in a *saraswat* brahmin family, he went to Elphinstone College and later to Grant Medical College. He was one of the city's first medical graduates with an influential practice. He played a prominent part in the setting up of the Bombay Association and had close links with Jagannath Shankarseth, its President. Bhau Daji was keenly interested in music and theatre and patronised troupes visiting the city. He was also associated with the Paper Manufacturing Company established in Bombay in 1854. Having invested heavily in the cotton boom of the 1860s, Bhau Daji suffered serious financial setbacks when the market collapsed in 1865. See Dobbin, *Urban Leadership in Western India*, p. 79 and p. 131 and A.P. Priyolkar, *Bhau Daji Lad: Vyakti, Kaal, Kartutva*, Bombay, 1971.

Native Press Initiatives After 1857

The press became an important site for this set of graduates and lawyers to demonstrate their critical intermediate position. As briefly noted earlier, unlike the previous generation of native newspapers that emerged in the 1840s, all the three major weeklies that appeared in the 1860s and the 1870s, *Indu Prakash*, *Native Opinion* and *Subodh Patrika,* were bilingual. The small circle of well-placed, university-educated, bureaucratic professionals mentioned were closely associated with each of these press initiatives. Although all these three newspapers, and from 1863 onwards the older *Dnyanprakash* too,[23] used both Marathi and English, they did so in a way that was quite different from what the *Durpan* was attempting.

In adopting a bilingual policy, a key aim was to reach a diverse readership. But in not rendering all published items in symmetrical and equivalent bilingual columns, as the *Durpan* had done, these later papers implicitly admitted the existence of two virtually discrete audiences to whom non-identical sets of messages needed to be directed, and who needed to be addressed simultaneously, but separately, in English and Marathi. The layout of these papers acknowledged an irrevocable ideological divide between the English and vernacular spheres. It was usual for these papers to publish the main news of local events and important announcements of government appointments in Marathi. The Marathi articles were mostly meant to show the intelligentsia's familiarity with the state of affairs in the provinces and articulate views on measures to improve the condition of subaltern sections. The important Marathi articles to appear in the *Subodh Patrika* over 1879-80 included pieces on '*Hindustantil shetkarkaryatil halli nikrusthavastha va tee sudharnaechi upay*' (the depressed condition of Indian agriculture and ways to improve it);[24] '*Lokanche agyan*' (the ignorance of the people);[25] '*Ingrez lok*' (which discussed the important qualities of the British character, including their enterprise and drive);[26]

[23]R.K. Lele, *MVI*, p. 96.
[24]*Subodh Patrika*, Vol. 7, 8 June 1879.
[25]Ibid., 22 June 1879.
[26]*Subodh Patrika*, Vol. 7, 3 August 1879.

and '*Deshi karkhanyas uttejana denyache avashyakta*' (the need to encourage native industries).[27] However, important policy measures and government decisions, important court cases and appointments of natives to positions of high rank, opinions expressed in the Anglo-Indian press (especially about the native papers), were all reviewed in English. As against this, important public events, especially those concerning the 'cultivated' sections of the Marathi community like the meeting of the *Marathi Granthotejak Sabha* (Meeting for the Promotion of Marathi Publications)[28] or the first annual prize distribution function of the *Pune Stree Vakrutatvatejak Mandal* (The Association for Promoting Elocution among Pune Women)[29] or the Governor's reception attended by two hundred and fifty native *grahasthas* (gentlemen) were reported in Marathi.[30] But a lecture delivered by Keshab Chundra in London was reported in English,[31] as was the report on the *Gujrati Dnyanprasarak Mandali*.[32] Similarly, Shivnath Shastri's discourse on the Hindu religion at the Bombay Prarthana Samaj was reported in the Marathi pages, but his lecture on moral education at Elphinstone College found mention in the English section.[33] What these simultaneous and selective uses of language in the public domain underlined was the fact that the intelligentsia were developing their role as mediators.

In trying to do this through the newspaper press their underlying strategy was not so much to aim for a wider audience for the radical discourses of modernity, and even less to seek alliances with popular bases of discontent towards colonial rule. Instead, they preferred to employ their privileged educational training to publicise their own particular assessment of colonial power as a way of securing political influence. As the *Native Opinion* put it:

> The task of the native newspapers and political associations is identical to the role of the Opposition in the House of Commons in Parliament

[27]Ibid., 6 July 1879.
[28]Ibid., Vol. 8, 22 February 1880
[29]Ibid., 29 June 1880.
[30]Ibid., 6 July 1880.
[31]Ibid., 20 July 1880.
[32]Ibid., 8 February 1880.
[33]Ibid., 14 October 1880.

in England. That task is of critically examining government policy to suggest improvements, by removing those parts that will not be to the benefit of the people, and also by ensuring speedy implementation.

These associations ought to carefully study the particular issues, gather diverse relevant information on the nation as well as on what are the possible and desirable improvements, and this will surely earn it considerable political influence.[34]

Several examples show that, from the 1860s, the main thrust of the intelligentsia's discourse sought to consolidate its own claims to speak with the colonial government on behalf of the 'entire' native community. A long essay on 'English and Native Rule in India'[35]—serialised in the *Native Opinion* during the first half of 1868 and presumably the work of Vishwanath Mandlik (the well-known Bombay lawyer who also edited the paper[36])—was published as a response to a proposal by the viceroy to initiate an official inquiry into his own dearly-held view that the Indian 'masses' were more prosperous and far happier in British

[34]Retranslated into English from a Marathi version of the original English item in the *Native Opinion*. See *Native Opinion*, 3 April 1870, quoted in Marathi in G.R.Havalder, *Raosaheb Vishwanath Narayan Mandlikyanche Charitra*.

[35]*English and Native Rule in India*, Bombay, 1868.

[36]Vishwanath Narayan Mandlik (1833–89) was born in a *chitpavan* brahmin family in Ratnagiri. He studied Sanskrit at home before going on to the local Marathi school and the Ratnagiri English school. He came to Bombay in 1848. He was active in the Students Literary and Scientific Society and held various positions in the bureaucracy of the Education Department before passing the High Court Pleader's examination in 1863. He was the Government Pleader between 1874 and 1884, the Chairman of the Municipal Corporation in 1879 and the Dean of Arts in the University of Bombay in 1889. As a well-established, legal professional and government bureaucrat of his time, Mandlik was an advocate of administrative reform that would allow the intelligentsia a greater influence in political affairs. Thus, although Mandlik's views conflicted with those of the *sethia* lobby in the Bombay Association, his stance on many social and political issues of the time tended to be quite conservative. He opposed the Khoti Settlement Bill of 1879, which aimed to hand over rights to tenants in the Konkan. Similarly, he had strong reservations about Malabari's Bill on the age of consent. In arguing against the use of legislation to regulate social conduct, Mandlik anticipated some of the orthodox positions Tilak would soon take.

territory than they were under states ruled by Native Rulers.[37] Mandlik's piece was a detailed, soberly-worded polemical exposition on the relative merits and defects of the situation in the territories administered by native princes and those under British rule. One of his main purposes in setting up this comparison was to initiate critical discussion on colonial government and invoke the possibility of self-rule. A criticism of the claims of colonial power was in itself not new to the native press, nor was the earlier criticism lacking in self-assurance. But it is interesting to compare the anti-colonial sentiment of the 1840s[38] with the thrust of these arguments advanced in the post-1857 period. As Mandlik's piece showed, the newness lay in the intelligentsia's willingness to temper and 'adjust' their critique of colonial power in ways that could advance their own potential to displace it. Their claims were to an intimate knowledge of 'native opinion' and a close familiarity with the forms of modern governance. Bilingual papers constantly emphasised their intention to work alongside the colonial administration, reiterating that their criticism was meant to acquaint the government with the views of the native community. Such an accommodating attitude towards the state was unlike the balanced but forthright criticism that pre-1857 native papers like *Prabhakar*[39] directed, both towards the administration and native practices. Such a conciliatory tone was not surprising. On account of their proximity to the administration and their elitist training, the intelligentsia could boast of few cultural or ideological means to forge concrete social and political bonds within native society. In keeping with their aim of questioning the legitimacy of the colonial state through their professedly representative opinions, all these papers appeared from the provincial capital, Bombay, even as they publicised their claims to be 'widely circulated in Bombay and the Mofussil'.[40]

[37]*English and Native Rule in India*, p. 3.

[38]Bhaskar Pandurang Tarkhadkar wrote a series of eight long letters under the pen name of 'A Hindoo' in the *Bombay Gazette*, between 30 July 1841 and 27 November 1841. For more details of Tarkhadkar's letters and the critical tone of the early vernacular papers, see chapter three, pp. 129–31 and fn. 39 below and chapter four.

[39]See chapter four, especially pp. 195–6.

[40]The full text of an advertisement for the *Native Opinion* read: NATIVE

Despite such proclamations, reading audiences were quite small and certainly not large enough to represent a sufficiently lucrative commercial possibility to attract substantial capitalist investment. And yet this generation of important post-1857 newspapers enjoyed a degree of longevity that had not characterised native ventures till then.[41] By the 1860s the intelligentsia had acquired a relative financial autonomy which allowed it to invest collaboratively in such a crucial series of important publishing ventures.[42] These papers were not commercially viable, self-sustaining ventures[43]—indicated by the fact that both *Indu Prakash* and *Native Opinion* changed hands several times because of losses. But they were able to continue without significant interruptions, besides being able to employ editorial personnel on a quasi-regular, contractual basis.[44] The papers were run by men of relatively inde-

---

OPINION, AN ANGLO-MARATHI JOURNAL. Published every Sunday Morning and WIDELY CIRCULATED IN BOMBAY AND THE MOFUSSIL, Terms of subscription: Annual subscription in advance ... Rs 15. This advertisement appeared on the back-cover of the above-mentioned booklet, *English and Native Rule*.

[41]See chapter four, p. fns 144–7 and preceding text.

[42]Writing to Col. Jacob in 1859 about the difficulties of sustaining a native public discourse, Mandlik observed that although the intelligentsia harboured such aspirations, they lacked the means to back their plans, whereas those who possessed the means had no interest in such matters. Paraphrased from Mandlik's letter dated 9 January1859, quoted in G.N. Havaldar, *Raosaheb Mandlikyanche Charitra*, p. 193.

[43]In the beginning each edition of the *Native Opinion* had a print run of 500 copies. According to Mandlik's biographer the total monthly cost for producing the paper was Rs 695, of which monthly salary expenses for the editor/manager, clerk and caretaker were Rs 200, Rs 15 and Rs 8 respectively, and printing costs amounted to Rs 474. See G.N. Havalder, *Raosaheb Mandlikyanche Charitra*, p. 195.

[44]In an entry in his personal diary dated 24 December 1863, Mandlik emphasised the need to bring out a standard native paper. He added that the financial cost could not be a deterrent in this important task. He argued that in order to administer India well, the wise and benevolent British Government needed information that only the natives could supply. To carry out this critical task of bridging the gap between the rulers and their subjects through the communication of an 'independent' and educated opinion to the government, the *Native Opinion* was even prepared to incur financial losses. Evidently, such 'public views were not synonymous with representative opinion. For, as Havalder

pendent means who were convinced of the political significance of their efforts and could keep these ventures going despite inadequate revenue.

While confirming Habermas' general insight into the interconnections between the literate and political spheres, this evidence challenges his implicit belief in the fundamental rationality and consensuality of such connections within a bourgeois liberal order. For it is evident that, despite the elitist limits of colonial reading audiences, the intelligentsia was not only able to assert a representative status but could do so even while declining the burden of cultivating a large readership. This rather wrong-foots Habermas' thesis about the exercise of modern political power being intrinsically founded on rational and consensual communicative norms.[45] The colonial public sphere could yield a relatively homogeneous discourse with potentially hegemonic dimensions less through the processes of discussion and accommodation, more through the virtual exclusion of counter-discourses in the domain of cultural production.

Despite occasional differences, the three main bilingual papers advanced a set of internally consistent ideological strategies. The similarity in background of the figures involved has been noted. In a politically uncertain situation, where the state often relied on judicial amendments to secure its position, lawyers, as semi-independent professionals, were in a particularly advantageous position to wield influence through their understanding of the intricacies of bureaucratic power. In particular, lawyers and subsidiary legal bureaucrats were closely associated with efforts to articulate and publicise a body of anti-colonial opinion from the 1860s. It was not simply coincidental that Ranade, Mandlik, Tilak, Agarkar, and G.V. Joshi all had varying degrees of training and experience in the legal profession, besides making critical editorial and entrepreneurial contributions as press-men. One of the self-pro-

---

argued, the *Native Opinion's* position was safeguarded mainly because its editors were men of independent means and the paper did not have to depend on revenue earned from readers, See ibid., pp. 195–6.

[45]'Political Functions of the Public Sphere' in J. Habermas, *The Structural Transformation of the Public Sphere*, esp. pp. 82–5.

claimed objectives of *Native Opinion* was to publicise the judgements of the Bombay High Court to provincial readers. This gave the paper an increased circulation among the *vakils* of subordinate courts in *mofussil* areas, especially after the Copyright Act had made it difficult for local papers to carry translations of reports first published in the Bombay papers.[46] The predominance of *moffussil vakils* among the leadership of the local-level political *sabhas* that soon emerged showed that such efforts to reinforce links between the elite and the provincial members of the legal bureaucracy had paid off. Given the circumscribed political space available to the intelligentsia, their preferred strategy for consolidating anti-colonial opinion was emerging as a textualist exercise which could, ostensibly, be approached and 'settled' through the presentation of learned arguments arrived at through meticulous research.[47] Much of the important writing in the native press during this period, including 'English Rule and Native Opinion', subscribed to this method. Whether or not this was inevitable within the formative circumstances of colonial modernity, the approach showed the potential to reinforce elitist anti-popular tendencies that informed the intelligentsia's discourse after 1857.

Textualist Strategies, Upper-Caste Hegemony

As many scholars have noted,[48] such moves to insinuate a predominantly upper-caste cultural bias into the agenda for the reform of native society according to modern principles alienated major sections which did not identify with the hierarchical preferences of brahmanical

[46]G.N. Havalder, *Raosaheb Mandlikyanche Charitra*, p. 200.

[47]*Native Opinion* 3 April 1870, quoted in ibid., p. 211.

[48]Practices like *sati*, prohibition of widow remarriage and seclusion of women were mostly customary to upper-caste groups, who used them as signs of their 'superior' status and exclusivity. However, both before and during the nineteenth century, such practices were adopted by upwardly-mobile groups while attempting to claim a higher ritual status. For an account of how such caste-specific practices were publicised through the upper-caste reformist agenda, see Rosalind O'Hanlon, *A Comparison Between Men and Women: Tarabai Shinde and the Critique of Gender Relations in Colonial India*, Delhi, 1994, and also Lata Mani, 'Contentious Traditions: the Debate on Sati in Colonial India' in Kumkum Sangari and Sudesh Vaid, eds, *Re-casting Women: Essays in Colonial History*, New Jersey, 1990.

Hinduism. At one level, the foregrounding of upper-caste norms within the reformist programme was meant to help new intellectuals secure their position *vis-à-vis* the traditional intellectual elite. In the absence of prior secularisation, and because of the limited spread of colonial-modern literacy, print had also helped to reinforce the authority of traditional brahmanical texts by making them more generally available. Additionally, the vernaculars needed to draw upon the linguistic resources of Sanskrit in developing standardised forms and lexical repertoires, which again renewed Sanskrit's normative influence. Moreover, realising the need to contest the authority of the traditional brahmanical elite to interpret *shastric* and religious texts, intellectuals engaged in frequent public debates on exegetical issues to 'demonstrate' that the high Hindu texts implicitly approved of specific issues on the reform agenda. Often, these colonial brahmins were also associated with efforts to produce authoritative versions and commentaries of such texts.

The emergence of modernity in the West, too, had seen analogous processes whereby the high texts of Christianity had been authoritatively reproduced in printed vernacular editions. But as colonial modernity had not led to the creation of large-scale reading publics, these processes of scriptural transfer from oral to printed forms did not correspond with the dissemination of the idea of a laicised knowledge into social commonsense. Textual production, whether of traditional texts or in the new vernacular forms, continued to remain largely in the hands of traditionally literate, upper-caste groups. In fact such groups were able to assume that their control over channels of textual and cultural production would be *sufficient* to re-negotiate their pre-eminence within the emerging public domain. Recognising that the audiences for new literate practices were small, and that their control over the new processes of textual production represented precious cultural capital, the intelligentsia aspired to rationalise the reform project almost exclusively on the supposed authority of 'ancient' texts. But if traditional Hindu texts were to provide a point of arbitration, this logic led to a reform agenda that would not fundamentally challenge the principles of hierarchical difference within traditional *jati samaj*. It was in this way that the traditionalist textualist strategy of the upper-caste reformist elite only served to further contain the possibilities of a laicised cultural order. Thus, by the late 1850s, upper-caste native discourse showed an increasing wariness of general access[49] and an unwillingness to critique the fundamentals of indigenous hierarchies.

After 1857, once the intelligentsia had renounced their nominal support to radical principles of general access, they were free to foreground 'secondary' issues like widow re-marriage, the issue of the appropriate education for girls, and the age of consent as important to the reform agenda. These and similar questions were crucial to the rearticulation of patriarchal power, and these debates surely opened up emancipatory spaces and even empowered social movements. But dealt with in this way, the questions largely remained problems to be 'worked' out without challenging the fundamentally hierarchical nature of the social structure. The 'reform'-oriented discussion in all the post-1860 weekly papers betrayed this reluctance to question the principles underlying *jati samaj*. It was not coincidental that those who owned or wrote for the press and those involved in the several, formally staged, protracted public debates with 'orthodox' *shastris* all came from a small but apparently highly-visible elite. Despite the small size of reading audiences, by virtue of their almost exclusive control over the channels for making and distributing the new discourses, a small homogeneous elite achieved a hegemonic influence for their opinions. It was thus that the absence of voices from diverse social strata within the colonial public sphere, the elitism of the colonial intelligentsia, and the excessively textualist and increasingly conservative biases of their discourse came to reinforce each other. All of this, while seeming like grist to the mill for Habermas' core insight into the nature of the links between modern culture and politics, also questions his model of the public sphere.

Advancing Hegemonic Claims and Disclaiming Difference

Even as native press initiatives after 1857 tried to circumvent the political consequences of bilingualism, native discourse showed signs of an increasing reluctance to discuss the bilingual divide in a forthright manner. The intelligentsia's growing self-consciousness coincided with

[49]See chapter three, pp. 136–7.

a tendency which moved from candidly analysing irreconcilable splits within the native literate community towards a reluctance in later writing to admit these ruptures. Increasing awareness of the conditions under which they could assume a representative position led colonial intellectuals to disavow the political significance of the linguistic divide, or even the asymmetry between educated and uneducated segments. Apparently, especially in the matter of access to privileges and opportunities, heterogeneity was seen as antithetical to the professed representativeness of their discourse. This shift is manifest in the writings of Moreshwar Kunte,[50] an interesting intellectual figure of the post-1857 period who deserves more attention. His ballad, *Raja Shivaji*, won a prize from the *dakshina* committee, almost at the same time that one of Phule's manuscripts was rejected by the committee.[51] Kunte published the first part of the poem in 1852, with the explicit intention

[50]Moreshwar Kunte (1835–88) was born in a poor family at Mahuli near Satara. He and M.G. Ranade were fellow-students in the Kolhapur English High School from where he matriculated in 1859. He completed his BA from Bombay University in 1864. He was appointed as the Headmaster to the Karachi High School, where he studied Sindhi. In 1867, he returned to Kolhapur, as the Headmaster of the Rajaram High School. While in Kolhapur, he studied Sanskrit, especially *alankaarshastra,* and music. He was the first Indian to be appointed as the Headmaster at the Poona High School, serving in that position for a total of sixteen years. During this period, he also did brief stints as Professor of Sanskrit, as the Acting Principal at Elphinstone College, and at the Ahmedabad College. Besides, he served on the Pune Municipality.

His ballad on *Raja Shivaji* was his first Marathi composition, which won a prize from *dakshina* committee. His poem *Dnyan Hech Mukhya Sukh* (On Knowledge being the Foremost Joy) was published in the *Dnyanprasarak* in 1862. His English poems included *The Rishi* and *The Famished Village*, the latter based on the experience of the famine of 1876–77. He also published his treatise on *The Reform Question* in 1871, but his main contribution to the nationalist discourse was his *The Vicissitudes of Aryan Civilisation in India*, Bombay, 1880. Not surprisingly, the *Kesari* paid rich tributes to Kunte's scholarship when he died in October 1888. This summary is taken from the Introduction, S.S. Bhonsle, ed., *Raja Shivaji,* Aurangabad, 1992, pp. 5–54.

[51]The manuscript of Phule's play, *Tritiya Ratna,* had been rejected by the *dakshina* committee in 1855. Similarly, the 'high' literary journals like *Vividhdnyanvistaar* pointedly ignored Phule's work, claiming it did not conform to current literary and linguistic norms.

of contributing to the paltry store of published literature in the vernacular, but significantly he prefaced it with an English account that analysed the state of vernacular writing.[52] His preface offered a perspicacious and detailed description of the cultural and linguistic ruptures created through colonial education and their implications for vernacular production, especially in introducing the possibilities of a laicised culture. In placing his literary efforts before the 'public', he felt impelled to reflect upon divisions in the literary 'taste of his countrymen'. He saw that contemporary ruptures did not correspond with traditional divisions along lines of *jati:* 'The inhabitants of Maharashtra, including Brahmans, shudras and others may be divided into three classes in reference to their taste (1) The Shastris and those whom they guide. This class is large.[53] (2) The educated, that is those who know English.[54] (3) The uneducated; *especially those who are indifferent to the Shastris or the educated'.* (emphasis added)

These boldly-offered schematic remarks led him to consider the possibilities of contact and conflict between pre-colonial and current literary practices and norms. In the process, he made some telling observations on the displacement of old norms through the entry of

[52]Moreshwar Kunte, Preface to Part One, S.S. Bhosle, ed., *Raja Shivaji*, pp. 1–15.

[53]Elaborating on the characteristics of this category of intellectuals, Kunte wrote: 'Our *shastris* have doubtless exercised an important influence on the literary taste of our countrymen; nor is their education contemptible. There is enough of excellent Sanskrit literature to enable our *shastris* to be acute critics. But their taste is affected. Instead of waiting to see how one large general argument or sentiment is developed, and how general arguments and remarks are brought to bear on the evolution of a particular feeling, they expect something artistic in every couplet; and they look for excellence and interest in the elementary subordinate ideas rather than in the combined effect. They also draw a broad line of demarcation between the *Puranas* and poems. The former are the Ramayana and the Mahabharata while the latter are by Kirata and Magha and others. ... [but] it is too late to attempt to write a poem on the model of Kirata or Naishada.' See ibid., pp. 2–3.

[54]About the English-educated, Kunte observes: 'Next to the *shastris* in numerical strength but far superior to them in intelligence and in such power as intelligence imparts, come our educated country-men. Their taste is improved; their understanding is enlarged; their judgement is generally correct and formed after consideration; and their minds are free from prejudices.' Ibid., p. 3.

English and the implications of new cultural norms and practices for vernacular writing:

> Accustomed to read English, thoroughly sensible of what English poetry is, and competent by their education to enter into the feelings of English authors. ... But such is not the case with Marathi; though it be their vernacular. Here they find raw materials, uncouth expressions and a versification to which, perhaps, their ears are not accustomed. A *shastri* does not consider a poetical line to be tolerable, till it is considerably stuffed with Sanskrit words; for pure Marathi grates upon his ears. Here there are two facts—*the fact that the educated do not find Marathi tolerable, and the fact of the Shastris looking down upon it. Nothing is common to these two classes except that they do not labour at Marathi and cultivate it; but that they look at it from a Sanskrit or an English point of view.*[55] (emphasis added)

However, the task of intellectual analysis was not identical with the challenge of advancing political possibilities. What could be acknowledged within the former exercise could jeopardise the representative claims that the intelligentsia wished to make. Thus, a few years later, writing about the strategies that the intelligentsia needed to adopt to manoeuvre its way across the cultural and social divides, Kunte was unwilling to admit the disruptive effects of colonial education. His remarks in Part II of his English treatise of 1871, entitled the 'Reform Question', form a striking contrast to the prefatory essay of 1852 discussed above. The later piece is an assessment of the benefits of British rule and deliberates upon ways to strengthen representative contact between British rulers and native society so as to minimise the political liabilities of a 'foreign government ruling over a dependency'. Like Mandlik's long essay in *Native Opinion,* Kunte acknowledged the intelligentsia's strength as being their ability to claim greater proximity to the 'native people' than the British government.[56] The prospect of consolidating their position when contesting the legitimacy of colonial rule made the intelligentsia unwilling to publicise the internal divisions

[55]Ibid., p. 4.

[56]Kunte, *Reform Question II*, Bombay, 1871, pp. 18–39.

within native society. Kunte's otherwise astute analysis of the political changes introduced through colonial rule is marked by a questionable disclaimer of the political advantages accruing to those who enjoy access to colonial education. Crucially, it was only in English that such a disavowal, asserting a dubious transcendental equality between those who had access to English and those who did not, between the uneducated 'many' and their educated spokesmen, could be made. Thus in 1871 Kunte claims:

> The class of educated has come into existence. I am not willing to make any distinction between the educated and the uneducated, so far as political questions are concerned; and a distinction is not tenable, for, an examination, based more on the strength of mind than on the amount of knowledge crammed, will not fail to discover that the uneducated in some cases really know more than many educated gentlemen. Whether educated or uneducated— the terms being used according to the flippant usage of the present time— there are many natives throughout India who strive for the good of the country, and the purity of whose conduct and the nobility of whose aspirations are ill-rewarded by the nation which does not understand them and by rulers who cannot condescend to appreciate them.[57]

The post-1860 press reported on a range of themes that had not been altogether absent from earlier native discourse. However, both university-educated intellectuals who were part of the English sphere and the class of vernacular intellectuals gave the impression that they were no longer seriously persuaded by ideas of egalitarianism and open access. This can be illustrated through references to the writings in Chiplunkar's *Nibandhmala*, considered the very epitome of the Marathi literary 'renaissance' of the 1870s. *Nibandhmala* acquired a reputation for its efforts to define and publicise the criteria for literary taste and modern prose style in Marathi. But alongside such considerations of the norms of 'high' literary taste and cultivation, a characteristic element in the discourse was the virulent attack on attempts by subaltern groups to mark their presence in the sphere of literate

[57]Ibid., p. 11.

production. Some of the tensions between attempts to articulate a homogeneous collective identity and the possibility of an inclusive discourse were echoed in the intelligentsia's efforts to create a regional network of political associations from the 1860s.

Colonial Bilingualism and Political Associations

A crucial tenet of liberalism, the principle of voluntary association had brought together individuals with shared interests to form the large impersonal collaborative networks characteristic of modern societies. Such bodies that enabled individuals to share and further a limited but identifiable set of interests have sustained the division of modern life into separable, cohesive domains such as the economic, intellectual, political or aesthetic. The ensuing division of knowledge into expert disciplines has been crucial to defining a space for modern intellectuals to articulate a hegemonic position.[58] Inevitably, associations show a different trajectory in the colonial world. The discussion on education policy[59] showed that modern principles of voluntary association were first invoked in the colonial world as part of the organisational design of the education project. These principles were employed by the Bombay Education Society to bring together natives and officials as part of a collaborative forum for ideological purposes. Liberal associational principles were thus introduced in the colonial context to formalise a sphere of ideological collaboration between native elites and the colonial government. These associations were important in determining the modes through which colonial power could be approached as well as how elites would relate to their social world. Alongside this extension of associational principles, colonial rationality introduced the modern disjunction between the economic/material domain and the sphere of ideology and intellectual production. Colonial discourse had worked with a number of powerful binary assumptions about native and Western social and cultural practices; the displacement of the complex differentiation characteristic of

[58]See Zygmunt Bauman, *Legislators and Interpreters: Modernity, Post-modernity and Intellectuals*.

[59]See chapter two, p. 63 and pp. 66–8.

capitalistic modernity only further complicated the legacy of the various hierarchical underpinnings of colonial discourse and policy initiatives.

Associations and Consolidating Links Between Upper-Caste Intellectuals

Voluntary associations helped the intelligentsia to consolidate internal bonds amongst themselves. These bonds helped set up a powerful discursive dynamic which identified large sections of their compatriots as the 'unreformed' Other, proceeding from which diagnosis colonial intellectuals could offer themselves as most qualified to take various social and ideological initiatives. These processes can be traced through reference to the Students' Literary and Scientific Society, the first important association of native intellectuals established in Bombay in 1848. At a later stage the intelligentsia was able to exploit the organisational possibilities of voluntary associations to create an extended provincial network of *sabhas* that would link them with their 'schooled' allies, especially *vakils*, teachers and newspaper editors in the *mofussil* areas, as well as native professional and trading classes tied to the colonial economy or state.[60] Such efforts resulted in the formation of the Sarvajanik Sabha, one of the earliest precursors of emergent nationalism, established in Poona by 1870.[61] Until then, the region-wide political alliance between the colonial-schooled public had only been implicit in the readership networks of native newspapers;

[60]There were eleven *vakils*, five *seths*, five schoolmasters and two newspaper managers among the forty names in the list of attendees at the Second Annual General Sabha of the Thana Zillah Association, held at the Government English School, Thana, on 20 February 1870. See Proceedings and the Report of the Managing Committee of the Thana Zillah Association in G.B. Joshi, *Gelya Tees Varshapurveeche Lok va Tyanchya Samjuti*, Baroda, 1896, pp. 188–93.

[61]Similarly, *vakils*, *sardars*, traders, money-lenders and school-masters figure prominently in the list of 139 members and officers of the Sarvajanik Sabha. The Sabha aimed to enlarge its representative scope; Rule No. 3 explained that only those who could obtain signatures of at least 50 adult men from any caste or community in a specified locality would be eligible as members of the Association. See *The Constitution of the Poona Sarvajanik Sabha and its Rules*, Poona, 1871, pp. 9–10.

the emergence of the Sabha was one of the first concrete manifestations of the extended network that backed the intelligentsia's representative claims.

The Students' Literary and Scientific Society, established as an extra-curricular forum between past and present students and the faculty of Elphinstone College, figures prominently in accounts of the emergence of a liberal imagination in Western India.[62] In these accounts it is not very apparent that such societies also demarcated boundaries between 'reformed' colonial intellectuals and the large 'unreformed' sections of native society. Colonial associations allowed this new, 'improved' intellectual elite to articulate lessons they had internalised through contact with colonial discourse into a pedagogic vision to reform the social practices of their 'uninitiated' fellow countrymen. The predominantly textualist approach that the intelligentsia adopted to political questions arising out of the processes of modern dissemination showed that the pedagogic emphases within colonial discourse had been firmly embedded into the intellectual make-up of native intellectuals. This pedagogic orientation seems clear in the objectives of the Students' Literary and Scientific Society: 'The objects of this Society are two-fold; first, the improvement of individual members in English Literature and Science, and secondly, the dissemination of knowledge, amongst the natives of this county by the establishment of Schools, especially GIRLS SCHOOLS, and by the publication of periodicals in the vernacular languages of the Presidency'. (Emphasis in original text)[63]

Mirroring the professedly apolitical postures of colonial ideology, the society's rules disavowed its transformative intentions by stating that the Society's activities would categorically exclude 'all subjects of a religious and political character'.[64] Yet in stating its aims thus, the

[62]Christine Dobbin, *Urban Leadership in Western India*; Jim Masselos, *Towards Nationalism: Group Affiliations and the Politics of Public Associations in Nineteenth-Century Western India*, Bombay, 1974; Ravinder Kumar, *Western India in the Nineteenth Century*, London, 1968.

[63]'Rules and Regulations of the Students' Literary and Scientific Society' reprinted in *The Report for the Session of 1862–63*, Bombay, 1863, pp. 50–5.

[64]Ibid., p. 54.

Society presumed a pragmatic and utilitarian orientation to the social world.

By 1856 the Society had acquired a total membership of 190, including 38 non-residents from outside Bombay. The Society's main constituency comprised individuals who had direct links with Elphinstone College, with a few members who belonged to mercantile offices on the island.[65] Despite its small membership, through its discussions and publications the Society intended to disseminate a normative discourse to the rest of native society. Bearing in mind its proximity to the colonial administration and the need to 'reform' native science and literature,[66] the Society was entrusted with the responsibility of 'voluntarily' supplementing official pedagogic efforts by producing an appropriate corpus of printed literature in English and the vernaculars. The English Society had two subsidiary vernacular branches, the Marathi Dnyanprasarak Sabha and the Gujarati Buddhivardhak Sabha, with their respective committees to solicit and examine vernacular contributions. These tasks were to be carried out under the strict and exclusive supervision of Society Members.[67] Although in principle contributions from 'all quarters' were to be welcomed, these would have to be ratified by a sub-committee appointed to 'examine the language of each paper before it [was] finally sanctioned for printing'.[68] Thus it would seem from the Society's Proceedings for 1852 that the basic moves to secure the active participation of the colonial intelligentsia as ideological intermediaries were already in place:

> It may naturally be supposed that we look forward with great interest, and with no small anxiety, to the result of this first attempt to supply

[65]'List of Members, Resident and Non-Resident on 10 June 1856' in *The Report of the Students' Literary and Scientific Society for 1856*, Bombay, 1856, pp. v–xi.

[66]*The Third Report of the Students' Literary and Scientific Society and of its Vernacular Branches*, Bombay, 1852, p. 18.

[67]On 18 August 1851, the Society adopted resolutions to form two vernacular committees. Two Europeans, Professsors Paton and Reid, were requested to guide the committees, 'as the present state of science and literature and the immediate requirements of the people of this country, may seem to demand'. See ibid., p. 18.

[68]Ibid., p. 18.

> the people of Western India with a series of papers designed and composed by individuals sprung from among themselves, who with correct ideas regarding the character of their tastes, and the state of their knowledge, combine a degree of interest and sympathy which Europeans cannot pretend to entertain.[69]

This association between official discourse and intellectuals endowed the latter with a tremendous sense of moral superiority *vis-à-vis* their brethren. To them, the Society represented an arena befitting their own aspirations as harbingers of a 'colonial enlightenment'. The strong pedagogic aspect within such elevated self-perceptions is exemplified in the following report:

> We have now located all the schools in clean airy apartments; supplied them with school furniture, with pictures, with maps, and with school books compiled expressly for the purpose; placed them under the instruction of intelligent and enthusiastic teachers; and appointed superintendents from among our own body to visit and examine them: and what have been the results? Disheartening beyond measure as far as the Hindu portion of the community is concerned. *The great majority of the indolent Marathas for whose benefit the greatest exertions have been made still allow their children to figure in those vulgar exhibitions that are so constantly to be witnessed in the island, of a few wretched urchins huddled together in a dismal room ... squatting around a puntojee, himself half-naked and stupid and jabbering away mysterious paragraphs in barbarous Marathi* [*of which*] *neither they nor the teacher, who professes to be able to enlighten them can explain two consecutive sentences.*[70] (emphasis mine)

Despite tensions governing the transfer of liberal norms through colonialism, such ideas of voluntary association between persons of equal status were opposed to the organisational principles of native society, especially the practice of *jati*. This clash between divergent social rationalities was played out over many sites, but, on account of its importance to the making of a hegemonic discourse and the vernacularisation of liberal principles, this applied most importantly

[69]Ibid., p. 19.
[70]Ibid., p. 21.

to the emerging arena of associational politics. As concrete means to create enlarged social networks, the associations could have extended the new cultural and political discourses to non-schooled or pre-literate audiences. But, as the story of associational politics showed, there was an almost complete identity between the colonial literate public and the membership of colonial associations. Associational principles in the colonial situation actually helped reinforce the divisive and exclusionary pressures generated through colonial education. This enhanced the sense of homogeneity and political purpose that members perceived in the Society's activity early on:

> These discussions, in addition to the obvious advantage which they afford students, in the way of mutual improvement, by inviting them to consider and to argue questions of immediate interest, and of great practical importance, have also the useful effect of bringing and keeping together the former and the present students of the college. We are convinced that many of our band—some of them gentlemen holding important public posts—who never would have joined us had we, instead of entering the arena of actual life, and oiling our limbs to struggle with obstinate facts, held formal meetings to discuss some obscure point in the international law of Europe or to consider the comparative merits of two or three dead men in ancient times.[71]

And yet, as suggested, the intelligentsia's increasing political self-consciousness went hand in hand with conservatism: as political bonds approached formalisation, the intelligentsia grew more protective about its exclusivity. A comparison between the ideological orientation of early associational fora like the Students' Literary and Scientific Society with that demonstrated by contemporaneous early vernacular publications like *Durpan* and *Prabhakar* bears out this point. Whereas the latter had shown a definite inclination to publicly criticise the principles of

[71]The following remark was added in a footnote: 'At the commencement of this Society in June 1848, many predicted that, as in former societies of a similar kind, our time would be wasted in such idle discussions as whether "Brutus was justified in killing Caesar?" a subject which excited keen debate in the old society on the ruins of which the present society was founded': quoted from ibid., p. 17.

jati,[72] colonial intellectuals within the arena of associational politics showed marked reluctance to take the critique of traditional hierarchies on board. The greater homogeneity within such voluntary organisations allowed the emerging intelligentsia to discern the political potential of designating the rest of society as constituting an 'unreformed' inferior; whereas, being a more open and public medium, the native press needed to show greater engagement with social reality. Thus anticipating the general trend that later native discourse would take post-1857, the Society showed a preference for 'secondary' issues that had more to do with the redefinition of native patriarchal structures—like the establishment of schools for (upper-caste) girls—rather than risk challenging the fundamental hierarchies of *jati*. The only organisation willing to challenge caste barriers in practice was the Paramhansa Sabha, which, despite having several branches in Bombay and the outlying areas, kept itself outside the public realm by deliberately working in a cabalistic way.[73]

The reformed intellectual elite being such a small set, participation in the clandestine Paramhansa Sabha, alongside association with the native press and membership of the Students' Literary and Scientific Society and its vernacular branches, was bound to overlap significantly. And yet, while the critique of *jati* could enter the public domain in a limited way in the pre-1857 vernacular press, it was not a part of mainstream native public discourse and never concretely entered upper-caste initiatives in the arena of associational politics.[74] These nuances and levels of political complexity cannot be accommodated within the Habermasian ideal conception of the bourgeois liberal public sphere. The evidence within colonial modernity seems to strengthen the case made by Habermas' critics, who have emphasised

[72]See chapter four, fn.130 and preceding text.

[73]For more on the Paramhansa Sabha, see chapter four, pp. 159–60, esp. fn. 25.

[74]The Paramhansa Sabha was disbanded in 1867, when some Bombay papers carried letters threatening to publicise its membership. Notably, the issue of caste distinctions entered the public domain only with the formation of the Prarthana Samaj in 1868, but only as a belief in the transcendental equality and brotherhood of all mankind.

that bourgeois notions of voluntary association actually belong to a wider social and historical context that saw the rise of plural traditions of reasoned exchange. The liberal model, in fact, sought to marginalise these through applying a strategic closure upon the range of possible participants in public arenas.

The ideological shift in the second half of the nineteenth century can only be explained as a trajectory of political choices made by the intelligentsia from among a horizon of communicative and ideological possibilities. The ideological trajectory of the Student's Literary and Scientific Society traced here reinforces the general argument about the links between the homogeneity in caste backgrounds of the new literate agents, the increasing closure and textualisation of the reform project, and the intelligentsia's repudiation of even a nominal endorsement of ideas of open access and general entitlement.

The Emergence of Political Associations

Efforts to organise ground-level networks of 'representative' opinion began from the mid-1860s. Well known for their contributions to the native press, prominent figures like Ranade and Vishnushastri Pandit attempted to mobilise region-wide support for the issue of widow remarriage through personal correspondence, visits, hand-bill campaigns, and lectures directed at groups which gathered in the local native library or in provincial schools.[75] These efforts were followed by the work of G.B. Joshi[76] who, in the late 1860s, travelled through the districts around Bombay, especially Thana, to form a network of provincial *sabhas* as the organisational basis for the intelligentsia's claims to represent public opinion. However, the pedagogic paradigm, with its implicit codes of hierarchy, remained the dominant metaphor

[75]N.R. Phatak, *Nyayamurti Ranadeyanche Charitra*, pp. 140–5.

[76]Govind Baba Joshi (1826–1906) was a Pleader from Vasai. He founded the Vasai Association in 1862, and the Thana Zillah Association in 1867. He maintained a journal as he travelled, explaining the importance of such a network and establishing local *sabhas* wherever possible. This diary was published in 1896 as *Gelya Tees Varshapurveeche Lok va Tyanchya Samjuti athva Majhe Pravasachi Hakikati (Rojanishi)*, translatable as 'A description of the views of people thirty years ago, or a daily account of my travels'.

within these efforts to produce larger, collaborative political networks. Moreover, these organisational efforts had to span ideological and linguistic divides; discussion of hegemonic strategies will show that these efforts did little to radically undo the markedly textualist character of the intelligentsia's approach until then.

Two significant pieces explained the need for and advantages of such organisational networks to the 'uninitiated'. Both these were in the form of a dialogue between educated, upper-caste spokesmen for liberal ideas and ordinary, 'unreformed *lok*'. The first is taken from a semi-autobiographical account by G.B. Joshi, based on a diary he maintained as he travelled tirelessly through the province to organise an extended associational network. The second is an article published anonymously, but possibly the work of G.V. Joshi,[77] secretary of the Pune Sarvajanik Sabha. Entitled '*Navin adhikar ani tyanchya sambandhane kalpilela samvad*', it appeared in the important vernacular journal published by the Sabha from Pune from 1881, the *Sarvajanik Sabheche Masik Pustaka* (the monthly journal of the Sarvajanik Sabha).[78] In the face of rising discontent on account of successive years of drought, in the late 1870s and early 1880s the colonial government came up with proposals for local self-government. Although the second piece was written a few years after the first, both can be viewed as a projection of the intelligentsia's self-perception and interests at a point when moves to establish a rudimentary structure for native representation seemed imminent. Forced to confront the provincial constituencies on whose behalf they had already been making representative claims, these writings provide telling insights into the mobilising strategies that the intelligentsia adopted. They also reveal the ironic meanings

[77]Ganesh Vasudev Joshi (1828–80) was born in a poor family in Satara. Not having gone to College, he had only a working knowledge of English. However, he had passed the Examination for Pleaders and was well-versed in colonial law. This helped him in establishing the Pune Sarvajanik Sabha in 1870. Joshi was active during the famines of 1876–77, sending out the Sabha's agents to collect information from the drought-hit districts, which was later publicised through the Sabha's journals. Joshi represented the Sabha at the Delhi Darbar in 1877. In 1879, he defended Vasudev Balwant Phadke for his part in the *ramoshi* insurrection of 1878.

[78]See fn.11 above.

that the logic of colonial liberal representation assumed, especially its claims to enable an egalitarian distribution of political power. Both articles show that initiatives to create such networks stemmed from the intelligentsia's need to acquire a notional familiarity with provincial conditions to back their claims for a greater share of senior appointments in the administration. In return the intelligentsia offered to explain various laws to the ryots and unlettered rural folk, thereby acquainting them with an unfamiliar and alien political regime. However, the vernacular intelligentsia was quick to realise the difficulties they would face in applying the logic of voluntary associations towards creating such a provincial network, the most important being that the logic of voluntary associations presupposed the emergence of departicularised identities, which could scarcely be presumed in the colonial context. This left intellectuals with no option but to enact their quest for hegemonic bonds as a displaced, symbolic staging of difficulties in their writings.

The first of such writings envisaged a meeting between an 'ordinary' but politically aware villager (*gramasth*) and an old-fashioned village elder (*gramsisth*), with the former trying to impress upon the latter the urgent need for *sabhas* uniting 'respectable' residents of the village. The argument is that there is evidence of even the lower orders, including the 'unlettered' and the 'ignorant', adopting such modern organisational modes.[79] The imaginary dialogue includes a *nibandh* (essay), written especially to be read out as the protagonist/Joshi moves from house to house to explain the nature and purpose of such *sabhas*. The piece was evidently intended to act as a pre-formulated response to anticipated questions. Given the radical disjuncture between the logic of *jati samaj* and associational politics, it would seem that attempts to bridge social divisions could only proceed from such deliberate explanations. Indeed, implying that having ready answers to possible objections was tantamount to reconciling the underlying asymmetries only reinforces the argument about the textualist approach adopted by the intelligentsia towards securing hegemony. The *nibandh* told its audience that *sabhas*

[79]'*Sabhyans vinanti*' in G.B. Joshi, *Gelya Tees Varshapurveeche Lok va Tyanchya Samjuti*, p. 15.

were needed to arrest the material, political and technological decline of the province and that their efficiency derived from their ability to express the considered opinion of the collectivity.[80]

Appearing in the context of the need to enlist support for the limited elections to local bodies, the second article valorised the influence of the public opinion / popular will, emphasising how modern political relations reversed the old master-servant relation between *raja* and *praja.*[81] Power now rested with the collectivity; both *satta (*legitimacy*)* and *shakti* (power) derived from *jamav* (unity).[82] In colonial society, such unity had to be forged through strong leadership. The question of appropriate leadership was thus all-important, and both the articles under discussion deal with it at some length. In the first dialogue the audience is told that discussions in the *sabha* would range from general administrative issues (*sarkari rivajsambandhi mahiti*) to local, village-related concerns (*gramstithi sambandhi vichar*). They would take into account ways of securing the advancement of knowledge/education (*vidyavruddhi vichar*) and consider social customs and practice (*lokrit*i *vichar*).[83] Given the range of matters that were bound to come up before the *sabha*, the leader (*sabhapati)* would need to be doubly equipped, he would need to be a scholar capable of resolving conflicts about dharma according to the authority of the *shastras.* He would also need to be qualified in matters pertaining to the present political situation and modes of administration.[84] Realising that it would be rare to find a person with such expertise in all these domains, the *nibandh* suggests it might be best to divide the functions between two separate 'executives': the *dharmashastradarshak,* who would be well-read in the *vedas* and *dharmashastras;* and the *vyavahaardarshak,* who would have a good

[80] '*Sabha sthapan honyachi avashyakta*' in ibid., pp. 4–7.

[81] *Baithak dusra-raja mhanje kaay va tyancha adhikaar. Hallincha raja va praja hyanchya samjuteet pharak-uttam rajyapadhathi konti*, in '*Navin adhikar ani svatantrasmabandhe samvad*', *Pune Sarvajanik Sabheche Masik Pustak*, Vol. 2, No. 10, August 1883, pp. 21–46.

[82] Ibid., p. 42

[83] '*Sabhet konkonte vishay nighanyache*' in G.B. Joshi, *Gelya Tees Varshapurveeche Lok Va Tyanchya Samjuti*, p. 8.

[84] '*Sabhyas vinanti—dusara divas*' in ibid., p. 21.

grasp of official procedures, in addition to being knowledgeable on commercial matters.[85] Clearly, one of the aims of such *sabhas* was to establish a hegemonic structure that joined the authority of 'traditional' brahmanical discourses with a command over modern modes of economic and bureaucratic power.

Posed in this way, the objective hardly seemed to be to extend the *sabha's* influence by making it more inclusive; rather the emphasis was on *conserving* control over access to political power. Thus, although in theory it was hoped that the local *sabha* would be a collective, representative forum open to anyone who wished to come, in effect we learn that in the interests of discipline and order the sabha proposed to proceed with 'at least five or six representatives from each [important] caste'—like the *prabhus, vanis*, and *gaud saraswat* brahmins.[86] Those who were likely to be unruly, disruptive or ill-equipped to speak would be kept out. Order and decorum would be maintained by following the system of nomination and by prescribing strict rules to govern the functioning of the *sabha* from start to finish. Almost parenthetically, a concluding remark expressed the hope that 'people from these and other *jatis* as well would form a *sabha*'.[87] Modernity's displacement as pedagogy is quite apparent here, because of which colonial associations could never mirror society in microcosm. As Phule was keenly aware,[88] they remained conglomerates of educated individuals.

Within the colonial situation, various institutions of civil society were first established as 'extensions' of the apparatus of state. The second dialogue gives insights into the nature of emerging political equations through which the intelligentsia hoped to become influential. The

[85] '*Sabhapateenche sadharan gun*' in ibid., p. 26.

[86] Ibid., pp. 7–13.

[87] Ibid., p. 13.

[88] Phule was severely critical of the representative claims of reformist organisations and political associations like the Pune Sarvajanik Sabha. He persistently drew attention to the fact that these organisations were made up of upper-caste lawyers and clerks, making it impossible for farmers, labourers and other under-privileged, lower-caste groups to participate or have their interests represented through such *sabhas*. See Phule, *Shetkaryachya Asud* (1873) and *Sarvajanik Satyadharma Pustak* (1891), reprinted in Phadke *et al.*, eds, *MPSV*, esp. pp. 306 and 492.

intelligentsia revealed its complicity with official colonial discourse most especially when, in the course of approaching 'unreformed' rural audiences, they endorsed the colonial government's paternalistic claims of having a benevolent interest in the political education of natives.[89] This dialogue as well as the other reports show that a large part of the activities of the Sarvajanik Sabha proceeded with the approval and support of the official machinery,[90] reinforcing the point that colonial associations did not open out possibilities for a more even distribution of power. They led to a consolidation of the authority and collaboration already in place through six decades of colonial rule.

One of the most interesting features of the second piece is its symbolic display of the position of urban intellectuals (*Pune va Mumbai shahratun vidvan lok)* within these provincial networks. Evidently these mediators of a vernacularised liberalism did not belong to the milieu they wished to represent. Rather, they materialised on the scene quite miraculously, falling into the midst of the exposition on representative government and staying just long enough to 'explain' new proposals from the government to 'ordinary' people (*ryots/lok).* [91] Despite internal divisions within colonial society, the intelligentsia's position to mediate between town and country, peasantry and bureaucracy, and agrarian and urban interests remained unique as well as virtually uncontested within the colonial public sphere. The dialogue also shows links in the ideological chain extending between the provincial capital, Bombay, and the remote village. It was Rambhau, the provincial intellectual,

[89]While speaking of the benefits of representative government, Raghunathrao, the city-bred intellectual, explained that it would be best if the entire body of subjects (*praja*) selected a few intelligent representatives to make and administer laws. The English had realised that the welfare of the peasants could not be assured under any other system of government. It was now the intention of the benevolent and wise colonial government to provide such a system for natives too. Translated from G.B. Joshi, *Gelya Tees Varshapurveeche Lok Va Tyanchya Samjuti*, p. 42.

[90]See the accounts on the efforts of the Sabha's agents to collect information on the various districts in '*Sabhene kelelya kamachi report*' in *Pune Sarvajanik Sabheche Masik Pustak*, Vol. 2, Nos. 6–7, February–March 1882, pp. 73–80 and in Vol. 2, No. 10, June 1883, pp. 178–82.

[91]'*Navin adhikar ani svatantrasmabandhe samvad*', *Pune Sarvajanik Sabheche Masik Pustak*, Vol. 2, No. 10, August 1883, p. 31.

recognised in the village as hailing from 'nearby' Pune, who initiated the general discussion with a handful of people on the provisions for popular sovereignty within modernity, carrying on until it was time for the urban intelligentsia to descend upon the discussion at a crucial juncture, accompanied by the full array of local government officials. At this point the actual elaboration of the government's proposals for limited native representation at the local level was left to English-educated intellectuals from Bombay, who also explained how the imminent measures were modelled on the principles of rule-of-law and consultative government followed by the British House of Commons.

Even if awkwardly, the colonial intelligentsia had, thus, successfully negotiated the complex disjunctions between secular/religious, pre-colonial/modern moral and political codes by apparently accommodating both indigenous and modern normative structures within their discourse, thereby rendering traditional scholars irrelevant to their hegemonic enterprise. The *vedas* and *dharmashastras* were no longer invoked as possible reference points to settle disputes over 'traditional' matters in the later article. By this time, *dnyanprasar* was no longer on the agenda; instead one of the main objects of the reformist discourse was what was perceived as the overwhelming fatalism or apathy (*daiyvavaad*) of the 'ordinary' native, especially the peasant. The peasant needed to be galvanised out of his apathy through a new philosophy of action and enterprise. The only 'traditional' text that seemed important at this point was the *Gita*—its exhortation to immediate and unceasing action was considered pertinent in arousing an unresponsive, indebted, depressed peasantry![92]

However, even within this controlled staging of the intelligentsia's mediatory functions, there were signs that its position was insecure. Faced with the inevitable question about why the full parliamentary system of government was not practised in India, the intelligentsia responded with the classic liberal-gradualist answer of the majority

[92]Ibid., p. 42. Tilak, too, was especially interested in the Gita, on which he wrote a detailed commentary, *Srimad Bhagvadgitarahasya athva Karmayogashastra*, Pune, 1915. Unlike their predecessors, such as Vishnushastri Pandit, Ranade or Mandlik, Tilak's generation did not find it ideologically important to engage with a larger corpus of traditional texts.

being as yet 'unprepared' for full political status.[93] Until then, the right to vote and the eligibility criteria for candidates for the small number of municipality seats to be opened up to native representatives would be restricted to university graduates, *vakils* who could produce a certificate of their status from the High Court, medical and engineering professionals, jurors, assessors, and those paying an annual tax or drawing a government pension of or above Rs 20. Similarly, in the case of *taluka* committees, these rights would be given to those paying an annual tax of at least Rs 38, local *patils,* and police personnel.[94] Given the adoption of such obviously exclusive criteria for defining the 'political' public, the government's main duty was described as maintaining law and order. The corresponding duty of the people was to recognise the legitimacy of the ruling power 'at all times'.[95]

By the 1880s the ideological collaboration embarked upon by the colonial state had yielded an influential region-wide network of interests that identified with the logic of the colonial-modern political and economic structure. As ideologues for this alliance of interests, the intelligentsia were the chief proponents of a discourse that internalised the disjunction between the material and ideological aspects of the colonial enterprise. The creation of an apparently separable ideological realm provided the space to establish other disjunctions that characterise modern discourses—the separation of the aesthetic, the political and the moral into discrete cognitive domains. Despite serious contradictions, these could apparently coexist, as will be seen below in the writings of Vishnushastri Chiplunkar.

The second article discussed above showed that English was indispensable for securing a position of control within colonial-modern politics, but a command of English was not a sufficient condition if this was to *translate* into a position of political advantage and hegemonic influence. This paradox was not lost even upon those who had to reconcile themselves to living without the means to acquire English.

[93]'*Navin adhikar*', *Pune Sarvajanik Sabheche Masik Pustak*, Vol. 2, No. 10, August 1883, p. 67.

[94]Ibid., pp. 54–7. Women could also vote if they fulfilled the above conditions, but they could not hold the office of commissioners.

[95]'Ibid., p. 27 and also p. 77.

Realising that ordinary folk would not be granted the vote as part of the current proposals, one of the peasants in the above dialogue is heard telling the city-bred *ingrezi vidvan* (English intellectual) with great poignancy that, 'in the present times, you people are [like] our eyes',[96] thus reminding the latter of the responsibilities they carried via their knowledge of English. The Sarvajanik Sabha's decision to start a monthly journal in Marathi in 1881, ten years after the Sabha first emerged and three years after it began publishing its quarterly English journal, pointed to the intelligentsia's realisation of the significance of the vernacular sphere and the need to maintain visibility within it.[97] But alongside, they had to acknowledge 'the great number of persons in this region who do not know English'.[98] By this stage there was precious little that the intelligentsia could do to make a concrete difference to the linguistic divide, but even less could they afford to ignore it. Neither the extension of the social base of the literate public through education and translation, nor a political resolution of conflicting interests through consensus and accommodation seemed concrete, realisable options any longer. That the upper-caste intelligentsia had given up any substantial commitment it might have had towards laicisation was borne out in the concerted campaign launched through the native press[99] in anticipation of the Education Commission's sittings in 1882

[96]Ibid., p. 70.

[97]See announcement entitled '*Jahiraat*', dated 1 September 1881, signed by the secretaries of the Sabha, back cover of the *Pune Sarvajanik Sabhache Marathi Pustak*, Vol. 1, No. 2, October 1881.

[98]Ibid.

[99]For a summary of opinions expressed in the *Dnyanprakash*, *Kesari*, *Maratha*, *Native Opinion*, the Gujarati weekly *Rost Goftar*, see weekly Native Newspaper Reports filed between February-July 1882. In an article entitled 'Primary Education and Indigenous Schools', the *Quarterly Journal of the Pune Sarvajanik Sabha* argued in favour of the greater claims of the middle classes to higher education saying, 'It is the middle, or rather the hereditary literate and mercantile about [*sic*] 10% of the whole population which appreciate the present system of instruction, and in the work of Indian regeneration, the real work belongs to this class of society. They alone can furnish the teachers who will undertake the work of popular education. India's present circumstances require that their class agencies should be allowed to operate freely in all directions, and it becomes as much the duty of government to help the middle classes obtain higher education as to assist the lower to secure

and in the depositions[100] made before it. The upper-caste intelligentsia unanimously disapproved of the government's plans to curtail the funds allotted to higher education for the purpose of extending primary education.[101] By 1885 the ostensibly 'moderate' Sarvajanik Sabha[102] joined the public protest by the upper-caste intelligentsia and the press[103] against

primary instruction.' *Quarterly Journal of the Pune Sarvajanik Sabha*, July 1882, quoted in *Native Newspaper Report* for week ending 21 October 1882.

[100]Many established, upper-caste figures asked to testify before the Commission were candid enough to admit that primary education had not spread evenly among all communities. But fewer were willing to admit that lower-caste students had to face discrimination from upper-caste teachers and students in the government schools. Moreover, all of them were unanimously opposed to measures that would affect the access of upper-caste students or government allotments to higher education. See '*Evidence taken before the Bombay Provincial Commission and Memorials Addressed*', Vol. II of the *Report of the Bombay Provincial Committee of the Education Commission,* Calcutta, 1884.

[101]Reviewing the report of the Education Commission, the views of the *Maratha* of 18 November 1883 were fairly representative of the intelligentsia's position at that point. The report was glad that 'the Commission has not committed the blunder of over-estimating the importance of primary education at the expense of collegiate education. We are induced to think that the spread of elementary education on any extensive scale is hopeless, unless great encouragement be given to Collegiate education. ... We must have a great number of Collegiate Institutions in order that the enlightened students turned out by them, from year to year, may carry the light of the education to the remotest and most secluded regions of popular ignorance.'

[102]The Sarvajanik Sabha came into existence on 2 April 1870, the Hindu New Year day, through an assembly called to look into the alleged mismanagement of funds of the *Parvati* temple in Pune. The meeting comprised of elected representatives supported by residents in and around Pune. Almost 6000 signatures had been obtained, allowing the Sabha to claim that 'the formation of the Sabha on an elective basis clearly shows that the principle is almost ingrained in the Indian mind and is not a plant of foreign growth.' The Sabha intended to act as a mediating body between the Government and the people. Ranade played a crucial part in the Sabha especially until it split in 1895, after which it came under Tilak's leadership.

[103]See 'Correspondence on the Subject of the New Free Studentship Rules', in the Letter from the Secretary of the Sabha, dated 25 November 1885 to Mr. Lee-Warner, to the Acting Director of Public Instruction, published as 'Proceedings of the Sabha' in the *Quarterly Journal of the Pune Sarvajanik Sabha,*

the Bombay Government's decision to reserve a quota of free studentships intended for students from lower-caste backgrounds. The hopes of consolidating public opinion were thrown back upon symbolically staged efforts through the discursive arena of the press, for those were less likely to be constrained by irreconcilable ground-level differences that impeded the making of associational networks. If anywhere, the power of colonial discourse was evident in its capacity to construct irreconcilable differences that defied any ultimate resolution, and which could only be displaced as antagonistic but contingent forces within the public sphere.

In emerging as a major figure, Tilak showed keen awareness of this potential of inflated publicity within colonial public domain, especially in the launching of *Kesari* and *Maratha* in 1881. Above all, control over numbers and publicity was crucial within colonial representative politics. The editors of *Kesari* and *Maratha* realised this only too well, which was the reason they claimed a large increase in readership every few months.[104] Despite the difficulties of establishing reliable estimates for the colonial reading public, these papers, acutely aware of the politics of publicity, were among the earliest in Western India to achieve anything like a mass impact.[105] But even before that, the

---

Vol. 8, No. 4, 1885, pp. 30–42. The Sabha protested that the recent decision to reserve a quota of the government free-studentships and reduced-fee studentships was 'impolite and unfair' for 'singling out brahmins, and setting them against other classes, as representing opposite interests.' It further noted, 'There is ...a higher consideration of principle involved. The Government schools are open to all classes alike under the noble policy that has hitherto been followed. This privilege implies that all the advantages of free and reduced-fee studentships shall be equally open to poor boys from all classes, without distinction of caste, race and creed. This is the cornerstone of the British system of government in all its branches, and the educational department cannot take on itself to lay down any rules by which particular castes or creeds shall be favoured or discouraged.'

[104]See fns.13 above and 105 below.

[105]It is not easy to estimate the actual circulation of these native papers. Being keenly aware of the politics of enumeration, native editors were wont to exaggerate the figures they submitted, a tendency seen especially in the case of the *Kesari* and the *Dinbandhu*.

Despite the *Kesari's* popularity, its claim for an increase in circulation by anywhere

political benefits of an assertively claimed, dominant collective identity, symbolically foregrounded through the press, had been clear to Vishnushastri Chiplunkar; it was no coincidence that Tilak and Chiplunkar were closely associated in forming the Deccan Education Society and the Aryabhushan Press.[106] There is a clear line of continuity from Chiplunkar's efforts to develop an apparently 'apolitical', liberal,

---

between 25% to 80% every few months seems less than plausible. Soon after its appearance, in the week ending 5 February 1881, the *Kesari's* output is given as 200 copies per issue, until the report for the week ending 7 January 1882, where the figure is up to a 1500. The report for the week ending 10 June 1882 sees the claimed readership jumping to 2800. By the week ending 30 September, 1882, the *Kesari* was claiming its weekly circulation to be 3500. By 16 January 1886, *Kesari's* output per issue was claimed to be 4800. During the same period, the average figure claimed by other weekly publications in Marathi was between 175 and 400, with the *Dnyanchakshu* published from Pune, consistently claiming an output of 1000 copies per issue. From a figure of 300 in the week ending 8 January 1881, by the week ending 21 December 1881 the non-brahmin *Dinbandhu* weekly was consistently claiming that its output was per issue 925, surely an optimistic estimate, given the dismal state of literacy among lower-caste groups. The Bombay Anglo-Marathi weekly *Indu Prakash* was the other paper to give its estimate per issue at over 1000 consistently. For a comparable period, the figures for the *Native Opinion* and *Subodh Patrika* fluctuated between 400 and 600 and 600 and 1600, respectively.

[106]Writing in the annual review at the end of *Nibandhmala*'s sixth year of publication, Vishnushastri discussed these developments as the main achievements of the past year. The New English School was the first privately-managed high school in the Bombay Presidency and claimed to have 400 students at the end of its first year. Eight out of the twelve students sent up for the Matriculation Examination were successful. The Deccan Education Society had been set up to disprove the government's claims that a native-run private school could not be self-sustaining. Similarly, Chiplunkar noted that until now, the printing business had been in the hands of uneducated (*avidvaan*) and uncultivated (*adaani*) persons, because of which the true potential of the press had not been realised. But the Aryabhushan press intended to change that. *Maratha* would compare with any renowned English paper or journal and therefore prove useful to all those posted on government jobs in far-off places. *Kesari*, on the other hand, would be useful mainly to ordinary (*saamanya*) people who were not in contact with English or those who lived in rural districts. See Annual Review for 1880 in *Nibandhmala*, No. 76, December 1880, reprinted in *Nibandhmala*, a Commemorative Volume, Pune, 1917, pp. 328–30.

literary discourse in the vernacular through his influential *Nibandhmala* and the emergence of Tilak as an important early nationalist voice. The vehement intolerance underlying *Nibandhmala's* aims was demonstrated by its most abusive and immoderate attack on Phule's *Gulamgiri*[107] and the Annual Report of the *Satyashodak Samaj*.[108] Evidently the need for ideological consolidation within the vernacular sphere and a concern with the creation of 'literary' discourse in Marathi impelled a shift away from the previous emphases on the production of a socially 'useful', critical discourse based on a theoretical acceptance of consensual communicative norms.

The first self-consciously 'literary' journal that signalled the aestheticisation of vernacular discourse was *Vividhdnyanvistaar*,[109] started in 1867, followed by *Nibandhmala* in 1876. By deliberately addressing and creating a 'literary' audience in Marathi, both these journals, published from Pune, took on the task of articulating a collective identity

[107]See review of *Gulamgiri* and the *Satyashodak Samajache Report* in *Nibandhmala*, No. 44, August 1877.

[108]See also pp. 255–6 below.

[109]*Vividhdnyanvistaar* was the first privately-owned, self-consciously Marathi literary journal, proclaiming to be a 'monthly magazine of Marathi literature for ladies and gentlemen', below which ran the vernacular equivalent, '*Kulastriya va grhastha yankarita*'. It was started by R.B. Gunjikar in 1867 from Pune, the same year that the government-owned *Marathi Dnyanprasarak* ceased publication. It was published until 1937.

The first issue carried an introductory editorial, which was clearly suggestive of the hegemonic aspirations underlying such an attempt to sustain a modern, 'cultivated', 'literary' discourse. It noted: 'We are glad to be able to prove what a great need there is among our people, especially women, for a monthly journal such as this. But our pleasure is equalled by our regret that in a vast and densely-populated province such as Bombay, there does not exist a single journal geared towards the welfare and recreation of approximately 70,000 students.' Similarly, the editorial in the opening issue of the second year reiterated its intentions to be useful to both women and men by publishing articles on three types of subjects: firstly, relating to education, including translation of many excellent books, literary criticism, lectures on grammar, patriotic lessons (*deshgyan*); secondly, essays on worldly and practical (*vyavahaarik*) subjects, including information on hygiene; and thirdly, entertaining and imaginative stories (*chamatkarik goshta*) and poems. Translated from W.L. Kulkarni, *Vividhdnyanvistaar: Itihaas ani Vangmayavichaar*', Bombay, 1976, p. 3.

for the 'Marathi' people and their past. Thus, implicitly, the literarization of vernacular discourse had a dual agenda: of defining a distinct, homogeneous identity that would symbolically represent the 'Marathi' public and signalling its exclusivity. As 'mature' vernacular discourse demonstrated, representativeness could be claimed even at the expense of tolerance and egalitarianism. In thus proving its ability to sustain this disjunction between the aesthetic and the political, liberal vernacular discourse had evidently come of age! The politics underlying *Nibandhmala* show its manipulation of the aesthetic-political divide through what can be termed the aestheticisation of political exclusion within colonial society. This political underside of Chiplunkar's concern with developing a modern 'high' literary-critical Marathi discourse cleared the ideological space for the emergence of Tilak as an important political figure and, generally, for the emergence of a nationalistic vernacular discourse in Western India by the 1880s. Several strands in our overall argument, about the links between the vernacular 'renaissance' and the distinct shift towards conservatism as anti-colonial thinking approached its overtly nationalistic phase, can now be seen in conjunction.

Aestheticisation and Intolerance in the Vernacular Sphere: Ideological Consolidation through Chiplunkar's Nibandhmala

The intelligentsia's attempts to lay down norms for a 'high' modern, literary style for Marathi in the 1870s showed they had successfully learnt the value of the liberal differentiation between the domains of the aesthetic and the political. Since its time (1874–81), Chiplunkar's *Nibandhmala* has been recognised as an important part of the Marathi literary 'renaissance' and crucial to the making of a vernacular, anti-colonial early nationalist identity. I shall look at some of the writings published in the *Mala*, as it was familiarly identified among its circle of readers, to examine the nature of ideological consolidation within the vernacular sphere and the relation with English posited in its pages. It is interesting to ask how, given the asymmetry between English and the vernacular spheres, especially in terms of access to the range of professional and political opportunities, *Nibandhmala*'s discourse showed few signs of explicit antagonism towards the English-educated section of the intelligentsia. Chiplunkar openly declared his admiration for

English, and detailed discussions of its great literary 'wealth' were common in *Nibandhmala.* Despite his impatient differences with liberal leaders like Ranade, who desired the reformist agenda through constitutional means,[110] there is little overt criticism of the English-educated university elite in the journal's pages. Yet Chiplunkar's enthusiasm for English literature did not extend to an endorsement of liberal ideas of consensual or critical rationality—indicated by the frequent and extreme hostility that the *Mala* directed towards those it considered its 'lesser' Others, the lower-castes. The *Mala's* ire was especially provoked by the efforts of these subaltern communities to seek education and organise themselves under the banner of the Satyashodak Samaj. This underlying political agenda within *Nibandhmala* provides insights into the ideological orientation of the vernacular sphere at the moment of its so-called 'literary awakening', especially as the intelligentsia advanced towards articulating a nationalistic position.

Although the most important, *Nibandhmala* was not the first journal of the time to take up the task of defining a Marathi literary audience. Edited and managed for the Education Department, first by Krishnashastri Chiplunkar and then by his son Vishnushastri, the *Pune Shalapatrak* and also the more 'moderate' *Vividhdnyanvistaar*, which started publication in 1867, were forerunners of *Nibandhmala's* objectives of providing an exemplary, instructive discussion to create a 'literary' audience for Marathi. But by all counts the *Mala* was able to create a niche for itself[111] and, from Vishnushastri's reputation as having definitively

[110]Vishnushastri had little patience with attempts to advance the reform agenda through political associations. The Sarvajanik Sabha came in for derisive comment in *Nibandhmala*, especially its petitions for concessions. Vishnushastri's criticism of the parochialism that prevailed at the Sabha's meetings was surely not baseless, but in denouncing its leaders through *Nibandhmala*, Vishnushastri showed his lack of appreciation of modern methods of political organisation, preferring to believe that an improved literary taste was the key to an enlightened public opinion. For an account of the *Nibandhmala's* satirical report on the Sarvajanik Sabha's Petition for Representative Government in 1874, see N.R. Phatak, *Nyayamurti Ranadeyanche Charitra*, pp. 216–17.

[111]The reports in the annual review for the second and third years mentioned a significant increase in circulation. See *Nibandhmala*, a Commemorative Volume, pp. 309–11.

moulded the style of modern Marathi, it is apparent that *Nibandhmala's* brand of literary politics struck a chord with its audience, filling an ideological gap within the vernacular sphere. What gave the journal its distinctive character and appeal was Vishnushastri's assertive flair in combining a liberal, expansive tone of discussion *vis-à-vis* literary matters with a trenchant, exclusionist upper-caste claim to define the collective identity and boundaries of the vernacular sphere. A major factor in *Nibandhmala's* appeal lay in its apparent knack for maintaining a bold and audacious public posture in the face of evident internal dissonance within the vernacular sphere. Its discourse kept up a militant posture against both colonial state and missionaries. But far from enjoying general acceptance within the articulate sections of the native community, the journal's positions often met with internal opposition from the upper-caste intelligentsia.[112]

Almost paradoxically, *Nibandhmala's* assertive style stemmed from a deeply fraught position; indeed, there were many signs that upper-caste attempts to assert their dominance in articulating a representative 'Marathi' identity were not backed by an underlying social consensus. For example, even *Nibandhmala* admitted the chaos that prevailed at the annual meeting of the Pune Vakrotejak Sabha in 1878, intended to promote skills of public-speaking within the Marathi community.[113] Similarly, even by the organisers' own admission, efforts to hold the first ever gathering of Marathi writers, the Marathi Granthkar Sabha, in the same year, were far from successful.[114] Chiplunkar's own writings

[112]Chiplunkar's abrasive style and anti-reform views had brought him into conflict with many of his contemporaries, including Moreshwar Kunte and Agarkar. See also fn. 110 above.

[113]A full account published in *Nibandhmala*, No. 21, found mention in the annual summary for 1878, published in issue No. 24, p. 307.

[114]See article entitled '*Marathi Granthotejan*' in *Vividhdnyanvistaar*, Vol. 10, No. 3, March 1878, published in anticipation of the Marathi *Granthkaaranche Sammelan* that eventually took place in Pune on 11 May 1878. For the full text, see Appendix in W.L.Kulkarni, *Vividhdnyanvistaar: Itihaas Ani Vangmayavichaar*, pp. 138–63.

The second conference in 1885 did not fare much better. Phule refused Ranade's invitation to participate on account of what he termed fundamental differences between the vision of the Satyashodak Samaj and *sabhas* seeking to preserve upper-

in *Nibandhmala* repeatedly alluded to serious difficulties encountered in producing a regular supply of standard articles to sustain a journal like his that sought to rely on 'original' composition in the vernacular. All this testifies to the vulnerability of such attempts to articulate an elevated literary discourse in Marathi. The confident tone and self-assured style of Chiplunkar's prose is in complete contrast to what one might expect to find against this background of internal contestation and discord surrounding the attempts to define a homogeneous vernacular literary public. This apparent paradox makes sense when seen against the disjunction underlying *Nibandhmala's* cultural politics, namely the coexistence of an ambience of 'progressive' commitment to the cause of vernacular production and literary taste with a simultaneous, aggressive attack upon lower-caste interests.

The logic of an aestheticised, exclusive vernacular discourse could apparently comfortably coexist with the renunciation of even the nominal possibility for the emergence of an egalitarian, laicised literate culture. This was borne out by the attack that Chiplunkar launched on Phule through the pages of *Nibandhmala* under the pretext of reviewing the recently published Report of the Satyashodak Samaj.[115] The occasion brought out the most intemperate side of the particular brand of the sarcastic, bitter humour that *Nibandhmala* had adopted as its trademark. The review turned out to be an excuse to berate the basic thrust of Phule's politics. In taking an anti-low-caste position publicly, the *Mala* was speaking on behalf of its readership and, presumably, for their 'benefit', thus betraying its own political interest and position. The immediate provocation stemmed from lower-caste attempts to organise themselves to petition the colonial state on their right to education and public access. The upper-caste intelligentsia saw this as likely to undermine their own attempts at securing a hegemonic position *vis-à-vis* state and native society. Not surprisingly, the

---

caste privileges. See Phule's letter in *Dnyanodaya* of 11 June 1885, reprinted in Phadke *et al*, eds, *MPSV*, p. 344.

[115]Review titled, '*Marathi Pustake: Satyashodak Samajacha Report*', *Nibandhmala*, No. 44, August 1877, pp. 1–19. For the full report see '*Pune Satyashodak Samajaacha Report*' for 24 Sept. 1873–24 September 1875 reprinted in Phadke *et al*, eds., *MPSV*, pp. 193–203.

establishment of the Satyashodak Samaj in Pune in 1873 was seen as an immediate threat to the precariously balanced, 'secondary' space in between university-educated intellectuals and the 'ordinary masses' that the vernacular intelligentsia had tried to carve out for itself. Chiplunkar's aggression was aimed at the whole range of Phule's activities, the publication of his anti-brahmanical *Brahmanche Kasab,*[116] and *Gulamgiri,*[117] including articles published in the missionary paper, *Satyadeepika,* from Pune and the organisational efforts of the Satyashodak Samaj.

The disparaging comments against *Gulamgiri* were made under a thin veneer of aestheticism. The Report was criticised for not conforming to the norms of current literary discourse and ridiculed for what Chiplunkar considered the inaccuracies of its fantastic coinages and historical imagination as well as its apparent grammatical deficiencies.[118] But the review did not stop there; it went on to criticise, in very coarse language, the attempts by lower-caste groups to take advantage of the education offered in missionary schools. These were seen as blatant attempts to conciliate the colonial administration and the missionary lobby, which, in Chiplunkar's view, amounted to a subversion of the upper-caste intelligentsia's attempts to extend a homogeneous character to the vernacular sphere.[119] Phule's allegations about the exclusionist and oppressive aspects of brahmanism were only answered with a derisive chauvinism which, at best, admitted with patronising arrogance that the question of brahmanical privilege would be gradually reviewed at the appropriate time.[120] Chiplunkar's hostility towards the Satyashodak Samaj was couched in language far from decorous and made no pretence of respecting the norms of liberal communicative reasoning:

> Under the present conditions [it needs to be considered] how wise and really courageous it is for fools like Jyotiba to shamelessly bark away at

[116]Phule, '*Priestcraft Exposed or Brahmanache Kasab*', Bombay, 1869 reprinted in Phadke *et al.*, eds., *MPSV*, pp. 81–107.

[117]Phule, '*Slavery or Gulamgiri*', Pune 1873. reprinted in Phadke *et al*, eds., *MPSV*, pp. 109–92.

[118]See review, '*Marathi Pustake: Satyashodak Samajacha Report*', *Nibandhmala*, No. 44, August 1877, pp. 5–8.

[119]*Nibandhmala*, No. 44, August 1877, p. 14.

[120]Review of *Dinbandhu* in *Nibandhmala*, No. 48, December 1877, p. 25.

> brahmins, and to vie for crumbs that may be thrown at them according to the convenience of those in power; similarly it is worth thinking about how becoming it is in the present political situation [*deshstithi*], to establish sabhas in order to trade abuse amongst ourselves.[121]

Interestingly, Chiplunkar remained unimpressed with upper-caste attempts to renegotiate their dominance through the religious sphere, especially the initiatives of figures like Dayanand Saraswati to publicise a reformed Hindu faith and practice. Thus, whereas the leaders of the Sarvajanik Sabha, including Ranade, were keen to welcome the Hindu leader to Pune and organise a ceremonial procession in his honour, the *Mala*'s reports[122] on the Arya Samaj and its leader's visit to Pune were consistently unfavourable. Vishnushastri's own attempts to foreground upper-caste hegemonic claims mainly through an asserted dominance in the literary sphere and his evident lack of sympathy for such claims as based on religious authority showed that, by the 1870s, processes of Weberian disenchantment already formed a significant element within the political imagination of the provincial, lower-middle-class intelligentsia. This is hardly unexpected when one considers the fact that Phule realised only too well by this time that the basis for the articulation of brahmanical hegemony was no longer tied to their exclusive authority to interpret religious texts, but rather to upper-caste dominance within the secular structures of educational institutions and colonial bureaucracy. As his English preface to *Gulamgiri* put it:

> Though the brahmin of the old Peshwa times is not quite the same as the brahmin of the present day, though the march of western ideas and civilisation is undoubtedly telling on his superstitions and bigotry, he has not as yet abandoned his time-cherished notions of superiority or the dishonesty of his ways. ... Perhaps the most glaring tendency of the Government system of high class education has been the virtual monopoly of all the higher offices under them by the brahmins. If the welfare of the ryot is at heart, if it is the duty of the government to

[121]Translated from Marathi, see review, *Nibandhmala*, No. 44, August 1877, p. 14.

[122]See the critical account of Dayanand Saraswati's visit to Pune in 1876 in a piece entitled '*Pratikhandan*', *Nibandhmala* No 36, December 1876, pp. 1–29.

> check a host of abuses, it behoves them to narrow this monopoly, day by day so as to allow a sprinkling of other castes to get into public service.[123]

It was this apparent renewal of brahmanical privilege through the colonial period that allowed Chiplunkar to boast:

> Mr. Phule is thus notified—that if he is indeed concerned about the uplift of his caste-brothers, then it is little use for him to be composing books like the 'Gulamgiri' to abuse those who are his superiors in every way. However unjust or wicked brahmins may be, one fact is incontestable: that they retain possession of the keys to the storehouse of knowledge. And there simply are no avenues for the other *jatis* to have access to education/knowledge [*dnyan*] without their help.[124]

In contrast, any suggestion of such contemptuous bravado was kept out from *Nibandhmala's* attempts to elaborate a high-literary critical discourse in Marathi. In its literary discourse, the *Mala's* tone was unfailingly decorous and expansive; the cordiality, no doubt occasioned by the homogeneity of the social position of *Nibandhmala's* readership and their interests. It was *Nibandhmala's* practice to publish an annual review where the editor also gave his assessment of the journal's work during the preceding months. The tone adopted in such pieces showed a modest and respectful attitude towards its readers. Often, the *Mala* would go to great lengths to explain its difficulties to its subscribers, humbly asking their forbearance for the numerous obstacles that came in the way of a colonial journal aspiring to be a standard, 'original', 'literary' publication, from keeping to its regular schedule:

> ... we humbly request our readers that the reasons for the irregularity of our journal are none other than those discussed above. Our chief intention being to serve our readers' interests, we ask them to bear with us if the work takes somewhat longer. They ought to remember that we do not as yet possess the skills to reel out five or six pages at a sitting like

[123]See Phule, '*Slavery or Gulamgiri*', in Phadke *et al.*, eds, *MPSV*, pp. 125–7.

[124]Translated from Marathi, Chiplunkar's editorial comments on the *Dnyanodaya* and the *Dinbandhu* in *Nibandhmala*, No 48, December 1877, p. 24.

[Samuel] Johnson, nor are the printing presses here efficient enough for books to be produced within a few days of the type being set.[125]

Our *malakaar*, as Chiplunkar was often referred to by his contemporaries, had perfected the strategy of adjusting his tone and manner of address, given the intellectual and social domain he sought to address. A cultivated, liberal tone of elevated deliberation was to be reserved exclusively for a discussion of 'high' literary matters amongst a like-minded audience. However, as we have seen, this like-minded and apparently cultivated audience was perfectly capable of relinquishing all norms of etiquette and tolerance in speaking of its 'inferiors', especially when they were seen to transgress 'rightful' privileges. Also, significantly, despite the overriding need to consolidate a strong collective, anti-colonial identity through the vernacular, *Nibandhmala* never sought to play down its unstinting admiration for the English language and its literature. Besides his somewhat immoderate and highly aestheticist reverence towards English, seen in his famous comparison of English *vidya* to the milk of a tigress,[126] Chiplunkar's writings were liberally annotated with quotations and references from the works of famous English authors and poets.

On both counts, a contrast with Balshastri Jambhekar's position as an early vernacular intellectual (discussed in chapter three[127]) springs to mind. Balshastri's preoccupation with the critical, rather than the literary, discourses of English enabled his engagement with the possibilities of modernity to be far less aestheticised than the vernacular writing of Vishnushastri Chiplunkar. *Nibandhmala* published three influential essays on '*Ingrezi bhasha*',[128] giving detailed accounts of English literary history, focusing especially on the emergence of a learned yet commonly-understood language in modern prose through

[125]Translated from Marathi, Annual Review for 1877, *Nibandhmala*, No. 48, December 1877, reprinted in *Nibandhmala*, a Commemorative Volume, p. 315.

[126]'*Amchya Deshachi Stithi*', *Nibandhmala*, No 78, reprinted in Dr Nirmalkumar Phadkule, ed., *Nibandmaleteel Teen Nibandh*, Poona, 1975, p. 107.

[127]See chapter three, pp. 128–34.

[128]These were serialised in *Nibandhmala*, Nos. 28, 29 & 32, April, May and August 1876.

periodicals and literary/critical journals like the *Spectator*, *Rambler*, *Edinburgh Review* and *Westminster Review*. These articles also tried to summarise, for the Marathi reader, an account of the emergence of the modern historical imagination as seen through the work of English historians. Vishnushastri was thus enthusiastically open to the literary possibilities of familiarity with English, even while he and other vernacular intellectuals showed signs of rejecting many of the political premises central to liberalism. Combining an admiration of English literature and history, an anti-colonial consciousness which was at once profoundly anti-liberal and a desire to advance 'autonomous' literary criteria for Marathi, *Nibandhmala's* discourse showed a sophisticated cognisance of the distinctive character and emphases within different literary trajectories, which colonial discourse on translation had sought to obscure by ignoring the distance between languages.

But again, in contrast to Jambhekar, alongside his great concern for vernacular standards Chiplunkar did not mind admitting that Marathi would probably never possess the range of expressive idioms developed through English, especially the specialised prose styles spanning the domains of science, technology and modern political thought. He argued that this gap ought to be treated as a simple and obvious difference and was not to be invested with implicit judgements about the vernacular's 'primitive' or 'deficient' state.[129] In thus asserting the relative autonomy of the vernacular, Chiplunkar was reflecting his awareness of how, by this time, the linguistic divide had actually widened so that English and vernacular intellectuals seemed to inhabit distinct worlds of cognitive, social and political opportunities. But also, in thus renouncing the hope of adopting the critical vocabularies of science into the vernacular, the 'mature' intelligentsia was conceding that the apprehension of modernity on the subcontinent would have a predominantly literary bias. Thus in South Asia, especially, the transfer of modern rationality through colonialism saw the displacement of its political impact on to the redefined realm of culture and language. The other great constitutive influence upon the vernacularisation of the liberal imagination in the subcontinent was the fact that modern cultural

[129]'*Bhashaantar'*, *Nibandhmala*, No. 12, pp. 29–31.

and political norms were appropriated through the pressures of making an anti-colonial discourse. Under these twin pressures, the modern Indian imagination emerged as a paradoxical blend of a hyper-aestheticised consciousness that was, simultaneously, profoundly subversive towards the structures of modern bureaucratic and state power.

Nibandhmala served as a prelude to a series of important cultural and political initiatives in which Chiplunkar and Tilak were closely associated, namely the formation of the 'autonomous' Deccan Education Society, the launching of the Aryabhushan Press, the New English School and book-depot, as well as *Kesari* and *Maratha* in Pune by early 1881.[130] Chiplunkar did not live to see all these efforts flourish, but he remained closely involved with them until his premature death in 1882.[131] And yet, despite all his bold and energetic efforts to articulate an anti-colonial literary style for Marathi through absorbing the inspiration of English, Chiplunkar could not ignore the discrepancy between on the one hand the ambience of heightened militancy that his discourse tried to sustain, and on the other the signs of subordination of the vernacular sphere and political subjugation that he saw around him. In the essay discussed earlier, where he spoke of the great promise of heroic empowerment 'implicit' in the English language, Chiplunkar claimed that anyone reared on English books could never be weak on account of the qualities of enthusiasm, courage, righteousness and independence that they would imbibe by such reading. But in reality there appeared little evidence of these qualities; instead, servility and subordination seemed to be the rule. Repeatedly, he was forced to admit the contrast between the ideal picture of valiant savants who could challenge the colonial state through the power of their discourse, and the subservient and petty ways of colonial intellectuals.[132]

This is not surprising when one considers the actual circumstances

[130]The last issue of *Nibandhmala*, which probably appeared only in early 1881, gave details of the plans for each of these steps. See *Nibandhmala*, No. 72, December 1880, and also fn. 12 above.

[131]Annual Review for 1879, *Nibandhmala*, No.60, December 1879, reprinted in *Nibandhmala*, a Commemorative Volume, p. 319.

[132]'*Amchya Deshachi Stithi*', *Nibandhmala*, No 78, reprinted in Dr. Nirmalkumar Phadkule, ed., *Nibandmaleteel Teen Nibandh*, p. 107.

of those who made up the readership of the vernacular press and periodicals. The journal mainly relied on semi-literate, poorly-educated readers drawn from among those who staffed the subordinate positions in the provincial bureaucracy or those employed in the severely under-funded vernacular schools. The *Mala* was priced at 4 annas per issue, or at Rs 2 per year if paid for in advance;[133] this meant that despite its aspirations to create a 'high' literary discourse, the journal's target audience typically comprised lower middle-class vernacular readers. This was the stratum over which the 'high' college and university-educated intelligentsia could hope to exercise little direct influence—on account of the latter's minimal capacities to contribute to a public vernacular discourse. It was this provincial, lower-class, semi-literate audience that had little English, which the vernacular intelligentsia aspired to cultivate as their particular sphere of influence. But given the prevailing linguistic and political hierarchy, they could not hope to do this independently of the English-educated, high intelligentsia. That is why even at the high point of its so-called 'renaissance', vernacular literary discourse showed little explicit hostility towards the English sphere, despite its subordination under the influence of the latter.

We have noted the continuity between the cultural politics of *Nibandhmala* and Tilak's ideological vision. The emergence of Tilak as a political leader is a large subject that cannot be taken up here, except in relation to launching *Kesari* and *Maratha* in 1881. This provides an appropriate point to conclude the story of the intelligentsia's attempts to acquire a hegemonic position within the bilingual colonial social order.

Tilak spent his early political career as a journalist and editor rather than as a full-time activist engaged in micro-level organisation and mobilisation. The simultaneous launching of his two papers revealed that the intelligentsia could not afford to ignore the public-political significance of either English or the vernacular, especially as anti-colonial thinking entered its overtly hegemonic, nationalist phase. But it also showed that, by this time, the bilingual relation upon which the very existence of the colonial-modern public sphere was premised had

[133]See subscription details on back cover, *Nibandhmala*, No. 32, August 1876.

yielded two separate, largely monolingual, literate communities within the native social world. Although Tilak himself wrote in both English and Marathi, and colonial intellectuals even after the 1880s possessed skills in both languages, the making of modern political culture in Western India showed a much sharper split between intellectual production in English and the vernacular than was the case in Bengal. The term 'monolingual' is used here not in an absolute sense, but to denote substantial discontinuities between English and Marathi audiences. The fact that *Maratha* continued to be published, despite running up losses and having to be subsidised through the revenue brought in by *Kesari's* substantially larger circulation, showed that neither of these largely monolingual audiences could be ignored. These reading publics were culturally and politically related, interdependent, and overlapped to some degree. But, as the success of Tilak's venture showed, they were also sufficiently discontinuous to exist discretely.

Tilak's emergence as a public figure is generally acknowledged as a turning point in the history of the Marathi press, besides also marking the emergence of an early nationalistic discourse in Western India. His career and writings reveal the strains of chauvinism, social conservatism and political militancy in countering colonial power that have been identified here as part of the public style first developed by Vishnushastri Chiplunkar. Tilak's brand of leadership also shared traits evident in Chiplunkar's writings, namely its strategic use of an abrasive assertiveness in challenging those in authority and a deliberate defiance of rational norms, especially while discussing social 'inferiors'. To both of them goes the credit of forging a political style of 'symbolic militancy' that frequently bordered on the insolent, and which sought to derive its effectiveness mostly from an aggressive posture that conveyed an impression of absolute intolerance towards any alternative or oppositional point of view within the public domain. The success of Tilak's early career as a journalist demonstrated the intelligentsia's realisation of the decisive importance of the symbolic manipulation of the avenues for publicity within modern politics. Tilak's importance lay in his insight that, despite the internal divisions and the small size of the colonial reading public, the avenues for publicity through the press had the potential to circumvent the severe difficulties of forging ground-level ties between disparate interests—because of which associational networks within the colonial world would never reflect society in microcosm. Such pragmatic calculations contrasted with the more liberal ambitions of the first generation of Marathi press-men of the 1830s and 1840s. Evidently, the aspirations of the early colonial intellectuals to construct a sphere of rational and equal exchange between different and opposing points through the vernacular press had not withstood the 'transition' to the emergence of full-fledged nationalism.

Conclusion

The Limits of Upper-Caste Leadership

This book has tried to clarify the links between the structures of colonial literacy and the peculiar nature of the dominance that the upper-caste intelligentsia established over the public sphere by the 1880s. It has traced the specific trajectory of options open to the upper-caste leadership through analysis of the ways in which the colonial literate regime altered structures of learning and modes of contestation. Upper-caste authority was largely foregrounded through the control these groups established over the structures of cultural production; alongside, the limits of the influence this upper-caste intelligentsia could assert outside the domain of literary production have already been noted. Important work by scholars like Sandra Freitag[1] has emphasised the need to take into account the collective actions of non-elite groups within public arenas. Bearing this in mind, I have underscored the belief that competing aspirations and strategies within the colonial-modern public sphere can only be delineated against descriptions of normative shifts and the nature of the intelligentsia's overall ideological influence within the new arrangements. It is apt, then, to conclude with observations about the long-term implications and limits of

[1]Sandra Freitag, 'State and Community: Symbolic Popular Protest in Banaras' Public Arenas' in S. Freitag, ed., *Culture and Power in Banaras: Community, Performance and Environment 1800–1980*, Delhi, 1989; Sandra Freitag, *Collective Action And Community: Public Arenas in the Emergence of Communalism in North India*, Berkeley, 1989.

the hegemonic strategies adopted by the upper-caste intelligentsia.

The virulence of anti-lower caste discourse in the mainstream vernacular press was as much a sign of upper-caste intolerance and dominance as an intimation of the fragility and weakness of the intelligentsia's representative position. Likewise, the liberal upper-caste leadership was aware of the need to register their presence and influence within the city's public arenas; but they also realised the tenuousness of their abilities to mobilise collective support. Their predicament was demonstrated by incidents during the visit of the reformist leader Swami Dayanand Saraswati to Pune in 1875. He had visited the city at the behest of the liberal reformist leadership. Several meetings and lectures were scheduled, at the end of which plans had been made for the Swami to proceed, in spectacular fashion, on elephant back, through the city streets. Ostensibly meant to honour the Swami, this procession was equally intended as a public staging of the upper-caste liberal leadership's moral authority.

Not unexpectedly, things did not go quite as planned. Rival groups of orthodox brahmins had been making alternative preparations to express their dissent, through a parallel procession to mock the efforts of the reformist upper-caste leadership. An official police escort did not prevent the anti-reformist groups from following the main procession, parading a gorgeously bedecked donkey, with much mock fanfare. Watched by delighted crowds, the episode ended in pandemonium and an ugly scene ensued where the reformist leaders had mud and other things hurled at them. The available accounts give conflicting versions about the course of events. Contemporary liberal autobiographical accounts emphasise that the upper-caste colonial-educated intelligentsia conducted themselves with the utmost dignity despite the unpleasant provocations.[2] Further, their criticism of the 'orthodox' party is suggested as implicit and muted rather than overt. These accounts fail to mention the fact that, in staging this public procession, upper-caste colonial intellectuals were forced to seek the help of lower-caste groups and leaders. Nor do they mention that the

[2]See Ramabai Ranade, *Amchya Ayushyatil Kahi Aathvan*, Bombay, 1938, p. 49; N.R. Phatak, *Nyaymurti Ranadeyanche Charitra*, pp. 230–7.

orthodox *shastris* were not the only ones opposed to the Swami's visit.

Interestingly, *Nibandhmala* published several utterly disparaging reports that drew great enjoyment from the discomfiture of the reformist leaders, who, as the journal put it, were not saved even by the presence of their 'newly-liberated', lower-caste 'brethren'.[3] As we saw, Phule had publicly expressed his scepticism of upper-caste organisations. Yet if the claims in non-brahmin accounts are to be believed, it appears that, depending on the exigencies of particular situations, Phule and his Satyashodak associates could still be persuaded to support liberal upper-caste leaders against the conservative '*bhat*-brahmin' party and their friends in the vernacular press.[4] These incidents demonstrate the dissonances between the English-educated and vernacular sections of the upper-caste intellectual elite which, nevertheless, did not grow into open antagonism.

Likewise, these events showed that, for all their representative claims, the English-educated intellectual elite remained dependent on the non-brahmin leadership for ground-level support. These requests echoed similar pleas for help in the late 1840s, when a small group of English-educated brahmins made their way through the city streets to Vishrambagwada to hand in a petition supporting their claims for state patronage.[5] Indeed, this dilemma has bedevilled the lower-caste leadership ever since. For, despite personal links that individual lower-caste leaders may have had with some liberals,[6] by and large the non-brahmin lobby has been justifiably wary of upper-caste reformist organisations and their claims to be genuinely inclusive. Such doubts have been typical to almost all subsequent attempts to forge alliances between the elite liberal-nationalist leadership and lower-caste/non-brahmin/dalit aspirations. Founded on their control over the sites of

[3]See *Nibandhmala*, No. 23, November 1875, quoted in P.S. Patil, *Mahatma Jyotirao Phule*, First pub. 1927, second edn., Bombay, 1989, p. 67; see also *Nibandhmala*, No. 24, December 1875 and No. 36, December 1876, esp. pp. 2–7.

[4]P.S. Patil, *Mahatma Jyotirao Phule*, pp. 65–6.

[5]See chapter two, pp. 86–7, esp. fn. 57.

[6]See letters by Mama Parmanand, petitioning for financial support for the ailing Phule, just before the latter's death in 1890, Appendix 2 in Phadke *et al.*, eds, *MPSV*, pp. 673–7.

cultural production and their pre-eminence within the sphere of ideological collaboration, the dominance of the upper-caste leadership was inevitably subject to the tension between their almost exclusive control over new cultural practices and the legitimative criteria of a laicised political sphere. Their limited ability to enunciate an inclusive discourse capable of accommodating subaltern and alternative viewpoints left these intellectuals vulnerable to challenges from groups that could combine a greater identification with non-elite cultural practices with the skills needed to negotiate the avenues for colonial-modern publicity. Not surprisingly, the upper-caste intellectual elite tended to be most suspicious of 'lesser' voices that were likely to make themselves heard in the public domain.

Western India saw the assertion of lower-caste voices within the colonial-modern public sphere much before other areas of the subcontinent. The pressure from non-elite agents demanding admission to the new public-political domain came mainly in the form of the Satyashodak Samaj, whose constituency has been rightly identified by Gail Omwedt[7] as comprising peasants, urban non-Maratha castes like the *malis*, etc., the small number of non-brahmin professionals, intellectuals and other semi-urban personalities who, despite little education, had benefited from links with the colonial economy as merchant-suppliers or contractors.[8] Nurtured partly by the small but important missionary presence, this coalition of non-brahmin interests represented an alternative trajectory to upper-caste attempts to consolidate their dominance. Not all actors within the colonial-modern public sphere had gained access to these arenas through the privileges of a colonial education, a fact that was certainly true of this alliance, which claimed to represent subaltern interests—identified variously as *kunbi*, non-brahmin, *shudra*, *magaslelya* or *bahujan samaj* at different points in the history of the Satyashodak Samaj and the low-caste movement.

Having acquired their knowledge of political modernity outside

[7]Gail Omwedt, *Cultural Revolt in a Colonial Society: The Non-Brahman Movement in Western India 1873–1930*, Bombay, 1976, pp. 148–53.

[8]Details about the various activities of the Samaj and its patrons are given in its annual reports for the years 1873–1874 see Phadke *et al.*, eds, *MPSV*, pp. 195–219.

the avenues for ideological collaboration and enjoying a greater proximity with popular practices, this alliance represented a potential counter-public. Its leadership had shown an astute grasp of the principles of colonial publicity and the emerging social hierarchy. Further, they had made some visible forays into the public-political domain in the 1870s and 1880s—e.g., Phule's nomination to the Municipality between 1876 and 1882; the concerted Satyashodak campaigns in and around Poona to develop alternative rituals that dispensed with brahmin priests; and efforts to promote institutions and arenas that would help the rise of a non-brahmin educated class.[9] Besides these initiatives, Phule's speeches and writings bear out the intentions of the Samaj leadership to contest the representative claims of the upper-caste elite and their organisations.[10]

Thus, by the late 1870s, when modern Marathi found its 'high' literary voice, lower-caste groups did not identify with the public defined by upper-caste vernacular intellectuals. As a result, lower-caste presence in the public sphere took the form of a distinct counter-public that contested upper-caste dominance over the new modes of publicity and political organisation, besides using innovative mobilisational strategies and popular expressive forms. Even during Phule's own lifetime it was clear that the constituency of the Satyashodak Samaj and the future of the low-caste movement lay in gathering support in rural areas rather than in the cities. Here, despite the attempts to distribute books

[9]A wealthy Pune merchant, Ramsheth Urvane, and Dr. Vishram Gholay provided a prize for the best essay by a *shudra*. Besides, other measures including special prizes for *shudra* students at the government schools in Pune, a school in Hadpsar's, plans to look into the feasibility of a boarding house for *shudra* students were also announced; see ibid, p. 210.

[10]This is especially true of Phule's speeches at Samaj meetings in the rural districts near Pune in the early 1880s. These were later collected as *Shetkaricha Asud*, which was partially serialised in the *Dinbandhu*, but published as a whole only in 1967. This text demonstrates Phule's intimate familiarity with peasant life and day-to-day tribulations. At several points, Phule mocks the claims of the Sarvajanik Sabha to represent and protect the interests of lower-caste, rural communities. See '*Shetkaricha Asud*' in Phadke *et al.* eds, *MPSV*, pp. 245–331. For an account of the activities of the Dinbandhu Sarvajanik Sabha, established in November 1884 by Bhalekar, specifically to challenge the Pune Sarvajanik Sabha, see O'Hanlon, *Caste, Conflict and Ideology*, pp. 282–7.

and pamphlets to popularise the Samaj's ideology and programme,[11] print was bound to have a limited impact among such sparsely-educated groups. Popular forms using oral performance had to be adopted to address this politically aware but 'non-reading' public. Although wanting firm evidence, it is tempting to speculate that Phule's hesitation in allowing Bhalekar use of the Samaj printing press in 1874–5 (to start the first non-brahmin newspaper) must have at least partially stemmed from such reasons.[12] Both Phule and Bhalekar used the popular narrative and verse forms like the *povada* and *abhang*. Besides, the Satyashodak influence was helped by a long line of low-caste poets who drew inspiration from the popular, non-elite performative idioms of *shahiri* and *tamasha*, including Umababa Sawlajkar to Gopalbaba Walangkar in the nineteenth century, to Kisan Phaguji Bansode and Bhau Phakkad who put their talents at the service of the low-caste cause in the 1920s and 1930s.[13] Omvedt has documented[14] that the years which saw the rise of Tilak coincided with the growth of rural support for the activities of the Satyashodak Samaj, garnered through newspapers like the *Din Mitra*, but even more so through tireless propaganda by leaders like Marutrao Navale, Narobaba Mahaghat Patil, Dharamji Dumbre Patil,[15] using oral performative forms like *jalsas* and *kirtans*. Similarly, the adaptation of the popular performative genre of the *tamasha* by Samaj activists like Ramchandra Ghadge and Phalke played a crucial part in creating the momentum for the anti-rent revolt that spread in the Satara region between 1918–1920.[16] Inspired by the Satyashodak *tamashas*, the young non-brahmin leadership that emerged in Pune in the 1920s devised performative strategies like the non-brahmin *mela* and procession songs during the Ganpati festival to challenge the brahmanical domination of these celebrations since the late 1890s.

These non-brahmin procession songs denounced upper-caste nationalism and, instead, celebrated the figures of Shivaji, Shahu

[11]O'Hanlon, *Caste, Conflict and Ideology*, p. 233.

[12]Ibid., pp. 243–4.

[13]K. Kirwale, *Ambedkari Shahiri-Ek Shodh*, Pune, 1992.

[14]Omwedt, *Cultural Revolt in a Colonial Society*, esp. pp. 141–2.

[15]Ibid., pp. 138–43.

[16]Ibid., pp. 210–21.

Maharaj, Phule and Gandhi as true patriots, while the *melas* laid claim to the city's public arenas, especially in areas regarded as strongholds of conservative brahmanical opinion. Although ephemeral, such performative statements powerfully and publicly affirmed the challenge represented by non-brahmin ideology and its new leaders. The mounting political pressure on the upper-caste, nationalist leadership was signalled by the fact that by 1916 Gandhi was already in contact with the Satyashodak Samaj.[17] Subsequent years saw a significant recession in the dominance of upper castes within the arena of nationalist politics, although their pre-eminence in the sphere of cultural and intellectual production continued unchallenged well into the 1960s, and even after.

This complex scenario meant that the room for conciliation between these divergent political forces was quite limited. An increasingly defensive brahmanical tradition within the political sphere found itself at odds with the norms of mass politics. One instance where this tension came to a head was the violent retaliation against the *chitpavans* that ensued in various parts of West Maharashtra in the aftermath of Gandhi's assassination.

Yet, the conditions for these violent clashes were prefigured within the cultural and ideological divisions and alternative trajectories evident in the public sphere by the last decades of the nineteenth century. Negotiating the structures of liberal politics through their proximity with colonial authority, the upper-caste intelligentsia had only partially internalised the norms of modern communicative rationality. Paradoxically, they could make representative claims that were not premised on any proven ability to enunciate an inclusive discourse.

Paradigms such as 'domination without hegemony' and 'collaboration' do not fully describe the complexity of the colonial intelligentsia's ideological manoeuvres. Contingent upon the initiatives of a penny-pinching colonial state, like so much else in the colonial world then, the attainment of a position of hegemonic influence was not exempt from the politics of scarcity. Within such a scenario, control depended not so much on the breadth of political vision or qualities of intellectual

[17]Ibid., 148

or moral leadership that new intellectual groups could display. Emerging intelligentsias realised that, at least equally, their dominance depended upon strategic calculations about a trade-off between demographic considerations, the politics of numbers and the management of exclusivity. Thus, the dominant discourses in the colonial public sphere owed their influence not so much to their accommodative potential, as to the exclusivity of the criteria determining access to the arenas of cultural and political debate. However, the limited potential of the upper-caste intelligentsia to develop an inclusive discourse found itself at odds with the logic of representative politics, resulting in the historic incompleteness of the hegemonic influence that they were able to establish.

Glossary

arya	a Marathi/Sanskrit term meaning noble, learned, cultivated, especially used to denote descent from the Indo-European tribes who invaded the subcontinent about two millennia BC.
bakhar	a term used for the extensive corpus of Marathi accounts of important episodes in Maratha history. The earliest *bakhars* deal with Shivaji's life, but most of them narrate later events and were composed between 1700 and 1820.
bhadralok	the Bengali term meaning 'cultivated elite' used by the Bengali intellectual elite of the colonial period to describe themselves.
bhakti	a term common to many languages on the subcontinent meaning 'devotion'.
bhat	a brahmin priest; also denotes a lower order among brahmins.
bhikshuk	a brahmin who lives by gathering alms.
chitpavan	a sub-caste of brahmins from the Konkan region; the caste of the Peshwas, the powerful rulers whose capital was Poona, and whom the British defeated in 1818.
dharmashastras	the Hindu texts containing prescriptions of an individual's duty, according to his caste status and social position.
harikathas	mythological narratives, stories of the Hindu divinities, usually recited by a *kathakaar* (story-teller) to audiences in temples or other public gatherings.
Hindu Buddhi Vardhak Sabha	The Society for the Cultivation of the Hindu Mind.

inam	reward, usually in the form of a land grant given in recognition of political services.
jati	an endogamous caste or sub-caste.
karkun/karkoon	scribe, clerk or copyist.
kavi	poet, composer of verses.
kavya	poetic composition, the classical tradition of Sanskrit poetry.
khot	revenue officers in the Konkan who were granted hereditary collection rights.
kirtan	oral narratives with religious themes, drawn from the stories of the Hindu epics, performed by trained *kirtankaars*, often accompanied by music, in front of audiences in temples or private households.
kshatriya	the second of the four *varnas* or divisions of *jati samaj* or the Hindu social order, whose members, in theory, are meant to be rulers and warriors.
lok	collectivity, people.
lokahitawadi	one who speaks for the general good, honorific of Gopal Hari Deshmukh.
mahar	a caste of 'untouchables'.
mali	the caste of gardeners and vegetable cultivators.
mandali	group, association.
mang	a caste of 'untouchables'.
matha	Hindu religious institutions established by disciples of well-known preachers (*swamis*) or religious philosophers (*acharyas*) for the propagation of their views and interpretations.
maulvi	a priest/scholar learned in Arabic, Islamic scriptures and law.
mofussil	a term for the rural hinterland of any large city, here used with respect to Bombay.
munshi	accountant.
panchang	almanac.
pandit	a brahmin learned in the traditional Hindu texts.
pantoji	village school teacher, often used with a disparaging connotation.
patil	hereditary head of a village.

peshwa — the term for the *chitpavan* brahmin chief ministers who served the Maratha kings after Shivaji, and who from the early eighteenth century exercised power in their own right from the new capital, Pune.

peth — market-place or market town, usually established through official sanction and dealing in specialised categories of commodities.

pothi — manuscript-books or a collection of manuscripts preserved by being loosely tied together.

povada — a Marathi ballad form.

prabhu — a group of sub-brahmin castes who were often employed as professional scribes.

praja — a collective noun denoting political subjects.

prasastis — eulogistic verses, either in Sanskrit or the regional textual idioms, composed or inscribed in honour of a king or other important political patron.

prastavana — introduction.

prayaschita — ceremonial repentance involving ritual punishment and/or fines.

puranas — the corpus of sacred Hindu mythological narratives, supposedly eighteen in number, often drawing from stories in the Hindu epics, and usually accorded a lower status than the *shastric* and *vedic* texts.

puranik — one who is trained to narrate and explain the *puranas* through recitation, usually a brahmin.

raja — king, ruler.

ryot — peasant.

sabha — meeting, organisation, society.

saivite — worshippers of Shiva.

sampradaya — sect, tradition, a community united by certain distinct religious beliefs or practices.

sardar — a title denoting political importance that was granted to aristocratic chiefs.

sarkar — government, administration, often used to denote the British government.

sarvajanik collective, pertaining to everyone or all, the title of the early nationalist association established in Poona.

satyashodak seeker of truth, the title of the society started by Phule and his colleagues.

seth/sethia merchant, banker, important trader, a person who commanded respect and influence on account of his wealth

shabdakosh dictionary, glossary

shastri one learned in the *shastras* or the Hindu religious texts.

shastri mandali the group of *shastris* employed by the Education Society.

shenvi a sub-caste of the *gaud saraswat* brahmins.

shetkari farmer.

shimpi the caste of tailors.

shudra the fourth and the lowest of the four *varna* divisions of jati samaj or Hindu social order, which provides, in theory, provides servants and labourers for the higher *varnas*.

sonar the caste of goldsmiths.

taluka an administrative sub-division, smaller than a district.

Upyukt Dnyanprasarak Sabha/Mandali The Society for the Advancement of Useful Knowledge.

vakil pleader, lawyer, legal representative.

veda the religious texts that are supposed to be among the most ancient of Hindu writing, in theory, four in number, supposedly uttered by Brahma and fit to be studied only by brahmins and the 'twice-born' castes.

vidvan scholar, learned gentleman.

vidya knowledge, education.

vidyakhata Education Department.

vydick a brahmin trained in the *vedas*.

zilla an administrative sub-division, district.

Bibliography

Government Archives

Bombay Presidency Proceedings: General Department
Bombay Presidency Proceedings: Education Department

Manuscript Sources

MSS. Eur. E 234: Chapman Collection, India Office Collections.
MSS. Eur. F.87: Elphinstone Papers, India Office Collections.
Journal of Vedaridasan Mudaliar 1839–1840, (Student of Elphinstone College), School of Oriental and African Studies.
Letterbooks of the Free Church of Scotland Mission, Bombay and Pune Mission, National Library of Scotland, Edinburgh.

Dissertations, Unpublished Theses

Roberts, A.J., 'Education and Society in the Bombay Presidency', unpublished thesis, London University, 1974.
Gumperz, E.M., 'English Education and Social Change in the Nineteenth Century 1858–1898', unpub. Ph.D. thesis, University of California, 1965.
Orsini, Francesca, 'The Hindi Public Sphere, 1920–1940', Ph.D. thesis, University of London, 1996.

Contemporary Newspapers and Periodical Publications

Bombay Durpan
Bombay Educational Record

Bombay Witness
Deccan College Quarterly
Dinbandhu
Journal of the Bombay Branch of the Royal Asiatic Society
Kesari
Maratha
Marathi Dnyanprasarak
Native Opinion
Nibandhmala
Oriental Christian Spectator
Pune Sarvajanik Sabheche Masik Pustak
Pune Shalapatrak
Quarterly Journal of the Pune Sarvajanik Sabha
Subodh Patrika
Vividhdnyanvistaar

Official Publications

Annual Report of the Board of Education for the years 1840/41–1854/55.

Annual Report of Department of Public Instruction for the years 1855/56–1880/81

Appendix to the Education Commission Report, Government Press, Calcutta, 1884

First Report of the Elphinstone Native Education Institute for 1840, Bombay, 1841

Gazetteer of Bombay City and Island, 3 Vols., Bombay, 1909

Grant, A., *Catalogue of Native Publications in the Bombay Presidency up to 31 December 1864*, Bombay, 1867

Grierson, G.A., *Linguistic Survey of India*, Government Press, Calcutta, 1919

Native Newspapers Reports: Weekly Summaries of Vernacular Newspaper Publications in Bombay Presidency

Reports of Bombay Native Education Society 1825–1839

Report of the Hunter Commission, Government Press, Calcutta, 1884
Vol. 1.: *Report of the Bombay Provincial Committee*
Vol. 2.: *Evidence taken before the Bombay Provincial Committee and Memorials Addressed to the Education Committee*

Non–Official Publications and Reports

Bombay University Calendar.

Papers relating to the Examination of Candidates for Senior Scholarships in the Elphinstone and Poona Colleges for 1855–1858.

Reports of the Students' Literary and Scientific Society for the years 1848–1870.

Transactions of the Literary Society of Bombay 1819–1823.

Other Contemporary Materials

Anon., *Dialogues on Geography and Astronomy*, translated into Marathee language for the Bombay Education Society, lithographed at the press of the Department of Public Instruction, Poona, 1832.

Bhai Narayan and Damodar Bhaskar, *Two Hindus on English ... being Prize Essays at the Elphinstone Institute*, Bombay, 1852.

Bhandarkar, R.G., 'Relations between Sanskrit, Pali, the Prakrits and the Modern Vernaculars' in *Wilson Philological Lectures on Sanskrit and the Derived Languages*, pub. Radhabai Atmaram Sagoon, Bombay, 1914

Cavelly Venkata Ramaswami Pandit, *Biographical Sketches of the Deccan Poets, being the Memoirs of the Lives of Several Eminent Bards, both Ancient and Modern*, Victoria Press, Bombay, 1847.

Chapekar, N.G., *Peshwaichya Sawleent*, Aryasanskriti Mudranalaya, Pune, 1877.

Crawford, Arthur, *Our Troubles in Poona and Deccan*, Westminster Archibald Constable and Co., London, 1897.

Cursetjee, Maneckjee, *A Few Passing Ideas for the Benefit of India and Indians, Addressed to the Bombay Association*, Bombay, 1853.

Drummond, Robert, *Illustrations of the Grammatical Parts of the Guzerathee, Mahratta and English Languages*, Courier Press, Bombay, 1808.

English and Native Rule in India, Native Opinion Press, Bombay, 1868.

Forrest, G. W., ed., *Selections from the Minutes and the Other Official Writings of the Hon. Mountstuart Elphinstone*, London, 1884.

Gavli, P.A., *Peshwekalina Gulamgiri Va Asprishyate*, 3rd edn, Kolhapur, 1990.

Godse, Vishnubhat, *Majhe Pravas athva San 1857chya Bandachi Hakikat*, first pub. 1907, repub. Pratibha Pratisthan, Bombay, 1992.

Halhed, Nathaniel, *A Grammar of the Bengali Language*, Hoogly, 1778, reprint Scolar Press, Menston, UK, 1969.

Hazen, William, *A Century In India: The American Marathi Mission 1813–1913*, Ahmadnagar, 1913.

Jambhekar, G.G., ed., *Memoirs and Writings of Balshastri Jambhekar*, pub. G.G. Jambhekar, Pune, 1950.

Joshi, G.B., *Gelya Tees Varshapurveeche Lok va Tyanchya Samjuti athva Majhe Pravasachi Hakikati (Rojanishi)*, Baroda, 1896.

Joshi, V.K., and Sahasrabuddhe, eds, *Darpan-Sangraha*, Mumbai Marathi Granth Sangrahalaya, Bombay, 1946.

Kunte, Moreshwar, Dr. Bhosle ed., *Raja Shivaji*, Sahitya Seva Prakashan, Aurangabad, 1992.

Kunte, Moreshwar, *Reform Question*, Bombay, 1871.

Lakshmanji, Ganpat, *Essay on the Promotion of Domestic Reform among the Natives of India*, Bombay, 1843.

Madgaonkar, Govind Narayan, *Mumbaiche Varnan*, first pub. 1863, 3rd ed. Varda Books, Pune, 1992.

Mitchell, J.M., *In Western India: Recollections of My Early Missionary Life*, Edinburgh, 1899.

Padmanji, Baba, *Arunodaya*, Tract and Book Society, Bombay, 1888.

Palande, M.R., ed., Bombay Government, *Source Material for a History of the Freedom Struggle*, Vol. II, Bombay, 1958.

Pandit, Bhavani Shankar Sridhar, ed., *Raosaheb Keshav Shivram Bhavalkaryanche Atmavritta*, Vidarbha Samshodhan Mandal, Nagpur, 1961.

Pandurang, Dadoba, A.K. Priyolkar, ed., *Raobahadur Dadoba Pandurangyanche Atmacharitra*, pub. by Keshav Bhikaji Damle, Bombay,1973.

Pandurang, Dadoba, *Maharastra Bhasheche Vyakaran*, 2nd edition, Bombay, 1850.

Parasnis, D.B., comp. and ed., *Shri Mahapursha Brahmendraswamiyanche Patravyavhar*, Bombay, 1900.

Parulekar R.V., ed., *Survey of Indigenous Education in the Province of Bombay 1820–1830*, Asia Publishing House, Bombay, 1945.

Parulekar, R.V., ed., *Selections from Educational Records of the Government of Bombay*, 1819–52, Asia Publishing House, Bombay, 1953.

Parulekar, R.V., ed., *Selections from the Educational Records of the Government of Bombay*, Part II: 1815–1840, Asia Publishing House, Bombay, 1955.

Phadke, Y.D., ed., *Mahatma Phule Samagra Vangmaya*, Maharastra Rajya Sahitya ani Sanskriti Mandal (first edition, eds. Dhanajay Keer and S.G. Malshe), Bombay, 1991.

Phadkule, Nirmalkumar ed., *Nibandmaleteel Teen Nibandh*, Pune, 1975.

Richey, J.A., ed., *Selections from the Educational Records*, Part II, 1840–1859, Government Printing Press, Calcutta,1922.

Sardesai, G.S., comp. and ed., *Aitihasik Patrabodh Marathashahitil Nivadak Patra, 1596–1839*, Pune, 1939.

Sardesai, G.S., comp. and ed., *Selections from the Peshwa Daftar*, Vols. 1–45, Bombay, 1931–4.

Sharp, *Selections from the Educational Records*, Part I, Government Printing Press, Calcutta, 1922.

Stevenson, Rev., 'Observations on the Grammatical Structure of Vernacular Languages of India', *Journal of the Bombay Royal Asiatic Society*, Vol. III, 1849–51

The Constitution of the Poona Sarvajanik Sabha and its Rules, Poona, 1871.

Vad, G.C., Mawjee, P.V., Parasnis, D.B., Joshi, Puroshottam, comp. and ed., *Selections from the Satara Rajas and Peshwa Diaries*, 9 parts, Deccan Vernacular Translation Society, Pune, 1902–1911.

Vishnubuwa Brahmachari, *Vedokta Dharmaprakash*, Indian Printing Press, Bombay, 1882.

Wilson, John, *A Second Exposure of Hindu Religion*, Bombay, 1834.

Wilson, John, *An Exposure of Hindu Religion in Response to Morobhat Dandekar*, Bombay 1832.

Secondary Works

Acharya, Promesh, 'Indigenous education and brahmanical hegemony in Bengal', paper read at the workshop on *The Purpose of Education and Information*', 16–18 December 1991, SOAS, London.

Ahmad, Aijaz, *In Theory: Classes, Nations, Literatures,* Oxford University Press, Delhi, 1992.

Alam, Muzaffar, 'The Pursuit of the Persian Language in Mughal Politics', *Modern Asian Studies*, Vol. 32, No. 2, May 1998, pp. 317–50.

Amin, Shahid, *Event, Metaphor, Memory: Chauri-Chauri 1922–1992*, University of California Press, Berkeley, 1995.

Anderson, Benedict, *Imagined Communities: Reflections on the Origin and Spread of Nationalism*, Verso, London, 1991.

Baldick, Chris, *The Social Mission of English Criticism: 1848–1932*, Oxford University Press, Oxford, 1983.

Banaji, J., 'Capitalist Domination and the Small Peasantry: Deccan Districts in the Late Nineteenth Century, *EPW*, Vol. XII, Nos. 33–4, special number, 1977, pp. 1375–1404.

Bannerjee, Sumanta, *The Parlour and the Street: Elite and Popular Culture in Nineteenth Century Calcutta*, Seagull, Calcutta, 1989.

Basu, Aparna, ed., *Indian Education in Parliamentary Papers, Part I,* Indian Institute of Education, Bombay, 1952.

Basu, Aparna, *The Growth of Education and Political Development in India, 1898–1920*, Oxford University Press, Delhi, 1974.

Bauman, Zygmunt, *Legislators and Interpreters: Modernity, Post-Modernity and Intellectuals*, Polity Press, Cambridge, 1989.

Bayly, C.A., *Empire and Information 1780–1870*, Cambridge University Press, Cambridge, 1996.

Bayly, C.A., *Rulers, Townsmen and Bazaars: North Indian Society in the Age of British Expansion 1770–1870*, first pub. 1983, Oxford University Press, Delhi, 1992.

Behram, Boman, *Educational Controversies of India: The Cultural Conquest of India under Imperialism*, Taraporewala & Co., Bombay,1946.

Bhabha, Homi, *The Location of Culture*, Routledge, London, 1994.

Bourdieu, Pierre and Passeron, Jean-Claude, *Reproduction in Education, Society, Culture*, trans. Richard Nice, first pub. 1977; English edn., Sage, London, 1990.

Bourdieu, Pierre, *Language and Symbolic Power*, Harvard University Press, Cambridge, Massachusetts, 1991.

Breckenridge, Carol and van der Veer, Peter, eds., *Orientalism and the Post-colonial Predicament*, University of Pennsylvania Press, Philadelphia, 1991

Calhoun, Craig, ed., *Habermas and the Public Sphere*, MIT Press, Cambridge, Massachusetts, 1992.

Cashman, Richard, *The Myth of the Lokmanya: Tilak and Mass Politics in Maharashtra*, University of California Press, Berkeley, 1975.

Chakrabarty, Dipesh, *Re-thinking Working Class History*, Princeton University Press, Princeton, 1989.

Chattopadyaya, B.D., *The Making of Early Medieval India*, Oxford University Press, Delhi, 1994.

Clancy, M. T., *From Memory to Written Records: England 1066–1307*, Blackwell, Oxford, 1979.

Chandavarkar, Raj, *The Origins of Industrial Capitalism in India: Business Strategies and the Working Classes in Bombay 1900–1940*, Cambridge University Press, Cambridge, 1994

Chandra, Sudhir, *The Oppressive Present: Literature and the Social Imagination*, Oxford University Press, Delhi, 1991.

Chartier, Roger, *Cultural History: Between Practices and Representations*, trans. Lydia Cochrane, Cambridge, Polity Press, 1990.

Chartier, Roger, *The Order of Books*, Stanford University Press, Stanford,1994.

Chatterjee, Partha, *Nationalist Thought and the Colonial World: A Derivative Discourse?*, Zed Books, London, 1986.

Chatterjee, Partha, *The Nation and its Fragments*, Oxford University Press, Delhi, 1993.

Chaudhuri K.N. and Dewey, Clive, J., eds., *Economy and Society: Essays in Indian Economic and Social History*, Oxford University Press, Delhi,1979.

Choksey, R.D., *Mountstuart Elphinstone: The Indian Years 1796–1827*, Popular Prakashan, Bombay, 1970.

Cohn, Bernard, 'The Command of Language and the Language of Command' in *Subaltern Studies IV: Writings on South Asian History and Society*, ed. Ranajit Guha, Oxford University Press, Delhi, 1994.

Cohn, Bernard, 'The Census, Social Structure, and Objectification in South Asia', in *An Anthropologist amongst the Historians and other Essays*, Oxford University Press, New Delhi, 1987.

Darnton, Robert, *The Business of Enlightenment: A Publishing History of the 'Encyclopedie', 1775–1800*, Cambridge, Massachusetts, Belknap Press, 1979.

Darnton, Robert, *The Kiss of Lamourette: Reflections in Cultural History*, Norton, New York, 1990.

Das Sisir, Kumar, *A History of Indian Literature, 1800–1910: Western Impact, Indian Impact*, Sahitya Akademi, New Delhi, 1991.

Das Sisir, Kumar, *Sahibs and Munshis: An Account of the College of Fort William*, Orion Publications, Calcutta, 1978.

de Certeau, Michel, *The Writing of History*, trans. Tom Conley, Columbia University Press, New York, 1988.

de Certeau, Michel, *The Practice of Everyday Life*, trans. Steven Randall, University of California Press, Berkeley, 1984.

Deleury, Guy, *The Cult of Vithoba*, Deccan College, Poona, 1950.

Deshpande, Madhav, *Sociolinguistic Attitudes in India*, Karoma, Ann Arbor, 1979.

Dinshaw Wacha, *Shells from the Sands of Bombay: My Recollection and Reminiscences 1860–75*, K.T. Ankleshwaria, Bombay, 1920.

Dirks, N., 'The Invention of Caste: Civil Society in Colonial India', *Social Analysis*, No. 25, September, 1989.

Dobbin, Christine, 'Competing Elites in Bombay City Politics in the Mid-Nineteenth Century (1852–83) in E. Leach and S.N. Mukherjee, eds, *Elites in South Asia*, Cambridge University Press, Cambridge, 1970, pp. 79–94.

Dobbin, Christine, *Urban Leadership in Western India: Politics and Communities in Bombay City 1840–1885*, Oxford University Press, London, 1972.

Duara, Prasenjit, *Rescuing History from the Nation: Questioning Narratives of Modern China*, University of Chicago Press, Chicago, 1995.

Eagleton, Terry, *Literary Theory: An Introduction*, Minneapolis, University of Minnesota Press, 1983.

Edwardes, S.M., *The Rise of Bombay: A Retrospect*, Times of India Press, Bombay, 1902.

Eisenstein, Elizabeth, *The Printing Press as an Agent of Change: Communication and Cultural Transformation in Early Modern Europe*, Cambridge University Press, Cambridge, 1980.

Fabian, Johannes, *Time and the Work of Anthropology: Critical Essays 1971–1991*, Harwood Academic Publishers, Amsterdam, 1991.

Febvre, Lucien, and Martin, Henri-Jean, *The Coming of the Book: The Impact of Printing, 1450–1800*, trans. David Gerard, eds, Geffrey Nowell Smith and David Wooton, London, New Left Books, 1976.

Foucault, Michel, *Language, Counter-Memory and Practice: Selected Essays and Interviews*, trans. D. Bouchard and Sherry Simon, eds, Donald Bouchard, Cornell University Press, New Haven, 1977.

Foucault, Michel, *The Order of Things: An Archaeology of the Human Sciences*, Tavistock Publications, London, 1970.

Fukazawa, H.K., *The Medieval Deccan: Peasants, Social Systems and States*, Oxford University Press, Delhi, 1991.

Gallagher, John, *Locality, Province and Nation: Essays in Indian Politics 1870–1940*, Cambridge University Press, Cambridge, 1973.

Gordon, Stewart, *Marathas, Marauders and State Formation*, Oxford University Press, Delhi, 1994.

Green, Andy, *Education and State Formation in England, France and United States of America*, Macmillan, London, 1990.

Guha, A., 'More about Parsi Seths: Their Roots, Entrepreneurship and Comprador Role 1650–1918.' *EPW*, Vol. XIX, No. 3, 21 January 1984, 117–32.

Guha, Ranajit, *A Rule of Property for Bengal: An Essay on the Idea of a Permanent Settlement*, Mouton and Co. & Ecole Pratique des Hautes Etudes, Paris, 1963.

Guha, Ranajit, 'Dominance without Hegemony and its Historiography', *Subaltern Studies VI*, Oxford University Press, Delhi, 1989, pp. 210–309.

Guha, Ranajit, *Dominance without Hegemony: History and Power in Colonial India*, Cambridge, Mass., Harvard University Press, 1997.

Guha, Sumit, 'Potentates, Traders and Peasants: Western India, *c.*1700–1870', Occasional Papers on History and Society, Second Series, Number LVIII, Nehru Memorial Museum and Library, Teen Murti House, New Delhi.

Guha, Sumit, *The Agrarian Economy of the Bombay Deccan, 1818–1941*, Oxford University Press, Delhi, 1986.

Habermas, Jurgen, *The Structural Transformation of the Public Sphere: An Inquiry into a Category of Bourgeois Society*, German original, 1962; English edn., M.I.T. Press, Cambridge, Massachusetts,1989.

Haynes, Douglas, E., *Rhetoric and Ritual in Colonial India: The Shaping of a Public Culture in Surat City, 1852–1928*, University of California Press, Berkeley, 1991.

Houben, Jan, ed., *Ideology and Status of Sanskrit*, Brill Academic Publishers, Leiden, 1996.

Inden, Ronald, *Imagining India*, Basil Blackwell, Oxford, 1990.

Johnson, Gordon, *Provincial Politics and Indian Nationalism: Bombay and the Indian National Congress 1880–1915*, Cambridge University Press, Cambridge,1973.

Kaviraj, Sudipta, 'State, Society and Discourse' in James Manor, ed., *Re-thinking Third World Politics*, Longman, London, 1991, pp. 72–99.

Kaviraj, Sudipta, 'On the Construction of Colonial Power: State, Discourse, Hegemony', in Engels and Marks, eds., *Contesting Colonial Hegemony*, British Academic Press, London, 1994, pp. 19–54.

Kaviraj, Sudipta, 'Reversal of Orientalism' in V. Dalmia, ed., *Representing Hinduism: The Construction of Religious Traditions and National Identity*, Sage, New Delhi, 1995.

Kaviraj, Sudipta, 'The Imaginary Institution of India', in P. Chatterjee and G. Pandey, eds., *Subaltern Studies VII*, Oxford University Press, Delhi, 1992.

Kaviraj, Sudipta, 'Writing, Speaking, Being: Language and the Historical Formation of Identities in India', in D. Hellman-Rajanayagam and D. Rothermund, eds., Nationalstaat und Sprachkonklifte in Sud-und Sudostatesein, Steiner, Stuttgart, 1992.

Kaviraj, Sudipta, *The Unhappy Consciousness: Bankimchandra Chattopadhyay and the Formation of Nationalist Consciousness in India*, Oxford University Press, Delhi, 1994.

Keer, Dhananjay, *Mahatma Jyotirao Phule*, Popular Prakashan, Bombay, 1964.

Kolte, V.B., *Mahanubhav Samshodhan*, Vol. 1, Arun Prakashan, Malkapur, 1960.

Kulkarni, A.R., *Medieval Maharashtra*, New Delhi, Books and Books, 1996.

Kulke, Herman, ed., *The State in India 1000–1700*, Oxford University Press, Delhi, 1995.

Kumar, Krishna, *The Political Agenda of Education: A Study of Colonialist and Nationalist Ideas*, Sage, New Delhi, 1991.

Kumar, Ravinder, *Western India in the Nineteenth Century*, Routledge, London, 1968.

La Volpa, Anthony, 'Conceiving a Public: Ideas and Society in Eighteenth Century Europe', *Journal of Modern History*, Vol. 64, No. 1, March 1992, pp. 79–116.

Lederle, M.R., *Philosophical Trends in Modern Maharashtra*, Popular Prakashan, Bombay, 1976.

Lele, J, ed., *Tradition and Modernity in Bhakti Movements*, E.J. Brill, Leiden, 1981.

Masselos, Jim, *Towards Nationalism: Group Affiliations and the Politics of Public Associations in Nineteenth-Century Western India*, Popular Prakashan, Bombay, 1974.

McCully, Bruce, *English Education and the Origins of Nationalism*, Columbia University Press, New York, 1940.

McDonald, Ellen, 'The Modernising of Communication: Vernacular Publishing in Nineteenth-Century Maharashtra' in *Asian Survey*, Vol. 8, July 1968, pp. 588–606.

McGregor, R.S., ed., *Devotional Literature in South Asia: Proceedings of a Conference held in Wolfson College*, Cambridge University Press, Cambridge, 1992.

Mehrotra, S. R., 'The Poona Sarvajanik Sabha: The Early Phase (1870–1880)', *Indian Economic and Social History Review*, Vol. 6, No. 3, 1969.

Mehta, Makarand, *Business Houses in Western India: A Study in Entrepreneurial Response 1850–1954*, Delhi, Manohar Publications, 1990.

Mehta, S.D., *The Cotton Mills of India: 1854–1954*, Bombay, Textile Association of India, 1954.

Mishra, B.B., *The Indian Middle Classes: Their Growth in Modern Times*, Oxford University Press, London, 1961.

Morris, M.D., *The Emergence of an Industrial Labour Force in India: A Study of the Bombay Cotton Mills, 1854–1947*, University of Berkeley Press, California, 1965.

Naik, J.V., 'Early Anti-caste Movement in Western India: The Paramhansa Sabha', *Journal of the Asiatic Society of Bombay*, Vol. 49, 50 and 51, 1974–76, New Series, pp. 136–61.

Natrajan, S., *A History of the Press in India*, Asia Publishing House, Bombay, 1962.

Niranjana, Tejaswini, *Siting Translation: History, Post-structuralism and the Colonial Context*, University of California Press, Berkeley, 1992.

Nurullah and Naik, *A History of Education in India During the British Period*, Macmillan, Bombay, 1951.

O'Hanlon, Rosalind, *A Comparison between Men and Women: Tarabai Shinde and the Critique of Gender Relations in Colonial India*, Oxford University Press, Delhi, 1994.

O'Hanlon, Rosalind, *Caste, Conflict and Ideology: Mahatma Jyotirao Phule and Low-Caste Protest in Nineteenth-Century Western India*, Cambridge University Press, Cambridge, 1995.

Omvedt, Gail, *Cultural Revolt in a Colonial Society: The Non-Brahman Movement in Western India, 1873 to 1930*, Scientific Socialist Education Trust, Bombay, 1976.

Pandit, Maya, 'Translation Culture and Colonial Discourse in Nineteenth-Century Maharashtra', in Madhav Apte, Milind Malshe, P.N. Paranjape, eds, *Explorations in Applied Linguistics*, Pune, 1995.

Pinch, William, *Peasants and Monks in British India*, Oxford U. Press, Delhi, 1996.

Patel, Sujata, &Thorner, Alice, eds., *Mumbai: Metaphor for Modern India*, Oxford University Press, Bombay, 1995.

Phathak, Yashwant, *Nachu Kirtanache Rangi*, Pune, n.d.

Pollock, Sheldon, 'India in the Vernacular Millennium: Literary Culture and Polity 1000–1500' in Shmuel Eisenstadt *et al.*, eds, special issue on 'Collective Identities and Political Order', *Daedalus*, Vol. 127, No. 3, 1998.

Pollock, Sheldon, 'Literary History, Indian History, World History', special issue, *Social Scientist*, Vol. 23, Nos. 10–12, October–December, 1995, pp. 112–39.

Pollock, Sheldon, 'The Sanskrit Cosmopolis, 300–1300: Transculturation, Vernacularisation and the Question of Ideology', in Jan Houben, ed., *Ideology and Status of Sanskrit*, 1996.

Priyolkar, A.P., *The Printing Press in India*, Marathi Samshodhan Mandal, Bombay, 1958.

Pusey, Michael, 'Jurgen Habermas: Reason and the Evolution of Culture' in Diane J. Austin-Broos, ed., *Creating Culture: Profiles in the Study of Culture*, Allen & Unwin, London, 1987.

Ranade, M.G., 'A Note on the Growth of Marathi Literature, *Royal Asiatic Society Bulletin*, Vol. 20, 1902, pp. 78–105.

Ranade, M.G., *The Rise of Maratha Power*, Bombay, Punalekar and Company, 1900.

Ranade, M.G., *The Miscellaneous Writings of the Late Hon. Mr. Justice Ranade*, Sahitya Akademi, New Delhi, 1992.

Ranade, A., *On Music and Musicians of Hindoostan*, Promila and Co., New Delhi, 1984.

Raychaudhuri, Tapan, *Europe Reconsidered: Perceptions of the West in Nineteenth-Century Bengal*, Oxford University Press, Delhi, 1988.

Reisner, I.M., and Goldberg, N.M., *Tilak and the Struggle for Indian Freedom*, Delhi, 1966.

Ringer, Fritz, Muller Detlef, Simon Brian, eds., *The Rise of the Modern Education System: Structural Change and Social Reproduction, 1870–1920*, Cambridge University Press, Cambridge, 1987.

Rutnagur, S.M, ed., *Bombay Industries: The Cotton Mills—A Review of the Progress of the Textile Industry in Bombay from 1850–1926 and the Present Constitution, Management and Financial Position of Spinning and Weaving Factories*, The Indian Textile Journal, Bombay,1927.

Said, Edward, *Orientalism*, New York, Pantheon, 1978.

Sangari, K. and Vaid, S., eds., *Recasting Women; Essays in Indian Colonial History*, Rutgers University Press, New Jersey, 1990.

Sangari, Kumkum, 'Mirabai and the Spiritual Economy of Bhakti', *EPW*, Vol. XXV, Nos 27 and 28, July 7 &14, 1990.

Sardesai, G.S., *A New History of the Marathas, 1606–1707*, Vol. 1, Phoenix Publishers, Bombay, 1946.

Scott, James, *Domination and the Arts of Resistance: Hidden Transcripts*, Yale University Press, New Haven, 1990.

Seal, Anil, *The Emergence of Indian Nationalism: Competition and Collaboration in the Later Nineteenth Century*, Cambridge University Press, Cambridge, 1968.

Simon, Brian, *Studies in the History of Education 1780–1870*, Lawrence and Wishart, London, 1960.

Small, Ian, *Conditions for Criticism: Authority, Knowledge and Literature in the Late Nineteenth Century*, Clarendon Press, Oxford, 1991.

Spivak, Gayatri, 'Can the Subaltern Speak?' in Cary Nelson and Lawrence Grossberg, eds, *Marxism and the Interpretation of Culture*, London, Macmillan, 1988.

Stock, Brian, *The Implications of Literacy: Written Language and Models of Interpretation in the Eleventh and Twelfth Centuries*, Princeton University Press, Princeton, 1983.

Stoler, Ann and Cooper, Frederick, eds, *Tensions of Empire: Colonial Cultures in a Bourgeois World*, University of California Press, Berkeley, 1997.

Subramaniam, L., 'Banias and the British: The Role of Indigenous Credit in The Process of Imperial Expansion in Western India in the Second half of the Eighteenth Century', *Modern Asian Studies*, Vol. 21, No.3, 1987, pp. 473–510.

Telang, K, *Gleanings from the Maratha Chronicles*, Manaktala and Sons, Bombay, 1961.

Trautmann, Tom, *Aryans and British India*, University of California Press, Berkeley, 1995.

Tulpule, S.G., *Classical Marathi Literature from the Beginning to AD 1818*, Vol. IX of *A History of Indian Literature*, ed. Jan Gonda, Otto Harrasowitz, Wiesbaden, 1979.

Vaidya, S. G., *Peshwa Bajirao II and the Downfall of the Maratha Power*, Pragati Prakashan, Nagpur, 1978.

Vaudeville, Charlotte, *Myths, Saints and Legends in Medieval India*, Oxford University Press, Delhi, 1996.

Vishwanathan, Gauri, *Masks of Conquest: Literary Study and British Rule in India*, Faber and Faber, London, 1989.

Wagle, N.K., ed., *Images of Maharastra: A Regional Profile of India*, Curzon Press, London, 1980.

Washbrook, David and Penelope Corfield, eds, *Language, History, Class*, Blackwell, Oxford, 1991.

Wink, Andre, *Land and Sovereignty in India: Agrarian Society and Politics in the Eighteenth Century Maratha Svarajya*, Cambridge University Press, Cambridge, 1986.

Marathi Printed Works

Anon, *Vishnushastri Chiplunkaryanche Charitra*, Pune, 1894.

Bedekar, D.K., ed., *Char Marathi Bhashetele Arthashastragnya*, Gokhale Arthashastra Samstha Press, Pune, 1969.

Bhagwat, Durga, ed., *Rajaramshastri Bhagwat Yanche Nivadak Lekh*, Abhinav Prakashan, Pune, 1950.

Bhagwat, Durga, *Rajaramshastri Bhagwat: Vyakti and Vangmayavichaar*, Swastik Publishing House, Bombay, 1947.

Bhave, V.K., *Maharashtra Sarasvat*, Pune, 1951.

Bhave, V.K., *Peshwekalin Maharastra*, Indian Council of Historical Research, Delhi, 1976.

Deshpande, A.N., *Prachin Marathi Vangmayacha Itihaas*, Vol. 2, Venus Prakashan, Poona, 1966.

Dev, V.K., *Javaji Dadajiyanche Charitra*, Bombay, 1897.

Dhere, R.C., *Santsahitya ani Loksahitya: Kahi Anubandh*, Venus Prakashan, Pune, 1978.

Havalder, G. R., *Raosaheb Vishwanath Narayan Mandlikyanche Charitra*, pub. by Havalder, Bombay, 1927.

Jadhav, Bhaskarrao, *Marathe ani Tyanche Bhasha*, Kolhapur, Dasram Book Depot, 1932.

Kirwale, K., *Ambedkari Shahiri—Ek Shodh*, Nalanda Prakashan, Pune, 1992.

Kulkarni, W.L., *Vividhdnyanvistaar: Itihaas Ani Vangmayavichaar*, Popular Prakashan, Bombay, 1976.

Kulkarni, W. L., *Marathi Dnyanprasarak: Itihaas Va Vangmayavichaar*, Popular Prakashan, Bombay, 1965.

Lele, R.K., *Marathi Vruttpatrancha Itihaas*, Pune, Continental Prakashan, 1964.

Phatak N.R., *Nyayamurti Ranadeyanche Charitra*, Bombay, 1924.

Narke, Hari, ed., *Amhi Pahilele Phule*, Maharashtra Govt. Publications, Bombay, 1993.

Pagdi, Madhavrao, *Shri Samarth Ani Samarth Sampradaya*, Bombay, 1985.

Parikh, G. *et al*, eds., *Lokahitwadi Samagra Vangmaya*, Maharastra Rajya Sahitya Samshodan Mandal, Mumbai, 1988.

Phadke, Y.D., *Vyakti Ani Vichar: Kahi Anubandh*, Shree Vidya Prakashan, Pune, 1979.

Potdar, D. V, *Marathi Gadyacha Ingrezi Avataar*, Venus Prakashan, Pune, 1922.

Priyolkar, A.R., *Paramhansa Sabha Va Tiche Adhyaksha Ramchandra Balkrishna*, Mumbai Marathi Granth Sangrahalaya, Bombay, 1966.

Priyolkar, A. P., *Bhau Daji Lad: Vyakti, Kaal, Kartutva*, Mumbai Marathi Granth Sangrahalaya, Bombay, 1971.

Sardar, G.B., *Aravachin Marathi Gadyachi Purvapeethika 1800–1874*, Modern Book Depot, Pune, 1938.

Vaidya, Dwarkanath Govind, ed., *Prarthanasamjacha Itihaas*, Prarthana Samaj, Bombay, 1927.

Index